From Reader to Reading Teacher

CAMBRIDGE LANGUAGE EDUCATION
Series Editor: Jack C. Richards

This new series draws on the best available research, theory, and educational practice to help clarify issues and resolve problems in language teaching, language teacher education, and related areas. Books in the series focus on a wide range of issues and are written in a style that is accessible to classroom teachers, teachers-in-training, and teacher educators.

In this series:

Agendas for Second Language Literacy *by Sandra Lee McKay*

Reflective Teaching in Second Language Classrooms *by Jack C. Richards and Charles Lockhart*

Educating Second Language Children: The whole child, the whole curriculum, the whole community *edited by Fred Genesee*

Understanding Communication in Second Language Classrooms *by Karen E. Johnson*

The Self-directed Teacher: Managing the learning process *by David Nunan and Clarice Lamb*

Functional English Grammar: An introduction for second language teachers *by Graham Lock*

Teachers as Course Developers *edited by Kathleen Graves*

Classroom-based Evaluation in Second Language Education *by Fred Genesee and John A. Upshur*

From Reader to Reading Teacher: Issues and strategies for second language classrooms *by Jo Ann Aebersold and Mary Lee Field*

From Reader to Reading Teacher

Issues and strategies for second language classrooms

Jo Ann Aebersold

Eastern Michigan University

Mary Lee Field

Wayne State University

CAMBRIDGE
UNIVERSITY PRESS

PUBLISHED BY THE PRESS SYNDICATE OF THE UNIVERSITY OF CAMBRIDGE
The Pitt Building, Trumpington Street, Cambridge CB2 1RP, United Kingdom

CAMBRIDGE UNIVERSITY PRESS
The Edinburgh Building, Cambridge CB2 2RU, United Kingdom
40 West 20th Street, New York, NY 10011-4211, USA
10 Stamford Road, Oakleigh, Melbourne 3166, Australia

First published 1997

Printed in the United States of America

Typeset in Times Roman

Library of Congress Cataloging-in-Publication Data
Aebersold, Jo Ann.
From reader to reading teacher / Jo Ann Aebersold, Mary Lee Field.
p.   cm. – (Cambridge language education)
Includes bibliographical references and index.
ISBN 0-521-49705-1. – ISBN 0-521-49785-X (pbk.)
1. Language and languages – Study and teaching.   2. Reading.
I. Field, Mary Lee.   II. Title.   III. Series.
P53.75.A35   1996
418'.4 – dc20   96-19711
                                                                              CIP

*A catalogue record for this book is available from
the British Library*

ISBN 0 521 49705 1 hardback
ISBN 0 521 49785 X paperback

Contents

Series editor's preface

The acquisition of reading skills in a second or foreign language is a priority for millions of learners around the world, and there is a growing demand for both effective reading courses as well as high-quality second language reading materials. Those involved in teaching reading or in teacher education for language teachers will therefore welcome this comprehensive introduction to the teaching of second language reading. In it the authors demonstrate that sound second language reading pedagogy draws on a variety of sources, including psycholinguistic theories of the nature of second language reading, information about the strategies employed by effective second language readers, and the accumulated knowledge and wisdom acquired from the study of effective teaching practices.

The authors treat a wide range of issues in second language reading pedagogy and demonstrate throughout the book that reading in a second language is a dynamic and interactive process in which learners make use of background knowledge, text schema, lexical and grammatical awareness, L1-related knowledge, and real-world knowledge, as well as their own personal purposes and goals, to arrive at an understanding of written material. At the same time readers' and teachers' views of the nature of reading are seen to be shaped by their own social, cultural, and personal histories.

In developing principles for the teaching of L2 reading, Aebersold and Field show how effective teaching strategies address both top-down and bottom-up dimensions of reading, help learners identify appropriate attitudes toward texts and purposes for reading, and develop readers' awareness of appropriate reading skills and strategies, at the same time being meaningful and engaging for learners. The tasks and examples they use to illustrate their discussion will help reading teachers acquire the knowledge and skills needed in designing reading courses, selecting and adapting reading texts, preparing self-made materials, assessing readers' abilities, and integrating the teaching of reading with other aspects of the curriculum. *From Reader to Reading Teacher* will therefore provide a valuable resource for teachers, teacher educators, and other language professionals interested in the teaching of reading in a second or foreign language.

Jack C. Richards

Preface

From Reader to Reading Teacher: Issues and Strategies for Second Language Classrooms is addressed both to those preparing to teach second language reading and to those already teaching reading. It will give the novice teacher thorough, detailed, practical information about methods, issues, and strategies for teaching reading. It will provide the experienced teacher with a broad theoretical basis for further developing effective methods and a flexible curriculum for a second language reading class. Although many exercises in the book have been designed for students in reading methodology classes, the book can also be used by individuals working alone to improve their skills at teaching second language reading.

Our basic assumption, as our book title indicates, is that all people who have learned to read can use their own experience as a foundation for developing the metacognitive awareness, strategies, and methods for teaching others to read in a second language. We use the image of a "learning spiral" to chart the process by which learners acquire, expand, and refine their knowledge. To do so, they review their own experience, reexamining it, and integrate new information. The Introduction elaborates upon this image, which reappears at various points in the book. Chapter 1 describes the basic elements of reader and text, and the interaction between reader and text, and Chapter 2 expands upon that base to encompass the factors that influence reading in a second or foreign language. In order to address the needs of teachers in classrooms, we devote Chapter 3 to the design of a reading course. Chapters 4, 5, and 6 provide practical, detailed information, including lesson plan segments, about issues and strategies for teaching reading, highlighting the stages of before, during, and after the reading of a text. In Chapter 7 we address the issue of learning and teaching vocabulary in the reading classroom. Chapters 8 and 9 provide ideas on teaching literature in the reading class and on assessing reading, respectively. We present guidelines for preparing a lesson plan for a reading class in Chapter 10, and we conclude in Chapter 11 by returning to the "learning spiral" described in the Introduction, which guided the organization of this book.

We owe special thanks to a number of people who have helped and encouraged us along the way: to Eastern Michigan University students who used an earlier draft of the manuscript as the reading methodology segment of their teaching methods course and whose annotations, comments, complaints, praise, and questions gave us direction and clarity on many issues; to Dr. Cathy Day, who was willing to use that draft version with those students, and who gave us feedback from a teacher's perspective; to Glenna Davis, Mark Booth, Alyce Howorth, and Trena Haffenden, who provided us with annotations and feedback on the manuscript that were invaluable in our revision process; to those students and colleagues who provided narratives and illustrations to make our book more grounded and lively; to David, Li-hua, Eddie, and Carol, who proofread chapters instead of going to the beach; and to Brad for every possible kind of support and encouragement. We also want to express our thanks to series editor Jack C. Richards, executive editor Mary Vaughn, assistant editor Mary Carson, and project editor Olive Collen at Cambridge University Press for their advice and encouragement. We owe a special thanks to Sandy Graham, copyeditor, for her thorough and thoughtful notes on the manuscript.

We sincerely hope that among these pages readers will find ideas and strategies that not only guide their thinking but also fire their creativity as teachers of second language reading. There is no set path to becoming an effective teacher – or to writing a book – as we can affirm. Despite one being a morning person and the other a night person, one using a Macintosh and the other an IBM, one working best just before deadlines and the other needing to plan ahead, we kept on talking and writing. The process of capturing the art of teaching second language reading and presenting it within the pages of this book has engaged us in a sustained, rewarding, wonderful exchange of information, views, opinions, and experiences, often in an unpromising assortment of malls, libraries, and restaurants halfway between our homes and universities. Through this book we invite you to join in that exchange, to explore your own ability as a reader, and to learn how readers can develop into teachers of second language reading.

Jo Ann Aebersold
Mary Lee Field

From Reader to Reading Teacher

Introduction

. . . comprehension from within.
 – Elaine Showalter (1985: 261)

As a reader, you bring a certain amount of knowledge to the task of reading this textbook. You have the ability to read in your native language, and you have knowledge about what reading is, even though you may no longer be conscious of what you do when you read or how you learned to read. In addition, you have been a student in classes where a teacher helped you learn how to read. Perhaps you have experienced learning to read in a language that is not your native or dominant language. You may even teach reading – either in the students' native language (L1) or in their second or foreign language (L2/FL). If you have taught others to read, you bring a teacher's insight to this text. All of your past experience informs the perspective from which you approach the information in this book.

Methodological basis of the book

The epigraph, ". . . comprehension from within," highlights our belief that true understanding begins with you, as a reader. Your experience and your knowledge are your primary sources of information, and this book attempts to show how you can use these resources. Other, external, sources of information highlighted in this book include our experience and expertise, developed during the years we have read, studied, and taught; the knowledge of your classmates and teacher in the class in which you are using this book; the students and teachers that you observe at work in other L2/FL classrooms; and the books, journals, and other professional publications that focus on learning and teaching reading in the L2/FL that are referenced in this book.

Given these various sources, we see learning as a circular rather than a linear process that repeatedly engages new information until it becomes internalized. This process can be envisioned as a learning spiral (Figure 1) that represents the recursive, developmental nature of learning. For example, as a reader of this book, you will move from step 1 through step 7 using various information sources. Then you will begin the process again, analyz-

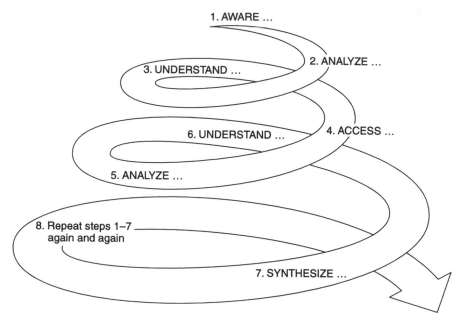

Figure 1   The learning spiral.

ing and evaluating your knowledge base in light of your new experience. The only difference is that each time you begin you will be starting from a base of greater knowledge. Each time you return to step 7, you will be working from a more informed and richer context when you make decisions about your teaching. We have used the image of the learning spiral because it includes the elements of growth, synthesis, incremental development, and an internal knowledge base. The teacher who understands and practices this process will be well prepared to use the same process as a guide to teaching students.

A description of the book

Because you bring a variety of abilities to the reading of this textbook and because we believe that people learn by starting with what they already know, we use an assortment of ways to make you aware of your knowledge of the reading process and the teaching of reading. We use questions that will help you clarify your thoughts on the topic. We ask you to recall past experiences that help you to remember what influenced your thoughts on the topic, through exercises called "Recalling Your Experience." We ask you to do activities that will cause you to reflect upon the process of reading and the teaching of reading called, "Building Your Knowledge."

In order to move beyond what you already know, we describe activities to use when teaching reading and ask you to understand the many choices involved in planning reading lessons through "Classroom Plans." We offer the reading and teaching experiences of others through interviews with students and teachers in the form of "Student and Teacher Narratives." We present ideas from theorists and researchers in the field, and we ask you to seek out information from others by reading academic articles on the topics being considered and discussing topics with other professionals in "Expanding Your Knowledge." In addition, we ask you to keep a "Teaching Portfolio" – a notebook of your work and ideas as you progress through this book. Participating in all of these experiences offers a range of opportunities for you to develop fully and to expand your understanding of what is involved in the teaching of L2/FL reading.

The Teaching Portfolio provides a place in which to record notes, activities, classroom methods, and resources. The portfolio is meant not only to aid you as you read this book but to serve as a reference for the teaching of reading throughout your career. We recommend these guidelines for setting it up: (1) Use a three-ring, loose-leaf binder so that you can insert pages, add items, and reorganize when necessary; (2) divide the portfolio into sections labeled "Notes and Exercises," "Classroom Activities," and "Resources"; and (3) add to the portfolio each time you develop a reading lesson, read an article about teaching reading, or come to some new understanding of the reading process.

From Reader to Reading Teacher first asks you to engage in the reflective, analytical, incremental process of examining your own understanding of reading. Then we present the views of others so that you may understand their perspectives and where they fit in the larger picture of L2/FL teaching. When you are secure in your own knowledge and informed about the knowledge of others, you can select the best way to teach reading to a given class, at a specific time, in a specific context. Teaching is often described as an art rather than as a science. To master the art of teaching reading you need more than a book of recipes. Instead of telling you what to do and how to do it, we want to present the principles and concepts that will inform your teaching throughout your career. In the spirit of Julia Child's *Mastering the Art of French Cooking,* we have designed a textbook that will give you *mastery* rather than presenting a collection of recipes. Our goal is to enable you to articulate the following:

- What you believe about the process of reading in second and foreign languages
- Why you believe what you believe
- How your beliefs shape your choices of teaching methods

Equipped with a deep understanding of these issues, you can become the kind of reading teacher who is flexible and responsive to student needs, who is able to draw on a wide variety of resources to create plans and materials that focus on class objectives, and who maintains a healthy, ongoing self-evaluation process in order to refine and renew and develop professionally.

1 *What is reading?*

Reading is like an infectious disease: it is caught not
taught. (And you can't catch it from someone who
hasn't got it . . .)
                                    – Christine Nuttall (1983: 192)

It seems only logical that a text about the teaching of reading would begin
with a definition of what reading is. However, the act of reading is not
completely understood nor easily described. In the most general terms we
may say that reading involves *the reader, the text,* and *the interaction
between reader and text* (Rumelhart 1977). Since our philosophy of learning begins with the individual, this chapter begins with you, the reader. The
first step is for you to become aware of yourself as a reader – your reading
skills and strategies, your assumptions about a text, your participation in the
interaction between the text and the reader – things you may have never
considered carefully before. Self-reflection is central to the learning spiral
that we described in the Introduction. It is the first step to becoming more
conscious of yourself as a reader and, ultimately, yourself as a teacher of
reading in the L2/FL classroom. In order to gain this higher level of con-
sciousness about your reading, we begin with questions and exercises that
challenge you to explore your own experience as a reader.

The reader

Readers' engagement in the reading process is based on their past experience, both in learning how to read and also in the ways reading fits into their
lives. What memories do you have about your experiences while learning to
read? What attitudes do you have about reading? Is it a pleasure or a bore?
Does it relax you or frustrate you? How did you feel about reading classes
when you were in the early years of school? In what ways is reading a part
of your life now? Our first exercise asks you to address those early memories. They may be difficult to recall, but whatever you can dredge up will
help you with the exercises that follow this one.

Exercise 1.1 Recalling your experience

1. Take no more than 3 minutes each to jot down some notes in your Teaching Portfolio on each of the following: (1) an early memory of reading at

home with parents or siblings, (2) a memory of reading in or for school, and (3) a recent reading experience. Write only enough to give you something to talk about with your classmates later.

2. Take another 5 minutes to reflect on these questions and jot down some notes: What are your emotions and feelings about these memories? Who were the other people who were involved in these memories? What value did the other people place on reading?

3. Analyze yourself as a reader by responding briefly to these questions: What role does reading play in your life now? Who helped shape that role? Has the role of reading changed for you over the years?

Note: You will use these notes for a later class discussion.

In Exercise 1.1 each reader will generate different answers to the questions from different knowledge bases, rooted in previous life and educational experiences. These bases are an important factor in how you as a reader approach, handle, think about, and understand written texts. You may also see more clearly where you "caught" the habit of reading, as Nuttall phrases it in the epigraph to this chapter. Reading experts generally agree that "more information is contributed by the reader than by the print on the page" (Clarke & Silberstein 1977: 136–7). That information comes from various sources in your life and, in turn, shapes your experiences of reading. The five most common sources include family, community, school, sociocultural environment, and individual differences.

The family influence

Despite their relatively small size, families foster a variety of experiences that affect reading. Family members, especially parents or other adult relatives in the house, model reading behaviors, habits, and attitudes. Children note why parents read – to gain information about their professions, about world and community events, about house maintenance; to relax; or to explore new interests. Reading for relaxation and enjoyment can be an individual or a family activity, such as the reading of bedtime stories. Homes that are filled with magazines, newspapers, and books send a clear message to children about the value of reading: Reading is a powerful activity that confers knowledge, insight, and perspective on readers. Those who grow up in homes where reading is seldom seen have a very different view of the value of reading (Heath 1983).

The community influence

Communities also provide readers with a set of varied life experiences that shape their individual bases of knowledge. To varying degrees, readers incorporate the knowledge and values of the community into their own perspective. The experiences of people growing up on farms, in urban ghettoes, in affluent suburbs, and in small towns will differ significantly. For example, going to dozens of weddings (or picnics, block parties, wakes, political rallies, parades, or other community events) as they are growing up enables readers not only to have memories of specific events but also to build mental concepts of an event by extracting the shared elements of those social events as they occur in that community. The more varied the community experiences and the more readers participate in community events, the richer the background knowledge readers will have to draw on when reading.

The school influence

Besides family and community experiences, readers bring their educational experience to reading. Schools can bring people into contact with communities other than their own, or they can be homogeneous institutions that reflect shared values. School experiences provides some common ground for people; they have all shared the experience of learning how to read. Nonetheless, there can also be very different experiences in the same school. Consider the students in these two classrooms:

Classroom A: In this room children are encouraged to read novels and stories, learning quite early about how a narrative unfolds and how a story is told. The teacher talks to them after they have read and they compare their ideas about the story, often connecting the events in the story to their own lives and experiences. The evaluation of the students' reading is qualitative, based on the teacher's observation and records of the children's participation in the tasks, their ability to discuss the stories, their ability to read aloud, and the amount of reading they do.

Classroom B: In this classroom reading is emphasized more as a read-and-recall activity in which students learn to remember details that may show up on a test the next day. The teacher consciously trains children to use certain reading strategies, such as skimming and scanning; repeatedly asks students to identify the main ideas; and requires them to summarize or paraphrase texts they have read. The evaluation of the students' reading is based on frequent tests and teacher-marked exercises.

The memories of reading in school that the students in these two classes carry with them for the rest of their lives are markedly different.

The cultural influence

Subsuming the important factors of family, community, and school is the larger context of cultural environment. Although many people associate the meaning of "culture" with the behaviors and artifacts that are produced by a given cultural group (e.g., art works, language, music, food), a cognitive definition of culture emphasizes that culture shapes a group's basic systems for seeing and interpreting the world around them (Robinson 1985: 10). While different social and economic groups within a culture may emphasize different uses for reading, overarching cultural values shape the general attitudes toward reading that a cultural group shares. Culture is like a filter, blocking or letting through a set of learned patterns and attitudes that form its core values. In a culture where reading is highly valued, the society as a whole will take great pains to promote reading among its members. A current example of that situation is the high literacy rates in Japan. Cultural notions about reading are implicit and hard to identify; people acquire them unconsciously. It is difficult enough to remember our early experiences of learning to read. Trying to analyze the cultural influences that shaped those experiences demands a knowledge of our own culture and cultural values in relationship to the values held by others.

The influence of individual characteristics

As people experience the influences just discussed – family, community, school, culture – each individual perceives these experiences and gains knowledge from them in different ways. The differences from one individual to another raise the question of nature versus nurture, a topic that has long been hotly debated in the field of education. Although L2/FL research investigates how motivation, learning styles, aptitude, and intelligence influence language learning, teachers need to consider how different readers read and how teachers can best facilitate that process. H. D. Brown (1987: 101–15) details several individual factors that influence language learning, including self-esteem, inhibition, risk taking, anxiety, and motivation. All of these factors operate in the reading classroom as well.

Home, community, school, culture, and individual characteristics all shape the life experiences that readers bring to reading. They help form the complex persona of reader and form the basis for understanding the reading process. The background information that readers bring to a text – including the knowledge of habits and beliefs from their own life experiences – is often referred to as **schema.** What people already know about the history, culture, habits, politics, sports, and music of any given place help them understand a reading about that topic. Also, the way they learned to read affects their degree of success in understanding a particularly difficult text.

Exercise 1.2   Recalling your experience

Gather in groups of three and share the memories you recalled in Exercise 1.1. Did you find that your experiences overlap? Where were there differences? similarities?

These discussions will provide rich material for much of what follows in this text. Make some notes (dated and labeled) in your Teaching Portfolio to help you remember some of the details.

The text

Although for many people reading texts means reading books, people read many different types of texts everyday, such as labels (on cereal boxes, medicine containers, clothes), instructions (street signs, directions for operating a VCR), advertisements (on TV, in magazines, on billboards), and notes (grocery lists, messages), to name only a few. Text can be anything from a few words, to one sentence, to thousands of words comprising thousands of sentences.

Readers know more than they may think about each of the text types they read and can categorize texts using various criteria. See what you already know about different types of text.

Exercise 1.3   Building your knowledge

1. Examine each of the following texts; some are excerpts and some are complete. Then write in the blank next to "Probable source" what kind of text you think it is and where it comes from.

Text A

Scientists have found that the Earth's lower atmosphere is laced with rivers of water vapor rivaling the Amazon in their flow.

Those rivers "are the main mechanism by which (atmospheric) water gets transported from the equator to the poles," said Reginald E. Newell of the Massachusetts Institute of Technology, who reports on the findings in the American Geophysical Union journal Geophysical Research Letters.

He said the concentrated streams, releasing not only moisture but latent heat in the higher latitudes, may turn out to be the main sources of hurricanes.

Climatologists have long understood that warm moist air rises from Earth's equatorial regions and drifts toward the poles along a course slightly offset by the motion of the Earth's spin. The surprise is that the moisture is confined in narrow streams.

A space-shuttle instrument spotted five rivers in the Southern Hemisphere, four or five in the Northern Hemisphere. Flowing at no more than 1.9 miles above Earth's surface, they stretch typically to lengths of 4,800 miles or so; widths ranged from 420 to 480 miles. The flow volumes typically measured 364 million pounds of water per second, comparable to an average Amazon flow.

Probable source: _____

Text B

Ideology is expressed in the educational systems of any society. Educational systems, like any cultural system, are always historically *situated,* that is, a product of particular cultural and historical forces. Thus, what students are taught about any subject necessarily values certain aspects of that subject over others. While this process of selection is inevitable, it is not uniform either across cultures or within a given culture at a particular time. Foucault argues in his essay "The Order of Discourse" (1971) that "any system of education is a political way of maintaining or modifying the appropriation of discourses, along with the power and knowledge they carry" (p. 64). Consequently, the education system can be as much a means of repressing certain groups of people as it is a means of empowering others. While many students and educators may be intuitively aware of the repressive as well as the enabling function of education, it is only when we begin to investigate systematically the ideological reasons underlying the way in which students are taught that we might possibly begin to change these educational inequities.

Probable source: _____

Text C

This was great! Thank you very much! I want my own copy – next time we go to Borders.
   Also – ordering from Penny's Tall, I finally found a pair of slacks that actually fit! I don't believe it!
   I am eternally grateful to you for those two discoveries.
   P.S. . . . We look forward to Sat. – see you soon

Probable source: _____

Text D

The high grey-flannel fog of winter closed off the Salinas Valley from the sky and from all the rest of the world. On every side it sat like a lid on the mountains and made of the great valley a closed pot. On the broad, level land floor the gang plows bit deep and left the black earth shining like metal where the shares had cut. On the foothill ranches across the Salinas River, the yellow stubble fields seemed to be bathed in pale cold sunshine, but there was no sunshine in the valley now in December. The thick willow scrub along the river flamed with sharp and positive yellow leaves.

It was a time of quiet and of waiting. The air was cold and tender. A light wind blew up from the southwest so that the farmers were mildly hopeful of a good rain before long; but fog and rain do not go together.

Across the river, on Henry Allen's foothill ranch there was little work to be done, for the hay was cut and stored and the orchards were plowed up to receive the rain deeply when it should come. The cattle on the higher slopes were becoming shaggy and rough-coated.

Elisa Allen, working in her flower garden, looked down across the yard and saw Henry, her husband, talking to two men in business suits. The three of them stood by the tractor shed, each man with one foot on the side of the little Fordson. They smoked cigarettes and studied the machine as they talked.

Probable source: _____

2. In the margin beside each text, jot down the characteristics that made you think the text came from the source you listed.
3. What features help you identify the kind of text you are reading? What do you know about the features of other types of texts not illustrated here? Make a list in your Teaching Portfolio. You will need to refer back to it.
4. In small groups, compare your answers on the possible sources for the texts. Then share your lists of text characteristics for each type of text that you thought of. Note any differences due to cultural factors. Take notes in your Teaching Portfolio.

The knowledge that readers have of text types allows them to adjust their reading expectations and skills to the text at hand. Readers' comprehension of a text may change as they reread the text, but the text itself does not change. Unlike readers, texts are static; once written, they cannot adapt to the readers who are reading them.

Texts exhibit various characteristics that can facilitate or hinder readers' comprehension. The following discussion of text features is limited to a discussion of expository, or informational, prose since most people spend more time reading that type of text.

Organization of information

Rhetorical structures is a term frequently used in writing to describe the organization of information in texts. These structures are fairly conven-

tional: description, classification, comparison, cont█████████████
process, argument, and persuasion, to name a few. F█████
as a whole is devoted to explaining how a new recy█████████████
its rhetorical structure is that of process. However, █████████
how the new recycling center functions but then shif█████████████
which it functions better than the old one, the struct█████████
contrast.

Look again at text A in Exercise 1.3. The rhetoric████████
newspaper article ("Climate clues lie below ocean'')
The writer describes the rivers of water vapor flo█████████████
atmosphere: what they are like, where they can be fou████████
One feature that helps identify this text as a newspape███████
the main idea is given at the beginning, followed by█████████
fact that paragraphs are short, consisting in most cas█████
sentences, is another text feature typical of newspape███████████████
is the use of a quote from an expert in the field.

Text B is a paragraph from an academic textboc████████████
Despite its brevity, it is evident that the organizatior███████
ment. The writer makes a claim in the first sentence██████
support that claim. In addition, the author quotes fro██████████
of an expert to support the argument. These are con██████████
demic texts. Text C is a personal note written to a fr███████
personal communication), and text D is an excerpt f█████████████
John Steinbeck (1954). Both will be discussed in mc████
chapter.

Syntax and grammar

Texts A–D also contain differences in sentence structu█████████
sentences of each text:

Text A: He said the concentrated streams, releasing ████████████
  latent heat in the higher latitudes, may turn out to be████
  hurricanes.
Text B: Thus, what students are taught about any subje████████
  certain aspects of that subject over others.
Text C: I want my own copy – next time we go to Borc███████
Text D: On the broad, level land floor the gang plows████
  black earth shining like metal where the shares hac███████

The difference in the lengths of sentences is striking████
the newspaper (A), the academic textbook (B), and th███████
longer than those from the personal note (C), with the████
longest. The newspaper and academic sentences are█████

more complex. The newspaper sentence contains more clauses or reduced clauses (two complete, three reduced) than any of the others. The sentence from the personal note has two clauses; the short story has three clauses (two complete, one reduced). The academic sentence contains two clauses, but its WH-clause, occupying the subject position of the other clause, is quite complex grammatically. Although the short story sentence has three clauses (one reduced), its compound verb phrase and WH-clause, modifying "black earth," are less complex and more readily understood. Thus sentence length and complexity are text features that can influence comprehension and can signal the type of text.

Another syntactic feature of texts is cohesion. **Cohesion** is the way the ideas and meanings in a text are related to each other. It is easy to understand this concept by looking at the first three sentences of text B; the words in boldface type provide cohesion:

Ideology is expressed in the educational systems of any society. **Educational systems,** like any **cultural system,** are always historically *situated,* **that is,** a product of particular cultural and historical forces. **Thus, what students are taught about any subject** necessarily values certain aspects of that subject over **others.**

"Educational systems" in sentence 2 repeats those words from the previous sentence; "cultural system" is a category that embraces "educational systems." "That is" announces that the information following it is a more specific way of restating the information before it. Although these types of cohesion have technical names (see Lorch & O'Brien 1995; Stoddard 1991), what is important is knowing how they work together to build meaning.

Words like *thus, for example, because, consequently, however, furthermore,* and *although* show relationships between ideas. When these words are used in a text, the relationship between sentences is *stated.* When these words are not used, the relationship between sentences is *implied.* Being able to understand the implied relationships between ideas is important to reading comprehension.

Vocabulary

In reading native language texts, readers are not usually aware of vocabulary unless they encounter unfamiliar words. If the number of unfamiliar words in a text is small and their content is not crucial to the basic meaning of the main message, they do not hinder reading comprehension. However, if there are many unfamiliar words that are key words, comprehension of the text begins to break down. For example, most readers would have some difficulty reading an article from a medical journal, written by a doctor for doctors, explaining how the hypothalamus functions. Although they would understand the **function words** (e.g., *a, an, the, of, in, on, through, by*), they would be unable to grasp the message of the text because of unfamiliarity with the **content words** (nouns, verbs, adjectives, and adverbs).

Another vocabulary factor that readers contend with is the several possible meanings of any one word. For example, notice how the definition for the word *ball* changes from one sentence to the next:

> The baby kicked the ball.
> The golfer kicked the ball.
> The soccer player kicked the ball.

> (adapted from R. C. Anderson & Shifrin 1980: 331)

In the first sentence we understand the ball to be soft and round, because a baby is playing with it. The golf ball is small, hard, round, and possibly white. The soccer ball is large, softer than a golf ball, round, and probably black and white. Now focus on the word *kicked.* Notice how the meaning of that word changes slightly from one sentence to the other. (*Hint:* Focus on the intention of the action.) Whereas the baby's kicking was probably done awkwardly and with delight, the golfer's kicking was surely done in anger. Kicking the ball is a normal action for a soccer player. The nuances of meaning are as important as knowing the primary meaning of vocabulary.

Vocabulary is a particularly important concern in literature. In text D, an excerpt of a short story (Steinbeck 1954: 56), there are various examples of unusual combinations of words. Thus, readers take note of phrases like "cold sunshine," since sunshine is usually associated with warmth. There are also some technical words, such as "gang plows" and "shares," which refer to machinery that most contemporary readers who are not farmers will understand only in a general sense. All of these vocabulary words help the reader to construct a mental image for the context of the story that follows.

Organization of information, syntax and grammar, and vocabulary are just a few important types of text features. The presence or absence of various combinations of these features affects the comprehensibility of a text.

The interaction between reader and text

The title of this chapter poses the question, "What is reading?" We have purposely not answered it, because we would like *you* to. What do *you* think reading is?

Exercise 1.4 Building your knowledge

1. In your own words, write a brief definition of reading in your Teaching Portfolio. (Don't use a dictionary!)
2. In your Teaching Portfolio, make a list of the influences you think have most shaped your understanding of what reading is.

In a general sense, **reading is what happens when people look at a text and assign meaning to the written symbols in that text.** The text and the reader are the two physical entities necessary for the reading process to begin. It is, however, the **interaction** between the text and the reader that constitutes actual reading. Granted, the meaning the reader gets from the text may not be exactly the same as the meaning the writer of the text wished to convey. Likewise, the meaning that one reader gets from a text may be different from that of other readers reading the same text. These variations occur because of influences on the reader by family, community, and cultural environment, and because of individual differences in motivation, aptitude, and other personal characteristics. Readers use their varying resources to differing degrees when they read. Thus, reading comprehension differs from one reader to another.

Interaction between purpose and manner of reading

When people read, they read for a **purpose.** They may read the instructions on a jar of instant coffee because they need to know how much coffee to put in the cup of hot water. They may glance at the newspaper headlines before they leave home to see if there are any major news items that they should know about. While driving to school or work, they may look for signs about road construction in progress so they can avoid traffic delays. They may notice a sign announcing a new store; they may read it because they want to find out what it sells.

Purpose determines **how** people read a text. Do they read the text slowly or quickly? Do they read to understand (reading for full comprehension), or simply to get the general idea (skimming), to find the part that contains the information they need (scanning)? Do they reread any parts? If so, why? People vary reading behavior according to their purpose for reading.

Interaction through reading strategies

Both teachers and researchers have attempted to identify the mental activities that readers use in order to construct meaning from a text (see N. J. Anderson et al. 1991; Devine 1988a; Hosenfeld et al. 1981). These activities are generally referred to as **reading strategies,** although they are sometimes called **reading skills.** Even though each reader has unique characteristics, successful readers also share much in common, and derive more or less the same meaning from the same text as the teacher or researcher does.

What do successful readers do, consciously or unconsciously, that enables them to comprehend the text well?

- Recognize words quickly
- Use text features (subheadings, transitions, etc.)
- Use title(s) to infer what information might follow
- Use world knowledge
- Analyze unfamiliar words
- Identify the grammatical functions of words
- Read for meaning, concentrate on constructing meaning
- Guess about the meaning of the text
- Evaluate guesses and try new guesses if necessary
- Monitor comprehension
- Keep the purpose for reading the text in mind
- Adjust strategies to the purpose for reading
- Identify or infer main ideas
- Understand the relationships between the parts of a text
- Distinguish main ideas from minor ideas
- Tolerate ambiguity in a text (at least temporarily)
- Paraphrase
- Use context to build meaning and aid comprehension
- Continue reading even when unsuccessful, at least for a while

(Anderson et al. 1991; Barnett 1989; Clarke 1979)

This list is not prioritized or complete. It continues to grow as more research into reading is conducted. Moreover, it is not clear which strategies are most important, which interrelate with each other, and who may be most likely to use a given strategy.

Interaction through schema

As noted earlier, schema (plural: schemata) refers to the knowledge readers bring to a text. Research on the theory of schema has had a great impact on understanding reading, and researchers have identified several specific types of schemata. **Content schema** provides readers with a foundation, a basis for comparison (Carrell & Eisterhold 1983; Carrell, Pharis, & Libretto 1989). For example, readers of a text about a wedding can compare it both to specific weddings they have attended and also to the general pattern of weddings in their culture.

In addition to content schema, researchers have also identified **formal schema,** which refers directly to the organizational forms and rhetorical structures of written texts (Carrell 1984a, b). When you guessed the sources of different texts in Exercise 1.3, you were making decisions based on your (perhaps unconscious) knowledge of formal schemata. You knew that a newspaper article was structured differently from a personal note; you knew that an academic text used language differently than a novel. The knowledge that you bring to a text about structure, vocabulary, grammar, and level of formality (or register) constitutes your formal schema (the items considered in the previous section on "The Text"). Your schooling and your culture have probably played the largest roles in giving you a knowledge base of formal schemata.

Linguistic schema is also being studied in the research on reading. While formal schemata cover discourse-level items, linguistic schemata include the decoding features we need to recognize words and see how they fit together in a sentence. Readers who have not actively studied a word or a grammar rule in their L1 cannot use that information when they read. They may, from repeated examples, be able to generalize a pattern or guess the meaning of a word, but it was not initially a part of their linguistic schema. The building of linguistic schema in an L2/FL proceeds in much the same way.

Schema theory research has been extensive since the 1970s. Some studies verify that students understand more of a text when they know the content schema (Steffensen & Joag-Dev 1984); some studies investigate "schema interferences" in reading (Carrell 1988); and some studies illustrate how schema theory can and should shape our teaching practices (James 1987).

Models of reading

In looking for ways to describe the interaction between reader and text, researchers have also created models that describe what happens when people read. So far, models have been confined to native language, and none has been comprehensive. Linguists and L2/FL professionals have, however, explored the similarities and differences between reading in the L1 and an L2/FL. A number of authorities have devised visual charts that model the reading process. Barnett (1989) provides a thorough summary of these models that includes L1/L2 issues:

There are three main models of how reading occurs.

1. **Bottom-up theory** argues that the reader constructs the text from the smallest units (letters to words to phrases to sentences, etc.) and that the process of constructing the text from those small units becomes so automatic that readers are not aware of how it operates (see Eskey 1988; Stanovich 1990). **Decoding** is an earlier term for this process.

2. **Top-down theory** argues that readers bring a great deal of knowledge, expectations, assumptions, and questions to the text and, given a basic understanding of the vocabulary, they continue to read as long as the text confirms their expectations (Goodman 1967). The top-down school of reading theory argues that readers fit the text into knowledge (cultural, syntactic, linguistic, historical) they already possess, then check back when new or unexpected information appears.

3. The **interactive school** of theorists – which most researchers currently endorse – argues that both top-down and bottom-up processes are occurring, either alternately or at the same time. These theorists describe a process that moves both bottom-up and top-down, depending on the type of text as well as on the reader's background knowledge, language proficiency level, motivation, strategy use, and culturally shaped beliefs about the reading. Two books, Barnett's *More than Meets the Eye* (1989) and the collection of essays *Interactive Approaches to Second Language Reading* (Carrell, Devine, & Eskey 1988), describe the interactive process in detail and provide useful resources to the reading teacher.

These theoretical models are rather abstract. Perhaps the following example will help to make the issues in this interaction between text and reader more concrete. Look at these sentences from the personal note (E. Tudor 1992) that we examined in Exercise 1.3:

> This was great! Thank you very much! I want my own copy – next time we go to Borders.
>
> Also – ordering from Penny's Tall, I finally found a pair of slacks that actually fit! I don't believe it!
>
> I am eternally grateful to you for these two discoveries.

This note demands some complicated interaction between the text and the reader. First, the reader will use some top-down strategies to figure out that the item the note refers to as "great" is something that can have copies. That leads the reader to think it is more likely a recording or book than an article of clothing or food. A reader, using only bottom-up strategies, could conclude that since the word "Borders" is capitalized it probably refers to the name of a place. Putting together these interactions, the reader could safely assume that something was borrowed, is now being returned, and the borrower also hopes to get a copy of it at a place called Borders. The next sentence demands similar interactions. If the writer has "finally" found some slacks that fit from "Penny's Tall," the reader may assume that this note-writer is tall. However, the text does not directly state all that information, and L2/FL readers, indeed even L1 readers, not familiar with J. C. Penny stores will have difficulty comprehending this text even when using all three models of reading.

Reading teachers need to develop the ability to analyze top-down and bottom-up components of the reading process. Understanding how you read and how your reading process may differ from others in your class is part of your preparation for teaching reading. By beginning with your own reading processes and understanding how they operate, you will eventually be able to anticipate the types of processes and potential problems that your students will experience.

Expanding your knowledge

Using the strategies listed on page 16, interview a student from another class (not yours). Find out how many of those strategies that student uses, or may use, when reading.

Chapter highlights

Understanding reading means understanding the way the reader acts, what the reader brings to the text, what strategies the reader uses, what assumptions the reader has about reading, and how reading texts can vary due to language and organization of information.

1. *The reader.* Each reader is unique – a sum of life experiences (from the family, community, school, society, and culture). Readers may differ in how they use their background knowledge due to individual differences.
2. *The text.* Most readers have an extraordinary amount of information about different types of texts: where they come from, what features each type of text typically exhibits, and how texts can differ due to language considerations (organization of information, grammar, cohesion, vocabulary).
3. *Interaction between reader and text.* Readers bring to each text areas of knowledge (content, formal, and linguistic schemata plus reading strat-

egies) that are crucial in shaping what happens in the reading process. While the text remains the same during each reading of it, the information the reader brings to that text fluctuates as comprehension grows; thus, the interaction between reader and text is constantly changing.

4. *Models of reading.* Top-down, bottom-up, and interactive are the three models of reading that have been recognized and researched. Most experts accept some version of the interactive model as the best description of the reading process.

2 Factors that influence reading in an L2/FL

Research into the nature of the reading process is
research into the unobservable . . .
– Christopher Candlin (1984: ix)

Our investigation of the reading process in Chapter 1 focused on the nature of reading in the native language. Although reading in the L1 shares numerous important basic elements with reading in a second or foreign language, the processes also differ significantly. This chapter examines those differences and investigates the key factors that influence L2/FL reading. Through an awareness of your own experiences, a consideration of the research conducted by others, and a sensitivity to the kinds of reading problems that L2/FL readers encounter, you will prepare yourself to teach L2/FL reading. Even without formally studying a second or foreign language, most people have had some exposure to other languages. The first exercise asks you to extract all that you can from your formal or informal past exposure.

Exercise 2.1   Recalling your knowledge

1. Describe briefly in your Teaching Portfolio a clear memory that you have of reading something in an L2/FL and realizing for the first time it was easy.
2. In a new paragraph describe how you feel when you read in an L2/FL. Compare reading in an L2/FL with reading in your L1. Do you feel tense, uncertain, somewhat hesitant, excited, pleased, powerful (from having access to another language), intellectually stimulated, relaxed? Use as many descriptive adjectives as you can.
3. Having described your experiences and your feelings, set up a page in your Teaching Portfolio with two columns. Label one column "Reading in L1," and the other "Reading in L2/FL." Begin by listing some factual information in these two columns: When did you begin to read in your L1 and in the L2/FL? How much vocabulary did you have before you began to read? What kinds of texts did you read first? How much support did you have for reading in that language? Add these facts to your L1 and L2/FL columns.

Having completed all the steps in Exercise 2.1, you will have a more conscious and accessible picture of your own L2/FL reading, an understanding of its elements, and a recognition of your own perspective on L2/FL reading. Perhaps you came up with some items similar to those identified by Grabe (1988: 57–8). He noted a variety of conditions that may influence the L2 reading of second language readers: Some are illiterate in their first language, some have little experience reading for academic purposes, some may not transfer abilities from their L1 to the L2, some must struggle with enormous differences in the writing systems of the two languages, and most try to read texts that are beyond their level of L2 proficiency.

Although research on reading acquisition since the mid-1970s has clarified the nature of L2/FL reading, questions still remain about how people learn to read, both in their L1 and in an L2/FL. Moreover, in a number of areas the studies have produced contradictory results. For example, some studies show that reading proficiency in an L1 has little influence on reading proficiency in an L2/FL; others show that there is a correlation between the two.

L2/FL readers, like L1 readers, share certain characteristics despite individual differences. Teachers may have some ideas about the shared characteristics based on their own close observations or based on their own culturally conditioned beliefs about the nature of the reading process. One of our students, a Chinese studying in the United States, gave us a particularly apt description of what reading English as an L2 is like.

STUDENT NARRATIVE

Let's talk about it this way. Let's say the words are the construction materials, like bricks, and the passage is the project. So, when I read Chinese, I feel there is somewhere in my nervous system . . . there are many blanks. These blanks are molded in certain ways, so that as soon as those ideas come in they fit into those blanks. But for English I don't have as many of those things. It's a process. I have to first build a mold, then, for the idea to stay. So I think that, that takes a longer time. So the result could be that, the result is that the reading of English is not as fresh as the reading of Chinese after the same amount of time.

A Chinese student in the U.S.A.

Teachers need to understand their students' reading behaviors and be able to help students understand those behaviors as well. Textbooks and materials designed for the L2 reading class, however, seldom detail the kinds of reading behaviors teachers might observe in class, much less explain the causes for those behaviors. Skilled teachers have to be careful observers and need to know as much as possible about the linguistic and educational backgrounds of their students. Sometimes teachers have to guess or to make assumptions. Even though the epigraph to this chapter reminds us that the reading process is "unobservable," research on the process of reading in an L2/FL provides us with some hypotheses about the factors that influence L2/FL reading.

Grabe (1991) identifies some of those factors in an article that surveys research on reading in a second language since 1970. He notes that students begin reading in an L2 with a different knowledge base than they had when starting to read in their L1. Most L1 readers know several thousand words before they begin to read, and they have some ability to handle the basic grammar of their own language. L2 readers have neither of those advantages. Grabe also notes that older beginning L2 readers have advantages over beginning L1 students, including more world knowledge, more highly developed cognitive abilities, the ability to use metacognitive strategies, and frequently more motivation (1991: 386–7).

Categorizing these factors makes them easier to remember and easier to recognize in student behavior. Some researchers develop overarching categories to describe them. Grabe (1991: 386), for example, identifies three: "L2 acquisition and training background differences, language processing differences, and social context differences." Scarcella and Oxford (1992), using the communicative competence framework of Canale and Swain (1980), discuss four areas: **grammatical competence** (knowledge of grammar), **sociolinguistic competence** (ability to use language appropriately in various social contexts), **discourse competence** (knowledge of acceptable patterns in written and spoken language), and **strategic competence** (ability to use a variety of language strategies to communicate successfully). Using current authorities on this topic (Alderson 1984; Grabe 1986, 1991; Scarcella & Oxford 1992), we have compiled a list of factors that influence reading in an L2/FL:

- Cognitive development and cognitive style orientation at the time of beginning L2/FL study
- Language proficiency in the L1
- Metacognitive knowledge of L1 structure, grammar, and syntax
- Language proficiency in an L2/FL
- Degree of difference between the L1 and an L2/FL (writing systems, rhetorical structures, appropriate strategies)

- Cultural orientation
    attitudes toward text and purpose for reading
    types of reading skills and strategies used in the L1
    types of reading skills and strategies used or appropriate in the L2/FL
    beliefs about the reading process (use of inference, memorization, nature of comprehension)
    knowledge of text types in the L1 (formal schemata)
    background knowledge (content schemata)

The research already completed on these factors encompasses numerous books and articles – far more than we can possibly survey here. We can begin, nevertheless, with a brief description of the factors, encourage you to compare these descriptions with your own experience, and provide you with references to the relevant research.

Cognitive development and style orientation

The best age to begin learning an L2/FL is part of an ongoing debate over the critical period of language acquisition. Reading teachers, however, have little control over when students begin to study an L2/FL. Likewise, cognitive, or mental, development levels at the time of beginning L2/FL study are beyond teachers' control. Both, however, are factors that may influence all the others on the list. The learning strategies of the 6-year-old who begins to study an L2/FL and those of a 20-year-old are quite different. Their L1 reading levels, world knowledge, reading strategies acquired in the L1, and most other aspects of the reading process will have been influenced by this difference. Hatch (1983) argues that these different factors related to the age of the learner can influence the success of language learning, and Segalowitz (1986) hypothesizes that L1 and L2 reading use different underlying cognitive processes. Thus all statements about the factors that shape L2/FL reading have to be considered in relationship to the age and L1 language level when the reader began the study of the L2/FL.

Somewhat less understood, but increasingly acknowledged and examined, is the issue of learning style, also called cognitive style orientation. Each person brings a preferred style, whether consciously or unconsciously, to the learning process. For example, the reflective learner tends to think about new information and process it carefully before going on to the next task. In contrast, a risk taker might make a guess and plunge into a new task without much reflection. In another style distinction, a field-dependent learner would tend to see contexts and relationships better than a field-independent learner, who would be able to pick out details but miss the larger context. The degree of ambiguity a learner will tolerate constitutes yet another style difference. H. D. Brown (1987) discusses learning styles in detail, and Reid's (1995) collection of essays on learning styles is a complete reference on the topic. Most learners have style orientation preferences for sensory input as well, preferring visual or auditory or kinesethetic modes (Scarcella & Oxford 1992).

The influence of cultural training on readers' strategies, both in the L1 and the L2/FL, is another major area of investigation. Readers from writing systems that differ from the left-to-right orientation of English, such as Arabic and Chinese, have an obvious adjustment to make (Hewett 1990).

Recognizing various cognitive style differences, seeing when students are using inappropriate strategies, and helping students adjust are all the reading teacher's tasks. The student whose style has always been to translate every word in a text will have a difficult time adjusting to skimming and scanning exercises. This same student may have a low tolerance for dealing with ambiguity in the meaning of a text. Whereas some may read through a passage and try to construct a meaning for it, the student with low tolerance for uncertainty will need to stop, look up words, ask questions, or get help (see Ehrman & Oxford 1990; Ely 1989).

Hewett (1990: 82) asserts that "the idea that individuals must be flexible in their cognitive style is a compelling one," even though there is not yet enough strong empirical evidence to support the idea. Few people become specialists on cognitive development or cognitive style, but the thoughtful teacher can become sensitive to this factor, recognize it when it appears in reading behavior, and help students modify their style or at least recognize how their cognitive style shapes the way they deal with a text.

Reading performance and competence in the L1

The level of reading proficiency that a reader has in the L1 also appears to be a factor in the development of L2/FL reading skills. Although the current research is far from definitive, a consensus holds that the skilled L1 reader has the potential (not always realized) for using L1 skills to enhance L2/FL reading. Royer and Carlo (1991) conclude that there is a transfer of reading skills from the L1 to an L2 and that teaching reading skills in the native language may facilitate the transfer. In other words, the more a person has learned to be a flexible, adaptable, questioning, comprehension-monitoring reader in the L1, the more likely it is that the same person will be an adaptable, questioning, and comprehension-monitoring reader in an L2/FL. The unskilled L1 reader, or the preliterate L2/FL language learner, clearly does not have that ability. Indeed the unskilled reader, like the student in the following narrative, may actually improve *L1* reading skills by having thorough training and increased awareness of reading processes in the L2/ FL. We asked this Japanese student if coming to the United States had changed his reading in Japanese.

STUDENT NARRATIVE

Ah, quitely changed! Yes, because I tried to read all sentences when I was in Japan, and I tried to catch all the meaning – every sentence or newspaper, or some other materials. I came here and I studied about how to read, how to read fast, so I tried to read in Japanese, very fast, to catch only the main sentence or main topics: So my speed of reading has become very fast.

A Japanese student in the U.S.A.

This student's comment illustrates that L1 competency is not the only factor in L2/FL reading.

Competence indicates a conscious understanding of language rules that govern language production; **performance** is the ability to produce language (Ellis 1986: 5). Performance is influenced by language situation. For example, the language a student displays in class in hastily answering a question may not illustrate the student's language competence or knowledge of rules. Given the opportunity to write out the answer, the same student might correct oral performance errors. Heath (1993) makes a powerful argument for the use of drama with L2 students, showing that community theater drama groups that were engaged in writing and producing their own scripts elicited from learners a much higher level of language performance than teachers usually get from students.

Metacognitive knowledge

In contrast to L1 **proficiency,** which constitutes the level of the student's language production and understanding in the L1, **metacognitive knowledge** consists of the student's ability to discuss, describe, give rules for, and comment on L1 language use. A 6-year-old learning to read in his L1 has a rather sophisticated but unconscious grasp of the syntax, pronunciation, and vocabulary of his own language – considerable proficiency but limited metacognitive knowledge.[1] If that child also begins to study an L2/FL, the language teacher cannot use complex grammatical explanations and linguistic terminology. A 25-year-old college graduate, however, may have a

1 In order to avoid such awkwardness as "s/he" or "he or she," we have chosen to refer to individual teachers with the feminine gender and individual students with the masculine gender.

good knowledge of grammar structures and other formal aspects of his native language – good proficiency and good metacognitive knowledge – that the L2/FL teacher may depend upon for making comparisons and for enhancing the learning process (see Devine 1993). This ability, moreover, is also shaped by cultural values, since some cultures devote relatively little study to the structure, grammar, and rules of their own language. Since learning an L2/FL often includes instruction in the grammar, structure, and rules of the new language, it is likely that those with a solid metacognitive knowledge of the structure of their own language will better apply such linguistic knowledge in L2/FL learning and reading.

Knowledge of language structures is only part of the issue, however, since the level of competency in the L1 may also be a factor. That level, sometimes called *threshold* or *ceiling* (Alderson 1984; Clarke 1980) or *underlying proficiency threshold* (Cumming 1981) may be the key to the amount of transfer that occurs. The factors that influence reading are – like reading itself – interactive. One series of texts for teaching ESL uses the overarching image of a tapestry to describe the language learning process (Scarcella & Oxford 1992). Like a tapestry, the process demands that many strands be woven together. The teacher needs to be able to pick out those different strands and see the relationships among them all.

L2/FL language proficiency

L2 language proficiency is another strong factor in L2 reading. In a well-known article published in 1980, Clarke argues that weaknesses in L2 language competence can "short-circuit" reading performance. Clarke maintains that there must be a basic level of L2 proficiency for the reading of any text, and that level – the threshold – varies according to the difficulty of the text. Indeed, many teachers and researchers would agree with Alderson that L2/FL readers "will not be able to read as well in the foreign language as in their first language until they have reached a threshold level of competence in that foreign language" (1984: 19). Devine's study of general language ability and second language reading provides an overview of the "hypothesis that L2 reading problems are due to inadequate knowledge of the target language" (1988b: 262–3).

L2/FL language proficiency influences the teacher's selection of materials for the reading classroom. Although it is important to challenge students and make sure that they continue to learn about the reading process (as well as about the content of the material they are reading), it is also important to avoid the frustration and despair that arise from constantly being required to tackle L2/FL reading texts that are far beyond one's language competence.

Degree of difference between the L1 and the L2/FL

The differences between the writing systems and rhetorical structures of the native language and the target language may be another factor in L2/FL reading. Orthographic systems vary widely, and some systems include strong aesthetic elements – for example, Chinese calligraphy is not only a communication tool but is also one of the most highly respected arts in that culture. Readers who use basically the same alphabet or writing systems in their L1 as they are learning to use in the L2/FL will have less to learn and be able to begin reading faster. Conversely, readers switching from a system with a limited number of symbols to a system with abundant characters will need more time to become proficient. Wallace (1992: 21–2) explains that "languages may be so different in the way they represent meaning in their written form that there is, arguably, no generalization from the first to the target language." It is prudent to keep in mind Haynes's (1989: iii) argument that mastery of the L2 writing system "is both harder and more important to L2 reading success than existing theory and research would suggest."

Exercise 2.2   Building your knowledge

Rank the first five factors which we have presented in this chapter in order of their importance in your own L2/FL reading, most important to least important. In your Teaching Portfolio write a sentence or two about what made one factor most important and what made one least important. Bring these to class for discussion with others.

Cultural orientation

Hard to identify, elusive to trace, complex, and subject to individual differences, cultural orientation influences a wide variety of reading behaviors, beliefs, and performance. The avalanche of students and observations that have examined the power of cultural orientation have sometimes produced conflicting results on specific experiments, but there is still agreement that cultural orientation is important. In fact, cultural differences are pervasive, and they constitute the largest category of factors that influence L2/FL reading. Generally speaking, the areas of L2/FL reading most influenced by cultural orientation fall into six groups.

Cultural orientation and attitudes toward text and purpose for reading

Cultural orientation shapes attitudes toward text. Those who learn to read by reading sacred scriptures, such as the Koran or Bible, absorb the belief that text equals Truth. Those who learn to read by having stories read to them and being asked to imagine, question, interpret, and answer queries develop the kinds of academic reading skills that are expected in an American university. Those whose culture emphasizes a more oral or storytelling tradition may use a text as the basis for creative or playful expression, but they may not share many of the assumptions about interacting with the text that will make them successful in school settings (Heath 1983).

Cultural orientation and the types of reading skills and strategies used in the L1

Each reader brings an individualized package of personal experiences, beliefs, cultural training, and educational experiences to the reading process. Certainly not all readers will have developed the same reading strategies, and the strategies they do develop will be partially (or substantially) dependent on the values and attitudes of their culture toward reading and toward reading in an L2/FL. Those who were preparing for a liberal arts college during their last years of secondary school may have had more emphasis on analysis, scanning for information, and reading academic texts, but little exposure to scientific works. Those who were headed for technical training or who wanted to move directly into scientific fields may have focused on math and science courses and had no experience with a variety of literary works. Although schools in the United States tend to keep a variety of courses in the college preparatory curriculum, European and other systems allow for early specialization. Even within the same culture different school systems may or may not emphasize tasks like recognizing main and minor points, understanding rhetorical structures and discourse patterns, outlining, and inferencing (see Field & Aebersold 1990). This student from Beijing reminds us that even students with high levels of academic training from other cultures may not be conscious of their use of various reading skills and strategies.

STUDENT NARRATIVE

We didn't have a lot of reading activities in the classroom. The teacher just asked us to read a paragraph out loud in class or sometimes silently in class, but we didn't have a lot of activities. Then, sometimes, the teacher asked

questions or chose some vocabulary and asked us to make a sentence with those
words. Usually we would sit at our desks and listen to the teacher. Sometimes
we may ask or answer a question. We didn't have activities to do. Our study
system in our country is different from here [U.S.A.].

– (Helen) Huailin Zhang, People's Republic of China

An even more obvious example of how culture may influence L1 strategies and skills is adults with little formal education who immigrate to
another country and begin to read in an L2/FL. Such adults may have done
very little reading in their own cultures and not be aware of language issues,
reading skills, or related matters. Some cultures encourage thinking about
these unconscious processes and try to make them conscious; others do not.
A study by Pritchard (1990: 2–3) shows that "cultural schemata . . . appear
to influence readers' processing strategies and the level of comprehension
they achieve." It is, therefore, the reading teacher who needs to watch for
and identify these influences, then make them clear to the students.

Cultural orientation and types of reading skills and strategies appropriate in the L2/FL

Demands for reading in another language vary widely. The skills and
strategies needed for success in an academic situation may include such
activities as being able to read long texts efficiently, being able to infer
meaning, being able to interpret and understand ambiguity, and being able
to recognize implicit meaning in texts. Survival reading skills necessary for
immigrants would include processing different types of texts, such as job
applications, checkbooks, forms, and other informational items. Moreover,
these tasks depend on the factors discussed earlier – age, L1 proficiency,
L2/FL proficiency, and the reading skills and strategies already learned in
the L1 – as well as factors that follow. With experience and careful observation, reading teachers are able to recognize these factors. Recent research is
beginning to identify these influences explicitly, even to the point of giving
a detailed analysis of the way culture influences specific reading strategies
like scanning, selecting, predicting, searching, regressing, and decoding
(Hewett 1990).

Both limited access to texts and different cultural attitudes about what
types of reading are important will shape the strategies that beginning
readers use and develop. A child whose classes in reading consist of reciting passages of a religious text, such as the Koran or the Bible, may be
especially proficient at decoding skills. A child who reads aloud by reciting
the eight syllable texts that Chinese students read in elementary school will
seldom practice the strategies of skimming or scanning. The children who

are questioned, at home and at school, about the characters, plots, and meanings of all the stories they read will probably learn to use predicting and selecting strategies. The emphasis on developing a variety of reading strategies seems to be a particularly North American and British cultural trait. One study that examined American and Palauan students found that American students used a "wider range" of strategies, used them more often, and were more willing to use strategies that required some flexibility and risk taking (Pritchard 1990: 289).

Cultural orientation and beliefs about the reading process

The pervasive influence of culture shapes teaching and leads to the learning patterns illustrated in the preceding paragraph. If teachers believe that learning many reading strategies is important, they will teach accordingly. Teachers who believe that memorization of texts and recitations of passages are important will instruct with that goal in mind. When teaching in China and Iran, we often saw some of our students walking around athletic tracks or pacing the flat roofs of houses to practice their reading assignments aloud before going to class. International students who come to study in the United States are often surprised at the lengthy reading assignments they receive in a history or literature class; American students abroad are amazed at the level of detail that is expected of them in university settings. In some cultures comprehension means the ability to explain the grammar and structure of a page of text; in others it means the ability to summarize the thesis and argument of a whole book in a few sentences. These cultural beliefs and attitudes about reading are transmitted by teachers in the early years of the education process and stay with students for a long time; to some extent, these attitudes are also transferred to the L2/FL reading process.

Cultural orientation and knowledge of text types in the L1 (formal schemata)

In the years since Kaplan's (1966) article on cultural thought patterns (which he revisited in 1987), researchers in anthropology, psychology, and linguistics have examined the types and organizations of text in different cultures. That work forms the basis for what is now called **contrastive rhetoric** (see Connor 1995 for a survey of research on this issue). Two studies argue strongly that beliefs about the organization and development of "good" writing are shaped by culture (Li 1992; Purves & Hawisher 1986). Those beliefs have an impact on the way students perceive the text they are reading. They value, for example, organizational structures common in the writing of their own cultures, evidenced by American students' impatience with French authors' theoretical or abstract essays that lack the details and development more familiar in the American essay tradition. Carrell (1982) found evidence of these beliefs about formal schema in L2 comprehension. For the reading teacher with a multinational group of students, understanding the text structures most common to all her students may be an impossible task. But teachers *can* be explicit about the structures of the materials the students are reading in the L2/FL lesson. Through in-class dialogue students can become aware of culturally shaped expectations about text. (Chapter 8 elaborates on teaching methods that address cultural differences and expectations in fiction.)

Cultural orientation and background knowledge (content schemata)

The impact of cultural orientation on background knowledge is perhaps the most obvious of the six influences examined here, and it has been discussed thoroughly by Barnett (1989), Carrell and Eisterhold (1983), Johnson (1982), Pritchard (1990), and Stefensen and Joag-Dev (1984). As a learner of an L2/FL, you may have struggled with this problem as well.

Steffensen and Joag-Dev (1984) conducted a study using two lengthy descriptions, both written in English, of weddings. One was a description of an American wedding, the other of an Indian (subcontinent) wedding. Both the Indian students, for whom English was an L2, and the American students, for whom English was the L1, read the descriptions and were later asked to recall each wedding. The hypothesis that readers would comprehend the texts about their own cultures more accurately than the other text was elegantly supported. The following sentences are a short excerpt from the Indian wedding text:

There must have been about five hundred people at the wedding feast. Since only fifty people could be seated at one time, it went on for a long time. The first batch with the groom and important in-laws started at noon. Since we were the bride's party, and were close friends besides, we ate in the last batch with her parents. We barely had time to get dressed for the reception. (Steffensen & Joag-Dev 1984: 58)

An American student was able to recall much of this part of the description. However, his own knowledge of American wedding culture crept into his recall of this part of the Indian wedding feast.

And the husband and bride and the in-laws ate first and we ate last since we're such good friends of them (whaat?). (p. 59)

The parenthetical "whaaat?" indicates that he is confused about this part. Although the words were easy to understand, the unfamiliar cultural protocol of an Indian wedding made the passage more difficult for him to remember.

Although all the variables and factors surrounding the issues of how culture shapes background knowledge and influences reading – both in the L1 and an L2/FL – are not fully understood, there is agreement among researchers that background knowledge is an important, thought not overriding, factor. Roller (1990) argues that background information is most helpful with a "moderately unfamiliar" text. The teacher's task is to be *aware* of the amount of background information necessary, to make the information available, and to see that the students are able to use that information.

Despite the emphasis in this chapter on the differences between L1 and L2/FL reading, recognizing the similarities between the two is equally as important. Haynes (1989), for example, illustrates that Chinese and American students have the same sensitivity to sequencing of letters in nonsense words. Some of the basic processes of reading do appear to be similar in all languages, and students' perceptions of their problems with reading are similar in many languages. Readers, especially L2/FL readers, are equipped to understand some of those similarities. When teachers see reading behavior that creates problems, they need to ask the students questions about what they do as they read. Even teachers who are not authorities on reading *can* trust themselves – having internalized the principles we present here – to make comparisons, ask questions, discover hidden assumptions, make issues conscious, and provide an environment in which students will learn and improve.

Expanding your knowledge

1. Interview an L2 reader (not one of your classmates) in order to learn about another person's L2 reading history: when he or she learned to read, attitudes toward reading, and the value of reading in that person's life. Use questions based on the experiences that you recalled in Exercise 2.1 at the beginning of this chapter. For example: What are your memories of first learning to read another language? What positive memories do you have of L2 reading? What people were influential in helping you learn to read in an L2? What is the place of L2 reading in your life today? Make careful notes on the interview and then compare them with your own answers in Exercise 2.1.

2. Pick one of the factors that influence reading in an L2/FL discussed in this chapter. Develop a list of questions that you can use to interview an L2/FL reading teacher. Interview the teacher, being sure to ask for examples or stories from personal experience in the classroom that illustrate this factor.

Chapter highlights

Teachers of reading in an L2/FL must understand the factors that influence their students' reading processes. Even though there are a number of factors, and their influences are not always fully understood or documented, L2/FL reading teachers who can recognize these factors at work are better equipped to help their students.

1. *Cognitive development and style orientation.* The age and level of cognitive development of L2/FL learners at the time they begin language study shapes their ability to grasp concepts, their willingness to use a variety of strategies, and their basic ways of approaching the text.
2. *Reading performance and competence in the L1.* Although the research is not yet definitive, there is agreement that those with higher levels of proficiency in the L2 are more able to transfer reading skills from their L1 to the L2, thus enhancing their L2 reading proficiency.
3. *Metacognitive knowledge.* Learners who are able to describe and discuss the features and rules of their own language appear to be more proficient at improving their L2 reading processes.
4. *L2/FL language proficiency.* The students' proficiency in the L2/FL is, perhaps, the greatest factor in L2 reading. Without certain threshold levels of L2 proficiency, reading does not improve. In addition, a careful assessment of the students' level is the teacher's first step in selecting reading materials for the class.
5. *Degree of difference between the L1 and the L2/FL.* It is generally true that the greater the differences between the native language and the target language (in writing systems, rhetorical conventions, and purposes for reading), the more difficult it is to acquire the target language and to become a proficient reader in it.
6. *Cultural orientation.* The most far-reaching and influential factors in L2/FL reading are those of cultural orientation. The students' attitudes toward text and purpose for reading, the types of reading skills and strategies they use in the L2, their beliefs about the reading process, their knowledge of text types in their L1 (formal schema), and their accumulated background knowledge (content schema) in the L2 are all major influences in their L2/FL reading.

3 *Designing the reading course*

> In language teaching, our methods and techniques have
> often failed to produce effective learning, however
> sound they may have appeared in theory. To discover
> why, we must study the learner.
>   – William Littlewood (1984: 1)

Many decisions and preparations need to be made before teachers actually step into the classroom. In this chapter we look at how to decide what to teach in an L2/FL reading course, or the course goals; how to structure the course in order to reach those goals, or the approach; and what considerations to keep in mind in selecting texts. The chapter closes with some initial considerations for a course evaluation plan and final course grade determination. The issues of assessment and evaluation are taken up again in Chapter 9.

Course goals

The most important information that teachers must have as they start to design a reading course is the **goals for the course** – the reading abilities that students should develop during the course. Teachers then use the goals to guide them as they decide about the structure of the course and about appropriate ways to evaluate the students' performance and thus the course's effectiveness. Goals are usually stated in a broad, general manner; they need not be long or complicated.

Exercise 3.1   Building your knowledge

Go back to the Introduction of this book and locate the statements that we used as our general goals for our students (you) in planning this book. How many are there? What are they?

Before developing reading goals, it is necessary to assess the needs of the students. J. D. Brown (1995: 37–8) identifies four groups that may be included in a needs analysis: the target group (those about whom information will be gathered), the audience (those using the information collected), the needs analysts (those gathering the information), and a resource group (those who provide further information about the target group). Although several groups may participate in determining the reading goals for a course, fundamentally, course goals must arise directly from students' needs, interests, and abilities.

Students' needs

Before goals can be written, teachers must consider what students will do with their L2 reading abilities. For instance, do they need to be able to read textbooks on other subjects, such as science or medicine? Do they need to be able to read newspapers or magazines? Do they need to be able to read literature? Do they need to be able to read schedules or forms? Do they need to be able to read letters or personal notes? In short, teachers should know why they are teaching reading to a particular group of students.

Because course goals need to be established well in advance of the first class meeting so that materials can be selected and course designs can be made, student needs as defined by teachers, administrators, and other groups are usually given greater weight than the needs defined by the students themselves. In addition, teachers are often more knowledgeable about what lies ahead for students academically than the students themselves are. However, since students who are involved in their own learning are better learners, teachers should and can include them in the process. Teachers always have some degree of flexibility to adjust and shape a course as it progresses. If feedback from students is collected throughout a course, the teacher can adjust the goals and activities selected to provide students with a meaningful and relevant course.

The most reliable way of finding out what students think they need is to ask them. A variety of ways can be used to collect information: questionnaires, individual interviews or oral reports, observations of small group discussions, and questions on quizzes or tests, to name a few.

One easy and useful way to collect information is a brief survey. **Surveys** usually consist of questions for students to answer briefly or an incomplete sentence that students must then finish. Surveys do not need to be long and complex in order to provide useful information. The level of language should vary according to the students' L2 proficiency. If students share a common L1, the survey could be done in that language for students at beginning and low levels. The following is an example of a survey that could be used with students at a low level of ESL/EFL proficiency.

1. Do you read anything in English now?
   a. If "yes," what do you read and why?
   b. If "no," what are you interested in reading in English?

2. What English reading materials are available to you?

Even if this survey were to come back with the answers "1. No 2. I don't know," a teacher would learn that this student did not have any established reasons for reading in English and had no awareness of what he might find to read in English. One of the first tasks this teacher faces is to build *with the student* a need or an interest to read materials in the L2/FL.

Assuming this response was typical for the class, an appropriate first assignment for these students might be to check local newsstands, book-stores, and libraries to see what is available in the L2/FL and where it can be found. This activity should produce some interest and excitement if the students are allowed to select texts according to their own interests. At this point the class is on its way to establishing its own purposes for reading. On the other hand, if students were to answer "Yes" to the survey questions, the teacher could begin immediately to build interest by asking students to elaborate on their needs, interests, and experiences. It is important that teachers involve students in establishing purposes for reading so that they understand why they are in a reading class and so that they make a genuine commitment to the reasons for reading.

By taking into account both teacher-perceived and student-contributed needs when planning reading goals, teachers and students work together to build a learning environment that is relevant to both. This environment optimizes the opportunity for learning. The more invested and involved students are in their learning, the more responsibility they will take for their learning.

Courses in which the students have some degree of control over what goes on in the course and how it occurs are considered to be **student-centered.** Courses in which the teacher has complete control are **teacher-centered.** Giving students some control over their learning process has many benefits: It makes them feel confident; it puts some of the decision making in their hands; it puts the responsibility for learning in their hands; and over the long term it builds independence and self-reliance so that they can read on their own without being dependent on teacher direction and supervision. It activates the students' own learning spirals.

Once the purposes for teaching reading are established, teachers can then begin to formulate goals for the reading course. **Goals** are broad, general statements about what students will achieve during the course. If a goal is expressed in specific terms, it is an **objective.** Objectives are specifically stated aims that teachers use in creating individual lesson plans. We examine objectives in more detail in Chapter 4.

Exercise 3.2   Building your knowledge

Read the following course description. Which sentences seem to state the goals for the students in this course? Identify three goals. Write them in your Teaching Portfolio.

Reading Course Description

The purpose of this 15-week course was to develop the students' ability and confidence to read a variety of real, nonsimplified texts in their L2/FL: academic textbooks, informative magazines, and short fiction stories. Academic texts were read for total comprehension while informational and fictional texts were read to whatever degree of comprehension satisfied the individual student. Throughout the course we did about a chapter a week in the textbook, which was a collection of chapters from various kinds of academic textbooks. There were reading exercises before, during, and after each reading text. Strategies for approaching the content of a text were developed. Vocabulary was dealt with in matching and paraphrase exercises at the end of the reading. Particularly complex grammar structures were examined one by one with opportunities for students to select their own sentences for class dissection. Each student completed the exercises for each chapter in the textbook, which were then checked either by the teacher or by the students in small groups.

In addition, students were assigned to a *Newsweek* reading group that met each week for the first 7 weeks of the course. At the beginning of the week they met to decide which article the group would read that week. Then they each read the article at home. At the second meeting, they again met with their group for about 15 minutes to discuss the article and ask any questions that they wished of the teacher. By the end of the week each student had to turn in a brief report (less than a handwritten page) to the teacher stating the main ideas of the article. These reports were read by the teacher for general comprehension, and no grammar or vocabulary was corrected. The teacher wrote responses on the reports that commented on personal experience, gave the teacher's opinions on the subject, etc. After half a term of this, the students were free to find their own magazines in the library. Each student read and wrote a report on his own, as an individual, turning in a copy of the article that he read along with his report.

Once every two weeks, the teacher brought in several copies of each of five different short stories and gave a brief summary of each story to the students at the beginning of class. Students could then choose which story they wanted to read at home. After they had read it, students were asked to make a brief oral summary on an audio cassette of what happened in the story and what their reaction to the story was. Midterm and final exams were given and the course grade was based on the results of those tests plus whether each student had completed the required number of written and oral reports.

Students' interests

We started this chapter by talking about needs (both teacher-perceived and student-contributed), but the reading survey introduced the issue of students' interests. It is possible that very few students have needs that motivate them to read in the L2/FL. However, they probably all have interests that could be used to propel them into reading in the L2/FL.

STUDENT NARRATIVE

When I was in college in my country, I tried to read fashion magazines, Vogue, Cosmopolitan. *They had a lot of information on beauty and skin care. I read an article, "Steps on How to Take Care of Your Skin." I bought a mask and some creams. Actually, my mother gave me something, like Clinique – with instructions. I wanted to know what to do but we couldn't understand the instructions! I still read those magazines here in the U.S.*

– Sung Hee Choi, Korea

Some students may have an established personal interest in certain topics and may like to read anything and everything that they can find on those topics. They probably already know a lot about the topic, but they want to know more. Thus a person who is interested in space exploration will automatically seek out articles on this topic when scanning the newspaper or perusing a magazine.

Another reason students are interested in certain topics is that the topic touches their lives in a personal way. An example of this is the interest that teenagers take in popular music and performers. They may become interested in that topic because their social peers are interested. They want to know what others around them know.

Another type of interest stems from the relevance a topic has to the larger community within which an individual functions. Americans have become focused on the connection between health and environment in recent decades as a result of being bombarded with information via magazines, newspapers, radio, television, and community meetings. To some degree readers' interest in this topic has been created for them. Readers have been made aware of issues that they might not choose to investigate on their own; thus, they recognize the need to become informed. An example would be the person who decides to give up smoking cigarettes because details of its harmful effects have been made available to the public.

The three types of interest (individual, peer group, community group) described in the preceding examples will occur to different degrees in different people. Degree of interest is an important factor in reading motivation. The more interested people are, the more they will persevere in reading. Intense interest motivates people to read materials that are beyond their range of language proficiency. It is important that students have some degree of interest in the materials they read.

Just as peer groups and communities can create interest on the part of readers, teachers, too, can create interest on the part of students. By using a number of activities and techniques (discussed in Chapter 4), teachers can create or heighten student interest in a topic before they read. By exposing students to new topics or new ideas about old topics, teachers can expand the bases of students' knowledge. Sometimes students are not interested in a topic until they know something about it.

STUDENT NARRATIVE

When I was in my country, I was aware that AIDS existed, but I didn't know much about it because there just isn't any information about it in public places. Since I took this course, I've learned a lot about it, especially from the readings I found. I'm really quite interested in it because it's a big problem and everybody needs to know about it. I went to the Art Fair last week and there was a lady there giving out information about it.

– Sung Hee Choi, Korea

Other times students may know something about the topic and think that they are not interested in it until prereading work in class has piqued their curiosity in some way. Being skilled at creating and heightening interest enables teachers to guide students toward topics that are important but that would not normally interest them.

A simple survey can be used to find out what topics students are interested in.

Exercise 3.3   Building your knowledge

Devise a simple survey that will investigate what topics your students might like to read about. Keep in mind that people are more likely to answer surveys when they can just check and circle answers. Of course, there should always be an opportunity for those who are inclined to give you their full opinion in writing to do so.

Surveys should be done periodically throughout the course to check on students' opinions about other things as well, such as quantity of work and techniques being used. They do not always need to be written – information can be collected orally as well.

TEACHER NARRATIVE

During the first meeting of an academically oriented ESL reading class for college students, I asked the students to introduce themselves and state what kind of books they read for pleasure in their native language. Almost half of the class did not read any books for pleasure at all! Since one of the goals of the course was for them to read unsimplified short stories in English that they had to go to the library and find themselves, I was apprehensive about how they would receive this assignment. On the basis of this informal, first-day, oral survey I decided to start them off on "pleasure" readings by providing them with short stories that I knew were short, humorous, and well within their language proficiency range. I continued to provide short stories until halfway through the term, when my mid-course survey on whether they wanted "more of, the same amount of, or less of" each type of reading showed that almost all of them felt the amount of short stories they were reading was "OK." From that point on, I sent them to the library to find and select their own short stories.

– Brenda Millett, U.S.A.

In addition to providing important information, opinion surveys reinforce the idea that students have some responsibility for their own learning. Using them throughout the course allows the monitoring of student thought on these matters as the course progresses. Students become more involved in the process when given the invitation (and the encouragement) to do so.

Students' language proficiency

The phrases "within their language proficiency range" or "beyond their language proficiency range" have specific meaning in a reading context. When students can understand enough of the text they are reading to make general sense of the message, they are reading **within their language proficiency range.** This means they may not know all of the facts and details, but they do understand the general topic, most of the main ideas, and several details.

When students try to read **beyond their language proficiency level,** they are overwhelmed. When a great deal of the vocabulary they are reading is unknown to them, they become frustrated. If the grammar structures of several consecutive sentences are long and complex, they get tired or lost, or both. If the topic written about is outside of their experience or base of knowledge, they are adrift on an unknown sea. When they have these feelings while reading, they may stop reading because they cannot understand the meaning of the text enough to satisfy their expectations, needs, or interests.

What degree of comprehension is necessary to motivate readers to read on? There is no fixed answer to this question. Other factors besides comprehension contribute to motivation. Readers who are very knowledgeable about the topic seem to tolerate a higher amount of unknown vocabulary and grammar because they have enough background knowledge of the topic to support their comprehension. Thus, those with more tolerance can read in the higher end of their range with more comfort than those with less tolerance can. Those with less topic knowledge will probably feel more comfortable when they are reading in the lower end of their range.

The parameters of students' language proficiency range are likely to vary even within one class. If students are placed in classes by their proficiency levels as demonstrated by tests, there should be a fair amount of overlap among their ranges. If, however, students are placed in a class because they have already completed one year of L2/FL study or they are in a certain grade, it is possible, even likely, that there will be greater differences among their ranges. An L2/FL classroom of this type is known as a multi-level classroom. It is a great challenge for teachers because it requires multiple lesson plans and a range of materials to address all the students. Indeed, different levels may need to study different skills at a given time. Planning for and teaching multilevel classes greatly increase the teacher's workload.

Approaches to teaching reading

Once course goals have been written, reading teachers need to decide what approach they will use to achieve their goals. **Approach** "refers to theories about the nature of language and language learning that serve as the source of practices and principles in language teaching" (Richards & Rodgers 1986: 16). Take a moment to clarify your own thoughts on how students improve reading in an L2/FL.

Exercise 3.4   Building your knowledge

1. Put a check in front of the sentences you agree with:
   _____ Students' L2/FL reading ability will improve greatly if they will read more than four texts a week.
   _____ Every L2/FL text needs to be completely and fully understood in order for students' reading comprehension to improve.
   _____ L2/FL reading ability improves when students read for real reasons: to get information to use for an argument, a report, to find out what is going on in the world.
   _____ Teachers know best which texts are appropriate for improving their students' reading.
   _____ Reading to get the general idea of an article or just the main ideas is sufficient to improve reading skills.
   _____ The quantity of reading is not as important as the quality of the comprehension of the text.
   _____ L2/FL readers should be able to select the texts that they read.

_____ Doing several language and comprehension exercises at the end of each reading greatly improves L2/FL reading ability.
2. Check your answers with those of your classmates. Discuss what each phrase you checked would mean for your class and the materials that you would need in order to teach reading that way. For example, if you selected the first sentence above, you might conclude that your students would need to read something for every class period, that they would need to read outside of class, that you would probably need more reading texts than those provided in a textbook, that you would not be able to require complete comprehension of each text read because there would not be enough time for them to read each text carefully enough to understand everything, and so on.

If you checked the first, third, fifth, and seventh statements and only those, you believe in a totally extensive approach to teaching reading. If you checked all the even-numbered statements and no others, you believe in a totally intensive approach. If you checked some of both, you probably feel most comfortable using activities that include both extensive and intensive approaches in your reading course.

An extensive approach

An **extensive approach** to teaching reading is based on the belief that when students read for general comprehension large quantities of texts of their own choosing, their ability to read will consequently improve. The emphasis in extensive reading courses is to use reading as a *means* to an end. In other words, reading is used to accomplish something else, such as a written summary, a written report, an oral report, a group discussion, a debate. In this type of course, students are usually given more freedom to choose reading materials that interest them and more responsibility in finding materials within their language proficiency range. The texts that they read may be completely of their own selection or to some extent selected by the teacher.

In an extensive reading course almost all of the reading is done outside of class, without peer support or teacher aid. The text is always to be read for comprehension of main ideas, not of every detail and word. The quantity of reading required of students each week prevents them from reading every text in depth, or from translating every text into their L1. Students are frequently asked to read more than one text on the same topic. The more texts they read on the same topic, the more they will understand because they will bring more background knowledge to each new text they read. Extensive readings are not generally used to teach or practice specific reading strategies or skills. Since students read authentic materials, the texts do not have accompanying reading exercises.

Since the idea of designing an entire reading course according to the extensive approach is still relatively uncommon, we asked a teacher who has taught such a course to write about her observations. Although she was an experienced L2/FL teacher, the extensive approach was a new experience for her.

TEACHER NARRATIVE

I've used the extensive reading approach two consecutive terms with a group of about 20 advanced ESL readers who would continue on to take regular college classes in an American university. Basically, the approach appeals to me for two reasons: It places the responsibility for developing their reading ability squarely on the shoulders of the students and it pushes them to read and make sense of a larger quantity of reading material than intensive ESL reading classes do. I sometimes feel that students are not asked to do the amount of reading that they will have to do in academic classes and thus they are not well prepared to do what they will need to do after they leave this class. An extensive approach also allows the students a greater degree of choice regarding which topics they read, and it encourages them to be more aware of what's available to be read in their surroundings.

This approach requires the teacher to be organized and stay current with the students' reading reports on a weekly or biweekly basis. I had to read, or skim, every text that each student read during the week in order to be able to evaluate their short written report of each text. Sometimes different students selected the same text and each week some students read short articles while others read long ones. However, it's a lot of work and if you get behind, it's impossible to catch up. Occasionally, I had to encourage students to read texts from a different source – one student continually read articles from the student newspaper. I always try to guide them a little towards different and more challenging materials to stretch them a bit. I also had to encourage some students to read texts whose language level was more appropriate to their range. I had one student who wanted to read the novel Shogun *in English, because he had read it in his native language! We negotiated and settled on him reading one long chapter. And, of course, there were a few students who couldn't quite organize or discipline themselves to meet deadlines. Students need to learn responsibility and this approach requires it, whereas in other approaches, the responsibility lies more with the teacher.*

The data I collected from students on their responses to this approach told me they were positive about the choice factor but not about the reading load. Because I saw each student individually for student conferences throughout the term, I got a fair amount of anecdotal feedback as well. I saw some of them the following term around campus, and they told me that they now understood why I had required them to read so much. Through the term I saw them grow in confidence as they successfully handled the work.

– Cathy Day, U.S.A

An intensive approach

In an **intensive approach** to reading – which currently reigns in most L2/
FL classrooms and books – reading the text is treated as an end in itself.
Each text is read carefully and thoroughly for maximum comprehension.
Teachers provide direction and help before, sometimes during, and after
reading. Students do many exercises that require them to work in depth
with various selected aspects of the text. Exercises can cover a broad range
of reading skills:

- Looking at different levels of comprehension (main ideas vs. details)
- Understanding what is implied versus what is stated
- Discussing what inferences a reader can reasonably make
- Determining the order in which information is presented and its effect on
  the message
- Identifying words that connect one idea to another
- Identifying words that signal movement from one section to another
- Noting which words indicate authors' certainty about the information
  presented

Exercise 3.5   Building your knowledge

Now that you have an understanding of the activities associated with both
approaches, look at the excerpts from the tables of contents from two
different advanced ESOL reading textbooks below. One exhibits an extensive approach, the other an intensive approach. Which is which?

Exercise 3.6   Building your knowledge

The complete tables of contents from each textbook are in Appendices A and B of this chapter. Examine each one carefully; make a list of the types of activities that each book asks the students to do.

It is possible – and common – to use a combination of both approaches in a reading course. For example, teachers who use a mostly intensive approach to teaching reading may ask students to read texts of their own selection and write a report on them, or to read something in the newspaper each week and report orally on it at the beginning of the class. Teachers who use a mostly extensive approach may have all the students read the same teacher-supplied texts from time to time so that they can discuss the same topic together or can learn how to write a report or make an outline.

Exercise 3.7   Building your knowledge

1. Reread the course description in Exercise 3.2. Examine which parts exhibit an extensive approach and which parts exhibit an intensive approach. Discuss your answers with your classmates.
2. What changes could be made in the course to make it (1) more extensive in nature? (2) more intensive in nature?

All of the examples given here of extensive and intensive reading courses assume a very high level of L2/FL proficiency. It is easier to use an extensive approach when the students have easy access to L2/FL texts in the culture at large. It is, however, possible to design an extensive reading course for students at intermediate or high intermediate levels of L2/FL proficiency; it requires a specialized library in the students' classroom, or the school, or the community, and some adjustment in the follow-up tasks that students do. Students need to have access to texts that are within their language proficiency range – texts that they can understand to a great degree without extensive use of a dictionary. In order to summarize the texts, they need to have a reasonable degree of comprehension. If students are asked to read texts beyond their language proficiency range, then the follow-up tasks for which they are reading should be adjusted to demand less of their comprehension – for example, students could be asked to present only the gist of the article or one prominent piece of information.

Content-based instruction (CBI) is a recent development in course designs. The approach underlying this design is the belief that students can improve their L2 language skills, including reading ability, while studying content material (e.g., texts on history, biology, computers, etc.). This course design is not discussed further in this book as the reading activities that teachers might select to use in the CBI classroom are the same as those used in the intensive reading course. The difference is that the CBI classroom focuses more attention on systematically presenting the content than the language skills (see Brinton, Snow, & Wesche 1989; Cantoni-Harvey 1987).

Selecting appropriate materials

When the course goals have been written and the dominant approach decided, the next task facing the teacher is to select appropriate materials. They may be expository, narrative, fiction – whatever type is necessary, as long as they fulfill course goals. Teachers using a mostly extensive approach in the reading course need to make sure that students have a readily available and sufficiently large supply of texts at their levels of language proficiency. Those using an intensive approach need to choose reading textbooks that provide the types of readings and reading skills they wish to cover in the course. Teachers using a mixed approach need to have both kinds of materials on hand.

Fiction or nonfiction texts?

The technical differences between fiction and nonfiction are not central to our purposes here. We can be content with the accepted distinction that **nonfiction** centers on the presentation of information. **Fiction,** on the other hand, centers on telling a story, a sequence of imagined events involving (usually) human characters whose emotional, physical, psychological, and spiritual experiences in life create empathy or response in the reader. People read informational texts, such as newspapers, magazines, instructional manuals, and reports, on a regular basis. Reading such texts is a life skill, whereas the need to read such nonfiction texts as textbooks and scholarly articles may end when formal education is finished. In contrast, texts that relate stories may not be a part of people's regular reading. Fiction can serve two important functions in the L2/FL classroom: to teach language and to introduce or reinforce human (social, cultural, political, emotional, economic, etc.) themes and issues in the classroom.

What is central to the role of L2/FL reading teachers is that these two types of texts often demand different kinds of focus, involving different teaching methods. Nonfiction works demand that readers understand the main points of the information the author is presenting. Fiction demands that readers follow the sequence of events, understand what happened to each person, understand the personalities (problems, emotions, ideas) of the main characters, and see what message or theme the author is illustrating through the people and events in the work. The way language is manipulated, while often sophisticated and subtle in both nonfiction and fiction, presents a wider range of challenges in fiction. (See Chapter 8 for further discussion on the use of literary texts in the L2/FL classroom.)

Authentic or modified texts?

There is an ongoing debate in the L2/FL profession about whether or not reading materials should be authentic. **Materials** in this case refers not only to types of texts found in magazines and books, but also to any item from everyday life that conveys meaning through written language, such as schedules, application forms, billboards, advertisements, labels, and so on. The texts in this latter category are generally referred to as **realia. Authentic materials** are taken directly from L1 sources and are not changed in any way before they are used in the classroom. Articles or advertisements from an L2/FL newspaper and train schedules are examples of authentic materials.

When a teacher creates a menu rather than using a real menu from a restaurant, the class is using simulated authentic materials that mimic the content, format, and language of authentic realia and are created solely for use in the L2/FL classroom. The teacher-created menu may not be quite as colloquial or complex as an authentic menu would be. The term **modified** is generally used to describe traditional text materials in which the language of the text and sometimes the cultural references have been changed so that L2/FL students can more readily comprehend them. Texts can be modified in several ways:

- The words used can be changed to more frequent, general usage vocabulary.
- The grammar structures of the sentences can be modified to be less complex than they are in the original.
- Transitions can be added so that the relationship between the ideas in each clause is made explicit throughout the text.
- Additional background or cultural information can be put into the text so that readers can have more access to what is being discussed.

The degree of text modification can vary greatly. In other words, just a few items in a text can be modified (a few words or idioms), or the complete text can be rewritten. In the latter case, the general message and usually the organization of the information in the text is kept, but the language (grammar and vocabulary) and, perhaps, the organization of the information is changed.

Exercise 3.8   Building your knowledge

Appendices C and D contain two different versions of a literary text, "An Occurrence at Owl Creek Bridge." Read each one and note what changes have been made in the modified version. Look for two or three specific examples of each of the four ways mentioned previously to alter text. See if you can add some items to the list of differences. (*Hint:* Find a partner to do this activity. One of you reads the first sentence of the authentic text and the other reads the sentence(s) from the modified text that convey the same information. Continue in this way until you have a solid understanding of the differences.)

The advantage and purpose of modifying texts is to allow students whose L2/FL proficiency is below that of the original text to read the modified text with sufficient understanding to comprehend the message.

Making texts appropriate to the level of the reader is a common phenomenon in materials produced for L1 readers as well. Materials for native children and young adults in the United States are written in modified English that is not only appropriate to their level of language mastery but to their degree of mental development. Audience factors other than age also play a role; consider the differences in language between texts found in *Reader's Digest* and *Scientific American,* or between a university freshman's psychology textbook and a graduate student's psychology textbook.

What is the place of authentic materials in the L2/FL reading classroom? The answer to this question is presently being explored. There has been a trend in recent years to introduce authentic materials into L2/FL reading classes at every proficiency level. This lets students know what is available to be read and demonstrates to them that even though they cannot yet read the material in its entirety, they can comprehend the text on some level by using their reading skills. The introduction of authentic texts in even low-level classes makes the purpose for reading real in a way that no modified texts can. Thus, using them to some extent in both the L2 and FL settings is useful. Mastering even a small degree of comprehension of authentic materials gives students confidence in dealing with reading for real purposes.

Types of textbooks

The most common type of L2/FL textbook teaches reading with a mixture of intensive and extensive approaches and contains both informational and story/narrative texts written in modified language. Each text has accompanying exercises that develop the use of reading strategies, vocabulary, and sometimes grammar comprehension. For a more detailed description of types of reading textbooks, consult Appendix E.

Evaluation and final course grade

We would be remiss in talking about the process of designing a reading course if we did not address the issue of evaluating students' performances and determining course grades. Teachers need to know how they will determine whether the course goals have been met. Therefore, they need to decide how they will evaluate their students' reading performances, when they will do so, and how those evaluations will figure into the students' final course grades.

To do this, they will start with the course goals and then convert them into statements that can be measured in some specified way. For example, one course goal might be for students to be able to read informational texts within their L2/FL proficiency range and comprehend the topic and most of the main ideas presented in the article. Thus, **an evaluative outcome statement** for this particular goal might read: "Students will be able to read an informational text on a topic of general interest within their L2/FL proficiency range under timed conditions and correctly identify the topic and 80 percent of its main ideas with 75 percent accuracy." One could add "in three out of five texts" or "in two out of three texts," or "in a text of approximately 500 words in 30 minutes," and so on. Another evaluative outcome statement might read: "Each student will read five informational texts of his choice each week of the term and submit on time a written report on each text that states the topic and contains 80 percent of the main ideas of each article." Whatever teachers decide upon as evidence of students' achievement should be written in specific, measurable ways so that (1) it will be clear whether or not students have achieved that goal and (2) these outcome goals can be used to measure students' achievement in the same course the next time it is taught. Precision in stating how goals will be measured allows for more consistency in evaluation (Chapter 9 deals more thoroughly with evaluation and assessment).

Teachers need to think about the types of evaluative tasks that will comprise the final course grade. Tests are one option. If a teacher has decided that she is going to use only tests to determine if course goals and evaluative outcome statements have been met, then the entire course grade will depend upon test scores. If, however, other evaluative tasks are used during the course, those too should be factored into the final course grade. In addition to test scores and grades on nontest work, many teachers also like to factor student preparation (including homework) and class participation into the calculations of the final course grades. Table 3.1 shows some typical distributions for determining the final course grade in three different courses. There is great variety in the composition of final course grades, depending upon course goals and the course approach.

Table 3.1   Sample distributions for final course grades

	Course 1	*Course 2*	*Course 3*
Quizzes	10		10
Reading tests	60	30	
Book report	20		10
Homework	10		
Reading reports		30	60
Final exam		20	
Reading journal		10	20
Preparation and participation		10	
Totals	100%	100%	100%

Exercise 3.9   Building your knowledge

Which final course grade distribution would be appropriate for an extensive reading approach, an intensive reading approach, and a combination of the two? What are some other breakdowns that reading teachers might use for a given approach? Why were they chosen?

The designing of a reading course is a time-consuming, but important, first step in teaching reading; the decisions teachers make at this point will establish the framework within which they and their students will work for the duration of the course. It is crucial that students invest in the goals of the course and in the means for meeting those goals. If teachers and students use materials that match their stated aims, the work of teaching and learning is greatly facilitated. Both teachers and students understand where they are going, how they are traveling, what instruments they are using for the trip, and whether they reach their destination.

Expanding your knowledge

1. Think of a time when your interest in a topic motivated you to seek out information about it. What did you do (that was out of the ordinary) to find or to read that information? Was the information that you found within your reading range? If not, what did you do?
2. Using the Reading Course Description in Exercise 3.2, devise a survey to be completed by your students at mid-course. You want to see how they are doing with the types of reading and assignments you have been giving.
3. Teachers who have previously taught the same course can draw on their knowledge about their former students. With these students in mind, they can begin to formulate goals for the current course. Write two major goals for a reading course based on this description of former students:

   > The students in this course are mostly refugees and immigrants in an adult community education program in an English-speaking country. They study English two days a week for 2½ hours at each class meeting. Their language proficiency level is intermediate; they can make themselves understood but with some difficulty. They speak haltingly and with many grammatical errors and inappropriate vocabulary. Typically, some of these students are already working and the rest hope to find work soon. Some have children in the public school system. Some parts of their lives are usually conducted totally in their native language, while other parts must be conducted in English because the people they come in contact with speak only English. They are, of course, interested in keeping up with the news in their home countries. They also want to know what is going on in the community in which they live.

4. Interview two L2/FL reading teachers. First, get enough information about the students in their course to write a course description, like the one in Exercise 3.2. Then ask them what goals they established for their students. Were those goals adjusted as the course progressed? Was student input sought? If so, how was that input collected?

Chapter highlights

Designing a reading course that will further students' knowledge and abilities demands that the course designer and the teacher keep many relevant points in mind so that the students will learn in the best possible way.

1. *Course goals.* Designers and teachers need to formulate goals based on what they as teachers know about the students' abilities and future academic needs as well as what the students themselves know about their needs, interests, and abilities.
2. *Approaches to teaching reading.* Reading courses can be conducted in an extensive way (believing that reading great quantities will build skills), an intensive way (believing that instruction and practice in specific skills will build skills), or a combination thereof.
3. *Selecting appropriate materials.* Teachers should be aware of what type of reading textbooks they are using so that they can use their texts in a manner that fits their beliefs about learning to read. Major considerations are the mix of informational texts with story-centered texts and whether the language in the text is authentic or modified.
4. *Evaluation and final course grade.* All decisions about how to evaluate student progress toward meeting course goals should be made before the course begins. Furthermore, those decisions should be made in concert with the course goals and the approach used in teaching the course.

Appendix A   Table of contents to *Reading on Your Own*

PART C

Appendix B   Table of contents to *Reader's Choice*

Reprinted with permission from E. Margaret Baudoin, Ellen S. Bober, Mark A. Clark, Barbara K. Dobson, and Sandra Silberstein, *Reader's Choice,* 2nd ed., © by the University of Michigan, 1988.

Appendix C   from "An Occurrence at Owl Creek Bridge" (authentic version)

A man stood upon a railroad bridge in northern Alabama, looking down into the swift water twenty feet below. The man's hands were behind his back, the wrists bound with a cord. A rope closely encircled his neck. It was attached to a stout cross-timber above his head and the slack fell to the level of his knees. Some loose boards laid upon the sleepers supporting the metals of the railway supplied a footing for him and his executioners – two private soldiers of the Federal army, directed by a sergeant who in civil life may have been a deputy sheriff. At a short remove upon the same temporary platform was an officer in the uniform of his rank, armed. He was a captain. A sentinel at each end of the bridge stood with his rifle in the position known as "support," that is to say, vertical in front of the left shoulder, the hammer resting on the forearm thrown straight across the chest – a formal and unnatural position, enforcing an erect carriage of the body. It did not appear to be the duty of these two men to know what was occurring at the center of the bridge; they merely blockaded the two ends of the foot planking that traversed it.

Beyond one of the sentinels nobody was in sight; the railroad ran straight away into a forest for a hundred yards, then, curving, was lost to view. Doubtless there was an outpost farther along. The other bank of the stream was open ground – a gentle acclivity topped with a stockade of vertical tree trunks, loopholed for rifles, with a single embrasure through which protruded the muzzle of a brass cannon commanding the bridge. Midway of the slope between bridge and fort were the spectators – a single company of infantry in line, at "parade rest," the butts of the rifles on the ground, the barrels inclining slightly backward against the right shoulder, the hands crossed upon the stock. A lieutenant stood at the right of the line, the point of his sword upon the ground, his left hand resting upon his right. Excepting the group of four at the center of the bridge, not a man moved. The company faced the bridge, staring stonily, motionless. The sentinels, facing the banks of the stream, might have been statues to adorn the bridge. The captain stood with folded arms, silent, observing the work of his subordinates, but making no sign. Death is a dignitary who when he comes announced is to be received with formal

Ambrose Bierce, "An Occurrence at Owl Creek Bridge," reprinted from *The Stories and Fables of Ambrose Bierce,* pp. 18–28 (Owings Mills, MD: Stemmer House, 1977).

manifestations of respect, even by those most familiar with him. In the code of military etiquette silence and fixity are forms of deference.

The man who was engaged in being hanged was apparently about thirty-five years of age. He was a civilian, if one might judge from his habit, which was that of a planter. His features were good – a straight nose, firm mouth, broad forehead, from which his long, dark hair was combed straight back, falling behind his ears to the collar of his well-fitting frock coat. He wore a mustache and pointed beard, but no whiskers; his eyes were large and dark gray, and had a kindly expression which one would hardly have expected in one whose neck was in the hemp. Evidently this was no vulgar assassin. The liberal military code makes provision for hanging many kinds of persons, and gentlemen are not excluded.

Appendix D   from "An Occurrence at Owl Creek Bridge" (modified version)

A man stood upon a railroad bridge in northern Alabama. He looked down into the river below. The man's hands were tied behind his back. A rope circled his neck. The end of the long rope was tied to part of the wooden bridge above his head.

2 Next to the man stood two soldiers of the Northern army. A short distance away stood their captain. Two soldiers guarded each end of the bridge. On one bank of the river, other soldiers stood silently, facing the bridge. The two guards at each end of the bridge faced the banks of the river. None of the soldiers moved. The captain, too, stood silent. He watched the work of the two soldiers near him, but he made no sign. All of them were waiting silently for Death. Death is a visitor who must be met with respect. Even soldiers, who see so much death, must show respect to Death. And in the army, silence and stillness are signs of respect.

3 The man with the rope around his neck was going to be hanged. He was about thirty-five years old. He was not dressed like a soldier. He wore a well-fitting coat. His face was a fine one. He had a straight nose, strong mouth, and dark hair. His large eyes were gray, and looked kind. He did not seem like the sort of man to be hanged. Clearly he was not the usual sort of criminal. But the Army has laws for hanging many kinds of people. And gentlemen are not excused from hanging.

Reprinted by permisson of Prentice-Hall, Englewood Cliffs, N.J., from D. G. Draper, *Great American Stories 1*, © 1993, pp. 86–101.

Appendix E   Types of L2/FL reading books

The following categories, although not comprehensive or mutually exclusive, make useful distinctions among types of textbooks.

INTENSIVE READING TEXTBOOKS

Intensive reading textbooks focus entirely on building reading comprehension abilities through reading texts from the book and completing exercises. Usually these texts will be written within the readers' L2/FL proficiency level. Several exercises will accompany each text, some focusing on reading skills, some on vocabulary, and perhaps some with other objectives. The exercises may or may not identify the skills they practice. The objectives are addressed within the confines of the book.

1. Informational

(a) Variety. This type uses predominantly informational reading texts covering a variety of topics and a variety of text types, including both formal and informal writing. Examples of text types include textbook excerpts, newspaper and magazine articles, pamphlets, schedules, notes, transcripts of conversations. To enhance the role of background in reading, there may be a series of texts on various aspects of one or more of the topics presented in the book.

(b) Content-based. This type of textbook strives to teach not only reading skills but content information as well. Generally, the exercises in this type of textbook focus on building content knowledge and perhaps on developing reading comprehension skills.

2. Story/Narrative.
Almost all the textbooks in this category include a variety of topics, although a textbook may specialize in a particular type of story reading, such as short story, mystery, American short story. The main difference among these textbooks is whether the language of the text is authentic or modified.

(a) Authentic. This type of textbook is generally a collection of literary works without modifications to the text. It contains exercises that focus on the main events and the significance of the story. It may also contain exercises that (1) build knowledge of the components of literary texts and criticism and (2) focus on aiding readers to comprehend any special language features of that text, such as dialect, euphemisms, double entendres, cultural references.

(b) Modified. This type of story or narrative textbook is written in language that differs to some degree from that of the educated native speaker. If the text is a rewritten version of an existing piece of literature, in all probability not only the language but also the story has been modified to some degree to make it accessible to the L2/FL reader. At this level of language, story or narrative textbooks usually contain several exercises aimed at developing language in addition to those aimed at promoting comprehension of the main events in the story. *Readers* is a term frequently applied to this type of textbook. Various publishers have readers series for L2 readers.

EXTENSIVE READING TEXTBOOKS

Extensive reading textbooks aim to improve reading abilities by having students read large quantities of texts outside of the reading textbook and report on them in some way. These books will usually have few reading texts in them; they will, however, usually have several presentations of (1) what types of texts exist in the real world to be read, (2) how to do the types of activities that readers can use to report on the outside texts that they read (summary, reaction, oral report, written report, etc.), and perhaps (3) what strategies readers might use to gain some degree of comprehension of those outside texts. The language used in these textbooks is within the readers' L2 proficiency range. There are few, if any, reading or vocabulary exercises accompanying the reading texts.

READING SKILLS TEXTBOOKS

Reading skills textbooks aim to improve reading abilities by focusing on the development of various reading strategies, such as skimming, scanning, finding main ideas of the paragraph, inferencing, summarizing. The book chapters, or sections, are clearly marked as to which reading strategy they practice. There are several short texts in each chapter or section to practice a particular skill. Answers are frequently provided somewhere in the book.

INTEGRATED SKILL AND SERIES TEXTBOOKS

The integrated skill textbook aims to teach language by using reading, speaking, listening, and writing skills. A heavy emphasis on grammar and vocabulary is easily recognizable in this type of text. Reading skill practice may be limited to having readers answer some questions on the text. These textbooks are frequently found at the beginning and intermediate levels of L2/FL readers. Integrated books can form a series. Series books, as the name suggests, are a set of integrated skill books that progress in difficulty. Each level attempts to move all skills along simultaneously by presenting new skills and reviewing previously presented skills. There may be as many as six to eight levels in a series.

4 Preparing to read

Every act of comprehension involves one's knowledge
of the world as well.
                        – Richard C. Anderson et al. (1977: 369)

This chapter focuses on the unconscious and conscious prereading processes that readers often use and the ways that teachers can make students aware of their use. The following narrative illustrates several prereading strategies and infers some of the problems that arise when readers ignore the clues available to them in the text.

TEACHER NARRATIVE

David, a serious and capable student, arrived at my office door one day holding a copy of Barbara Tuchman's historical work The Proud Tower *and asked if I could answer a couple of questions for him. He said he had enrolled in a class about World War I this term, eager for a chance to learn about events that took place before his time. He began reading the Tuchman book, assuming it would be full of military details, battles, strategies, biographical sketches of great officers, and so on. But to his dismay he wasn't learning anything about battles or officers. He simply couldn't understand why this book was required for the course.*

Although I was familiar with some of Tuchman's historical works, I had never read this one. After a quick skim of the Preface, the Table of Contents, and the last paragraph in the Epilogue I had an answer for him. Tuchman's book is a description of the economic, social, political and cultural conditions that existed before *the war! The subtitle was* A Portrait of the World before the War, 1890– 1914. *In the Preface she stated that the war itself would not be mentioned in her book. Her sole concern was to set the stage, describe the cast of characters, and identify the factors operating before the war. By not reading the subtitle or the Preface, by not checking to see if his expectations for the book fit with the purpose the author had in mind, David was thrown into confusion and frustration. He made the rather common mistake of assuming that the book would tell him what he* wanted *it to tell him – not what the author set out to tell him. Shaking his head as he left, he commented that my three minutes of previewing had given me more information than his first two hours of reading.*

                        – Mary Lee Field, U.S.A.

Many readers engage in a variety of prereading practices in their native language, having learned from experience that omitting basic prereading

65

activities can add to or create comprehension problems for them (Graves, Cooke, & Laberge 1983). This chapter focuses on methods for knowing and improving prereading strategies and provides explicit training in pre-reading skills and in transferring those skills from the L1 to an L2/FL. Such training gives students the chance to learn, practice, and internalize habits that will make them better L2/FL readers, especially of academic or informational materials (see Johnson 1982). Most researchers agree that "when the goal of reading is in-depth comprehension and good recall of information from expository text, previewing (surveying, overviewing) facilitates the process because it familiarizes a reader with the basic content and organization of the text and helps to activate relevant prior knowledge" (Shih 1992: 301). There are three major reasons for preparing students to read: (1) to establish a purpose for reading a given text, (2) to activate existing knowledge about the topic and thus get more out of reading the text, and (3) to establish realistic expectations about what is in the text and thus read more effectively. Note that these reasons illustrate steps 1 through 3 of the learning spiral. In addition, teachers usually do vocabulary work before reading in order to make more conscious and familiar the relevant vocabulary students already have, and to build new vocabulary that will prove valuable to them when they begin to read.

Establishing a purpose for reading

Establishing a purpose means taking into account the students' language and proficiency levels and determining the appropriate tasks for them to complete (see Chapter 3). Purpose influences reading at all levels; even beginning and low-level learners can successfully complete some tasks with authentic L2/FL texts, such as ascertaining the topic, scanning for specific information, and getting information from charts and graphs. At least three considerations influence the process of establishing purposes for reading.

One is the match between the content of the text and the readers' familiarity with that content. For example, a highly technical text, written by an expert for other experts in the field, is quite difficult for nonexperts to read, even in the L1. Asking students to read such a text for a *thorough* understanding is unrealistic. However, if the text is for the educated layperson and the readers are educated laypeople with an advanced or high-intermediate level of L2 proficiency, then reading for thorough understanding would be appropriate. If a text is written for the general public, the writer often provides the background and the definition of terms necessary for those readers to comprehend the message. Thus, the match between the text and the reader in terms of language and content is an important consideration when setting purposes for reading.

A second consideration is the teacher's purpose for having students read a text. If the teacher wants students to look for specific pieces of information, then it makes sense to scan for particular items rather than read the whole text. If students need to know what the text is about in general, then skimming or sampling the text (explained in a later section) is appropriate. If students are to have a good but not detailed understanding of a text, perhaps one reading of a text is enough. However, when a thorough understanding is the purpose for reading, two or sometimes three readings of the whole text are essential. Purposes in reading classrooms, like in real life, vary from text to text.

A third consideration is getting the reader to establish reasons for reading. Although it is the teacher in the L2/FL classroom who usually establishes the purposes for reading, it can be beneficial for readers to establish their own purposes, especially in a class using an extensive approach. Students can be asked to identify the purpose in a written report on each text so that the teacher knows how the text was read and can respond accordingly.

The activities we present in this chapter are designed specifically for the intensive reading class focused on reading informational texts, with some variations for beginning and low-intermediate students in a later section. Activities for students reading literature are presented in Chapter 8. We have elected to use the intensive reading approach as the central illustration because we believe that teachers need to be aware of reading strategies in order to facilitate their students' reading, regardless of the approach they choose to use in the classroom.

Activating and building background knowledge

Both L1 and L2/FL reading comprehension research tells us that readers benefit in three main ways from having an introduction to the topic of an informational text before they begin to read. First, an introduction helps students to recall any information that they may already know about the topic (content schema), either from personal experience or other reading. If the students keep this knowledge in mind as they read, they increase their opportunities to make sense of the information they find in the text. An introduction may also bring to mind cultural factors that help them understand the new material, thus enhancing comprehension. Second, getting the students to start to think about the topic should increase their interest in the topic and thereby motivate them to read the text. Third, if the introduction activity is conducted in the L2/FL, it will also review or introduce the relevant vocabulary for that topic.

We give specific illustrations of various methods for teaching reading by providing a number of descriptions of classroom interactions between teacher and students called Classroom Plans. Each Classroom Plan focuses on selected activities, that is, the specific actions that students and teacher will engage in during the class time (the what) and the steps in which these actions will develop or occur (the how). Activities grow out of objectives, those statements that further specify course goals. These can be written to state what students will be able to *do* after a class session or what students will *know* after a class session. Both types of knowledge are important to the development of an effective reader. Even more specific task- or behavior-oriented objectives are referred to in this book as *Students Will Be Able To* (or **SWBATs,** pronounced /swɑˈbæts/). Classroom Plan 4A shows typical sets of activities designed to activate content schema. These sets of activities (which are extracts from actual lesson plans) are samples of the types of exercises commonly used in the prereading class (see Barnett 1989; Grellet 1984; Mikulecky 1990; Oxford 1990).

CLASSROOM 4A   INTERMEDIATE LANGUAGE PROFICIENCY

Objectives for this lesson
- Activate students' (Ss') background knowledge about the topic of the reading
- Make the reading of the text more efficient
- Increase Ss interest in the topic
- Internalize (or transfer from L1) these prereading activities for more efficient independent reading in the future

Students Will Be Able To (SWBATs)
1. Tell others what an earthquake is
2. Describe the kinds of damage that earthquakes may cause
3. Explain in general terms the causes of earthquakes
4. Describe any experiences they have had personally in an earthquake
5. Recognize and understand words often associated with earthquakes that appear in the text (e.g., *tremble, Richter Scale, aftershock, epicenter*)

CLASSROOM 4A   INTERMEDIATE LANGUAGE PROFICIENCY
continued

Maria's class	*Karl's class*	*Beth's class*
Step 1 (5 min.) Teacher (T) states that California has frequent earthquakes and writes *earthquake* on the board. T then asks Ss if any of them have experienced an earthquake. If so, T has Ss describe what it felt like. T supplies and defines any words that Ss grope for, writing important topic-related words on the board.	*Step 1 (2 min.)* T shows videotape of an earthquake in progress to Ss. There is no sound, just pictures.	*Step 1 (3 min.)* While T hands out a short (half page) written description of what it felt like to be in an earthquake, T tells Ss that they will have 2 min. to read it so that they can do the next activity.
Step 2 (10 min.) T asks questions (which anticipate the kinds of information that will be mentioned in the text) to bring out more information on the topic (still writing important words on the board as they come up). For example: What causes earthquakes? What parts of the world have frequent earthquakes? Etc.	*Step 2 (2 min.)* When the video is finished, T tells Ss to take a sheet of paper and write down what they just saw. They should write quickly, not worrying about spelling or grammar.	*Step 2 (3 min.)* T puts Ss in groups of 3–4 and asks Ss to discuss what they just read. T circulates to groups, answering Qs as they come up.
Step 3 (1 min.) T tells Ss that these questions will be answered in the text and to look for the answers as they read.	*Step 3 (3 min.)* When the Ss have finished writing, T calls on a few Ss and asks them to tell (not read) the whole class what they wrote.	*Step 3 (5 min.)* T has the class as a whole describe what they read. T calls on a S from each group if no one volunteers. T repeats the key idea and words as the Ss bring them up.

CLASSROOM 4A   INTERMEDIATE LANGUAGE PROFICIENCY
continued

Step 4 (6 min.) T then asks Ss to form small groups (3–4) and discuss what they know about earthquakes. They have one person in the group write down questions (Qs) they have about earthquakes. T tells Ss that some of the information might (or might not) be mentioned in the text.	*Step 4 (6 min.)* T then puts Qs (which will be answered in the text) about earthquakes on the overhead projector and instructs the groups to discuss possible answers to these Qs.
Step 5 (12 min.) T collects Qs and reads them to the class to see if anyone can add other information about earthquakes. T takes notes on the board or transparency so Ss can see the important ideas and key words. T tells Ss that this information might (or might not) be mentioned in the text.	*Step 5 (1 min.)* T tells Ss to keep the Qs in mind as they read and to look for answers.

Five prereading exercise types are most evident in Classroom 4A:

Exercise type	*Maria*	*Karl*	*Beth*
Recalling information	step 1	steps 2, 3, 4	step 3
Generating new ideas	steps 1, 2	steps 1, 4, 5	step 1
Sharing or solidifying information		steps 2, 3, 4, 5	steps 2, 3, 4
Building key vocabulary	steps 1, 2	steps 3, 5	step 3
Establishing a purpose for reading	steps 2, 3	steps 4, 5	steps 4, 5

Not all the activities used in Classroom 4A are aimed at activating students' background knowledge. The next-to-last steps in both Maria's and Beth's classes aim to provide a framework for the kind of information that students will read in the text. There are a variety of activities that students can engage in to recall information on the topic. In Maria's class students generate information on earthquakes from what they recall from their personal experience with earthquakes. This type of free recall is sometimes known as **brainstorming.** It assumes that students have some knowledge base from which to work. Of course, if no one in the class has had any personal experience with earthquakes, the teacher will have to adjust her plan, asking them what they know about earthquakes from television or newspapers and magazines. In Karl's and Beth's classes (step 1) it is the teachers who provide information to their students, Karl via video and Beth via a short reading, so that all students will have some base of knowledge from which to complete later activities. The writing activity that Karl has his class do in step 2 is known as **structured writing.** The degree of structure provided by the teacher can vary. In this activity the video provides structure. Students may choose to recall it as it was presented to them, thus maintaining the same structure, or they may choose to disregard that structure and recall the information in any order they wish, thus making this a free recall activity. Other activities that can be used to activate students' background knowledge include:

- Field trips
- Role plays
- Word association activities (students connect words that have a similar meaning)
- Content mapping (students write down any information that comes to mind on the topic, then mark the sentences in the reading with content similar to what they wrote)
- Semantic mapping (students write down any words that come to mind on the topic and then circle and connect the words that are closely related)

Exercise 4.1 Building your knowledge

1. Look again carefully at the SWBATs for Classroom 4A and at the activities. Match the activity the teacher planned with the appropriate objective. For each step of each class, write the number of the SWBAT that the activity aims to accomplish. For example, for Maria, step 1, you would write SWBATs 1, 4, 5. Continue in this way until each step has a least one SWBAT listed.
2. Now look to see if each class addresses each SWBAT. Are there some SWBATs that are not addressed by any of the steps in a class plan? Does one class address any one SWBAT more thoroughly than the other classes? Discuss your findings with your classmates.

As Exercise 4.1 clearly demonstrates, teachers should be careful that their activities carry out their objectives. This matching exercise should be carried out repeatedly in the minds of teachers as they write lesson plans.

In addition to building content schema, intermediate and advanced level students also need to be aware of the structural, or formal, writing pattern of the text they are about to read. Knowledge of how information can be organized helps readers to understand and anticipate information in a text. Students who are preparing to take academic courses, in particular, benefit from an introduction to the type of text they are about to read. Classroom 4B presents two ways that formal schemata might be introduced to a class, after the class has done sufficient work to activate background knowledge, to heighten student interest, and to build key vocabulary. These kinds of activities are useful for L2/FL learners in an academic situation, who are expected to develop higher-level reading skills, such as activating or building formal schemata. One is experience-based (Bev's), the other is text-based (Roz's). They may not be appropriate for other populations of L2/FL students, such as children in refugee programs or adults in survival skills programs.

CLASSROOM 4B   HIGH-INTERMEDIATE LANGUAGE PROFICIENCY

Objectives for this lesson
- Activate Ss' background knowledge of comparison and contrast texts
- Increase Ss' ability to apply their structural knowledge of comparison and contrast texts

SWBATs
1. Recognize words commonly used in comparison and contrast writing
2. State the two common comparison and contrast structures for organizing paragraphs

Bev's class	*Roz's class*
Step 1 (5 min.) T writes the words *compare* and *contrast* on the board. Ss are asked to discuss what those terms mean.	*Step 1 (8 min.)* T puts a list of words on the board that are commonly used in comparison and contrast writing (*in contrast, on the other hand, another difference, similarity, likewise*) and asks Ss to talk about the meanings of these words.

CLASSROOM 4B HIGH-INTERMEDIATE LANGUAGE
PROFICIENCY *continued*

Step 2 (1 min.) T asks Ss if they have read essays or magazine articles that compare and contrast two things – movies, rock stars, books, philosophies, anything.	*Step 2 (10 min.)* T has Ss look for those terms in a text on the overhead projector (OHP).
Step 3 (8 min.) T and Ss discuss the way a comparison and contrast article is usually written and the signposts to look for while reading such an essay. At this point, T writes some common terms that often appear in this type of writing on the board (*on the other hand, another similarity, in contrast,* etc.).	*Step 3 (5 min.)* On the OHP T shows the structure of the text they are about to read, making explicit the comparison and contrast structure.

Previewing the text to build expectations

In addition to recalling one's own knowledge of the topic and of types of text structure, **previewing a text** before beginning to read is another useful preparation activity (Dole et al. 1991). Previewing enables students to establish their own expectations about what information they will find in the text and the way that information will be organized. The previewing process provides an orientation in order to avert the kind of problems that David had in the Teacher Narrative at the beginning of this chapter.

Previewing introduces various aspects of the text, helps readers predict what they are going to read, and gives them a framework to help make sense of the information. Several features in the text, which are usually distinct from the running text, aid the reader's ability to predict. These are particularly useful when previewing long texts:

- The title
- The author, source
- Subtitles
- Subheadings
- Photographs, drawings

- Graphs, charts, tables
- Spacing (e.g., extra space between paragraphs)
- Print that is different in size, darkness, or style

For each of the items listed, there are various previewing activities that students may do. Examine the activities in Classroom 4C and think about *how* each one will be done. Identifying what to do is sometimes much easier than plotting exactly how to accomplish it in class. The activities in Classroom 4C introduce text titles and parts of the text for "Our Future Stock," in Sample 4 of the Reading Textbook Samples at the end of this book.

Working with the title of a text is one previewing activity for establishing expectations about the content of a text. Others involve reading selected parts of the text in order to sample the ideas presented and to establish a mental framework for reading (see Barnett 1989; Devine 1988a). All of the following involve some reading beyond the title of the text:

Prereading strategies
- Read the introduction (all the paragraphs that comprise the introduction) and identify the key issues to be discussed.
- Read the conclusion paragraph, if present, carefully.
- Skim the text.
- Read the first sentence of each of the body paragraphs (the paragraphs after the introduction and before the conclusion) to see what ideas are mentioned in them.
- Scan parts of the text for specific information.

There is some evidence that reading strategies transfer from the L1 to an L2 (see Benedetto 1985; Royer & Carlo 1991; Sarig 1987), a condition that reading teachers need to exploit as much as possible. In informational texts, especially academic essays, technical books, college textbooks, and specialized scholarly writing, the introduction sets up the main issues and gives the reader clues to the main parts of the argument; the conclusion frequently repeats some or all of those main ideas. Thus, reading both the introduction and conclusion of academic texts will often give the reader useful clues about the main ideas the writer is making. In contrast, newspaper articles tend to give the reader the main idea at the beginning but seldom indicate the types of details that follow. They rarely have conclusions.

Another useful skill is skimming. **Skimming** is usually defined as a quick, superficial reading of a text in order to get the gist of it. Although

CLASSROOM 4C   ADVANCED LANGUAGE PROFICIENCY

Objectives for this lesson
• Practice (begin to internalize) the habit of reading the title and other visually prominent text information carefully, thinking about it, and using it to help predict content

SWBATs
1. Predict the topic of the text by using information in the title of the reading
2. Predict main ideas in the reading by using the title and any subtitles

Terry's class	*Chiang's class*
Step 1 (5 min.) T tells Ss to look at the title and any subtitles. Then T provides each S with a one-sheet "anticipation guide," which contains a list of various kinds of information that *might* appear in the assigned reading text (some items will appear in the text, others will not). T tells Ss to put a check by each idea they think will appear in the text, given the title and subtitle.	*Step 1 (3 min.)* T and Ss talk about the title of the reading for a few minutes to ensure that everyone understands all the words. T tells Ss to look for the subtitle. T calls on a S to read it out loud and then asks the whole class what each term means. T groups Ss into groups of 3–4 and tells Ss to come up with several ideas that they expect to find in the text. Each group lists their ideas on a sheet of paper. T then calls on each group to give one or two of their ideas.
Step 2 (5 min.) T has Ss form small groups to discuss their guesses. T tells Ss to save the "anticipation guide" sheet so that they can return to it after they have read the text.	*Step 2 (8 min.)* Working as a whole class, the Ss agree on a short list of the information they think will appear in the reading. That list is put on the board for future reference.
Step 3 (3 min.) T asks Ss why it is useful to look at the title and subtitles before they actually read a text.	*Step 3 (5 min.)* T asks Ss why it is useful to look at the title and subtitles before they actually read a text. T asks what else there is to look at before reading and why it might be helpful.

there is some question about exactly what readers do when they skim, it does appear to be a strategy for getting clues to the main ideas, divisions, points, or steps in an argument. Barnett (1989), Grellet (1984), Hosenfeld et al. (1981), and Jensen (1986) give instructions on teaching this strategy. Some teachers, however, substitute another, more defined technique, called sampling. Students are **sampling** when they read the first sentence of each main paragraph in the body of a text as a way to get an overview of the information. It is most useful with shorter texts, such as an article or a chapter.

Scanning is looking quickly through the text for a specific piece of information. It involves these steps:

1. Determine what key words to look for.
2. Look quickly through the text for those words.
3. When you find each word, read the sentences around it to see if they provide the information being sought.
4. If they do, do not read further. If they do not, continue scanning.

Scanning is useful in the prereading stage to build knowledge. Teachers can have students zero in on one topic by asking them a specific question and having them scan to answer that question. This familiarizes them with the text. Another possible prereading use of scanning is to check predictions that students make about the contents of the text to be read (see Jensen 1986). Scanning is also a useful strategy after having read a text as well. The process is still the same: Students can review the text to find a specific piece of information. The difference is that as a post-reading activity, readers have the advantage of having read the text and thus remembering various parts.

Exercise 4.2   Recalling your experience

What previewing activities did you engage in before you began reading our book? Did you read the Table of Contents and the Introduction? Did you skim the text? If so, did you change any of your expectations about what you would find?

Different texts lend themselves to different previewing activities. One of the jobs of the reading teacher is to find the right match between the text and the most useful previewing activity. When teachers are conscious of their own practice, they have a foundation to work from in planning activities for students.

Exercise 4.3 Building your knowledge

Look at each of the reading chapters in Reading Textbook Samples 1–5 at the end of this book. What activities, if any, do they provide for activating or building content or formal schema?

Prereading activities for lower levels of language proficiency

Students at beginning and low-intermediate levels of L2/FL proficiency need to do prereading work for the same reasons as students with higher levels of language proficiency. Even though these students come to a text with some degree of knowledge about text type and content schema, their knowledge of the L2/FL is minimal to nonexistent. Thus, many of the activities that have been discussed in this chapter will not be useful with this particular level of student. For example, it would not be productive for beginners to form groups and discuss in the L2/FL what they know about earthquakes, because they would not understand what the others were trying to say and they would not have the language to express their ideas to other students. The result would be a short, frustrating activity of little value. Lower-level students can, however, ask each other teacher-provided questions and report the answers to the whole class. This section addresses some of the major issues of doing prereading activities with beginning and low-level students (see also Bruder & Henderson 1986).

One issue at this level is which language, the L1 or the L2, the teacher uses in class. Those who teach in the FL setting and speak the L1 of the students have the option of using that shared language for some prereading activities, allowing students to use their L1 to access their topic knowledge. In order to facilitate reading in the L2, teachers must interject the L2 as the discussion progresses in the L1. For example, when there is an opportunity to introduce a relevant phrase or word in the L2, the teacher should present it and immediately reinforce it in the students' awareness. The teacher can (1) ask the students to repeat it, (2) write the language on the board and have the students scan the reading for it, noting where it appears, or (3) have the students copy the language on a sheet of paper for future reference. All of these activities contribute toward the goal of learning the L2. Without such activities, schema has been activated but learning the L2 has not been facilitated.

In either the L1 or L2 setting, the teacher who uses only the target language with students should choose activities that require students to produce very little of the L2 from memory. The activities need to provide the language for the students but still ask them to do some thinking about the topic. Obviously, activities that are visual and that use the receptive modes (listening and reading) lighten the language production load on the students while still allowing them to complete activities that ask them to participate and act, thus building comprehension and promoting the learning of language at the same time. This type of work is sometimes referred to as **literacy activities.** Such activities teach vocabulary and establish context almost purely through visual, nonlanguage means. "The Neighbor's Kitchen" in Appendix A at the end of this chapter has minimal text for the students to read; students are asked to listen and think about the story and then to write.

Exercise 4.4   Building your knowledge

1. Carefully examine each activity in Appendix A, "The Neighbor's Kitchen."
2. In your Teaching Portfolio, draw a line down the center of a page. In the left column, write the implied SWBATs for Activities A–H. In the right column, write a prose description of the activity and point out how that activity will help students achieve those SWBATs.

Example:

SWBATs	Activity
A. 1 To activate the vocabulary and grammar needed to retell and to talk about this story.	A. 1 Talk about the story using whatever language they can generate among themselves. This discussion will demand that they pronounce words in the story and that they hear those words spoken by others.
2 To practice recognizing the sound of the words.	2 Listen to a taped reading of the story. This activity will reinforce their word recognition skills and will provide models of correct pronunciation. It will also provide the vocabulary for items they see in the pictures but may not know the names of.

3. Compare your descriptions with those of your classmates.

Recognizing the students' need to build language, many beginning-level reading textbooks have numerous illustrations that link the new words with actions or objects. There may be lists of useful vocabulary so that students using their bilingual dictionaries can look up the unknown word in the vocabulary list or so that teachers will teach those words. However, most reading texts do not have much more in the way of prereading exercises than a question or two for students to read, think about, and answer before they read. Frequently it is up to the teacher to activate or to build students' background knowledge.

Exercise 4.5   Building your knowledge

Examine the Reading Textbook Samples 1 and 2 at the end of the book, both of which involve beginning texts. Note the prereading exercises to access background knowledge.

All the texts in Sample 1 were written in modified English using simple sentences, with a very high frequency of useful everyday words. Since the language is both the object of instruction as well as the medium of instruction, it is controlled to be within the range of the students. Thus they can comprehend a majority of the text and learn enough new vocabulary to further their language learning and develop their L2/FL reading ability.

It is also possible to use authentic texts in the beginning and low-level proficiency reading class, but teachers need to remember to ask students to do only what they are capable of. Authentic texts can be used to make students aware of the value of reading skills by previewing the text (reading the title and subheadings, using visuals, etc.) or scanning for specific words or kind of information. These activities teach students that they can get a general sense of the texts even when they cannot understand the whole text. Using an authentic text in such ways in a beginning-level proficiency class builds students' confidence and skills in approaching texts. Authentic texts can more readily be used in the foreign language classroom, where teacher and students share a native language. The activities that these students do will be the same as in the second language classroom; however, more elaborate instructions and faster discussions can be conducted in the L1.

Exercise 4.6   Building your knowledge

Look at the reading exercises in Appendix B, which is from a beginning-level, integrated skills text for use in the foreign language setting (in this case, Spanish for native English speakers). We have provided only the reading section of that chapter so that you can see how the issues we have been considering are implemented in classroom materials. Identify and list in your Teaching Portfolio the reading skills that these materials promote. Discuss your list with your classmates.

Keeping in mind the principal factors that affect planning reading lessons for beginning and low-intermediate language proficiency students, look at Classroom 4D and Exercise 4.7.

CLASSROOM 4D

Bob's class	Stephanie's class
Step 1 (6 min.)	*Step 1 (6 min.)*
T tells Ss to look at the picture on the first page. T points to the picture as she gives directions. T asks the two Qs in the Prereading section. T repeats Ss' responses as they answer, perhaps making complete sentences.	T puts a list of key vocabulary words on the OHP and has Ss pronounce them after her. T points to each word as she carefully pronounces it. T goes through the list two or three times, depending on how well Ss repeat. Then T calls on individual Ss to pronounce the words she is pointing to.
Step 2 (15 min.)	*Step 2 (3 min.)*
T continues asking Ss Qs, helping the conversation along as needed. (T asks the same Q to many Ss.) T writes words on board.	T takes a bottle of lemon-scented dish soap and gives it to Ss to look at. T has Ss smell the soap and asks what they smell. T has them look at the words "lemon-scented" on the label.
T shows a picture of real dishes and says "dishes." Then, pantomiming, T asks:	T continues to have Ss look at the product and notice the words on the label. T asks:

Do you wash dishes?
    What do you use to wash dishes?
    Does it smell good? like lemons?
    Do you eat dish soap on your salad?
    What do you eat on your salad?
    Where do you get your salad dressing?
    Do you sometimes use lemon on your salad?
    Is it good?
    Do you get salad dressing at the supermarket?
	What is this?
	    What is it for?

Class repeats the vocabulary words on the board after the teacher.	

CLASSROOM 4D *continued*

Step 3 (5 min.)
T divides Ss into pairs and gives a list of the first 8 Qs she asked to one of the people in each pair. T tells Ss to ask these Qs of the other person and then has them change roles.

Step 3 (1 min.)
T asks Ss if they would put this on a salad. When Ss says "No," T asks: "Why not?" Ss answer.

Step 4 (8 min.)
T calls on various people to report to the whole class about the other person in their pair.

Step 4 (3 min.)
T tells Ss that in this reading, a man put lemon-scented soap on a salad and ate it. T asks: "What do you think happened to the man?"

Step 5 (4 min.)
T asks the following:
If you eat dish soap, how do you feel?
Do you feel well or sick?
(*pantomine*)
If you are very sick, where can you go for help?

Step 5 (1 min.)
T tells Ss to read the story and answer this Q: "Why did Joe eat dish soap on his salad?"

T tells Ss that sometimes in the U.S. when companies make a new soap or new toothpaste, they mail it to people. They want people to try the new product. T asks if any S has received a product through the mail.

Step 6 (3 min.)
T tells Ss to read the text and to answer the Qs. What happens to Joe?

Exercise 4.7   Building your knowledge

Which one of the plans in Classroom 4D, developed for the text in Reading Textbook Sample 2, would be most successful for low-level students? Analyze each step carefully with respect to the issues discussed in this section. Be prepared to explain your choice to your classmates using specific details.

Since providing repetition to reinforce learning is essential in the beginning-level classroom, the set of activities that gives students more practice with language and content before reading is preferable at this level.

As you plan

Having examined specific issues, strategies, and classroom activities for prereading, we conclude this chapter with a look at the overarching concerns to keep in mind when planning the reading class. With course goals and objectives in mind, teachers plan *what* the students will study in class – that is, the sequence of activities the students will engage in to achieve those objectives. Teachers plan *how* activities are done – the details about the time, grouping, instructions on how to proceed, and debriefing. In order to make these decisions, teachers need to know *why* – the reasons behind the decisions. In general-to-specific order then, teachers are responsible for course goals, objectives, and activities.

Specifying SWBATs

In addition to objectives, the Classroom Plans also list SWBATs. In order to understand the value of SWBATs, teachers must recognize the difference between general and specific statements of objectives.

Exercise 4.8   Building your knowledge

1. Read each of the following phrases and determine which are more general in nature and which are more specific. Write G in front of the more general and S in front of the more specific.
   _____ Look at the text they are going to read before they read it
   _____ Activate their personal experience regarding the topic of the text
   _____ State in the L2/FL what personal experience they've had with the topic, if any
   _____ Write questions about ideas that may be in the text based on the title
   _____ Use the visual information in the text to guess about its contents
   _____ List what they've read or learned before on this particular topic
   _____ State the theme or focus of the text after reading the introductory paragraphs
2. Compare answers with some of your classmates. Discuss what makes you think some statements are more specific than others.

Four of the statements in Exercise 4.8 are more specific than the others. Any of them could be used as a prereading objective; however, the four specific statements pinpoint what behavior is expected of the students, and could thus be used as SWBATs. The more specific the objectives, the easier it is for teachers to stay focused when developing activity plans. SWBATs also make it easier to assess how much students can achieve after engaging in the planned activities.

Varying modes of activities

Even though the activities in this chapter all have the same general objective – to introduce students to the topic of the text – they go about it in different ways. In planning teaching activities, note which modes (oral, aural, visual, tactile) are being used for each activity. For example, in Classroom 4A, step 1 of Maria's plan is primarily an oral-aural activity from the students' point of view, with the visual mode used only slightly. Both the teacher and the students speak and listen, and the students see vocabulary on the chalkboard.

Exercise 4.9 Building your knowledge

1. Make a chart like the one below and complete it. Write a brief note about what is done. There may be more than one mode for an activity. Remember to fill in the chart from the Ss' perspective.

Activity	Oral	Aural	Visual	Tactile
Maria's class Step 1	Ss speak about their experiences	Ss hear Qs (T starts/ maintains discussion with Qs)	S sees key vocabulary on board	None
Step 2, etc.				
Karl's class Step 1, etc.				
Beth's class Step 1, etc.				

2. Working in small groups of 3–4, discuss the modes used in these activities. Do any of the modes facilitate remembering better than others? Do any of them promote more interest than the others? What advantages are there to using a variety of modes in one plan? Use your common sense to answer these questions.

These activities show a variety of modes – some more than others. Not all activities need to engage all four modes. However, teachers need to be aware of what they are doing with an activity and to make the choices that will best facilitate their students' learning.

Exercise 4.10 Building your knowledge

Working in small groups, develop a description of one more activity that could be added to, or substituted for, one of the activities that introduce the topic of earthquakes in Classroom 4A. Be sure you are clear about which general and which specific objectives your activity is trying to meet. Try to think of an activity that uses a combination of modes different from those already given (e.g., pictures).

Eventually, teachers develop their own styles and preferences, but all plans need to include variety for the sake of the students' different learning styles and orientations. Because learning is enhanced by increased involvement of all the senses, the more activity modes that can be involved, the better.

Planning activities to reach objectives

Activities group together to form whole lesson plans (see Chapter 10). A **lesson plan** is a written guide to one class meeting that includes these elements:

1. Class objectives and SWBATs
2. What will be done in class (activities)
3. How those activities will be done (mode)
4. How long each activity will take (time)
5. Which objective(s) and SWBATs each activity is built upon (reason)
6. How information will be assessed (SWBATs and evaluation)
7. The work the students are expected to do by the next class meeting (homework)

Each lesson is based on objectives that are derived from course goals. Richards (1990: 3–8) identifies four types of objectives: behavioral, skills-based, content-based, and proficiency scales (see also J. D. Brown 1995). Even when focusing on one of these types, attention can be directed toward the others as well. For example, the objectives in Classroom 4A are a mixture of skills-based and proficiency-oriented, while the SWBATs are behavioral. Selecting an appropriate activity for a given objective and for a particular class of students evolves from the initial decisions made regarding the design of the reading course:

- Course goals
- Approach (intensive/extensive/a combination)
- Materials

However, other issues arise in planning daily lessons and selecting appropriate activities for given objectives:

- Students' level of knowledge about the topic and the structure (How much of the information in this text will be new to them? is already known?)

- Students' level of interest in the topic of the specific text (Is their interest strong enough to carry them forward even if the language is out of their range?)
- Students' level of language proficiency, given the individual text you are using (How hard will it be for them to read and understand this text?)
- Students' knowledge of the organizational features of this type of text (Are they familiar to them? What do the students know about this type of text? Will they recall this as they read?)
- Students' ability to transfer L1 strategies to reading in the L2 (How much transfer will the students make as they read?)
- Time available (How much time does the class have to devote to achieving this objective?)
- Most useful methods (Given all of these above issues, which methods will best facilitate achieving the objective?)

Decisions about one factor have ramifications for the other factors. For example, if time is tight, teachers may choose a teacher-centered rather than a student-centered activity simply because the teacher can control how quickly the class progresses from one step to another. Different activities may create different long-term and short-term results in learning to read. Dole et al. (1991) found better comprehension levels in a group of students who had a teacher-centered prereading exercise than students who had an interactive (more student-centered) exercise. On the other hand, the same study found that the interactive exercises prepared students better for future reading tasks by aiding them to become independent readers. Thus, the choice of activity may have effects that go beyond that particular lesson. More research on how methods affect learning is needed to inform teachers' choices.

The requisites for planning activities include (1) how the activities fit the objectives, (2) the differences between the *what* and the *how* of each activity, and (3) which activities demand oral or written work, which have visual, and which have tactile elements. Whether prereading activities focus on text content, text features, text structure, or vocabulary in the text, the ultimate purpose of having students do them is to enhance their ability to comprehend the texts they are going to read. The strategies of activating background knowledge, previewing the text, and establishing purpose for reading are useful preparations for reading. Not all types of prereading strategies should be done with each text. Instead, teachers should present a strategy and practice it enough so that students are reasonably knowledgeable about what that strategy involves and why it is useful for them. As students gain confidence with one strategy, others can be taught. Revisiting previously studied strategies strengthens students' memories and the use of all strategies; eventually, the strategies become automatic and function as part of the students' own resources whenever they read.

Expanding your knowledge

1. Pick Classroom 4B or 4C and match the SWBATs with the objectives. Compare your results with those of your classmates. Then examine the activities in each classroom to determine if they guide students to achieve the SWBATs listed. If not, make changes.
2. Write a SWBAT for each of the objectives for the prereading part of a lesson:
   • Introduce the reading text
   • Increase students' interest in the text
   • Preview the text
   • Predict the content of the text
   • Establish a purpose for reading
   Be specific about what the students will be able to do as a result of the activity.
3. Examine Classroom 4A. Each class ends with students having lists of questions. Where does each list come from? Who provides the list? Which list (or lists) of questions might the students be more interested in? Why? Which list will provide more guidance as students read the text? Why? Which list more closely reflects a real, out-of-class reading experience (how the reader reads when there is no teacher intervening in the process)? Which list might you prefer if the language level of the text were significantly above the students' language proficiency range? Why?
4. Select one of the individual classes in Classroom 4A and write an additional step (or two) that has the students continue to make predictions by using yet another text feature (subtitles, subheadings, photos, spacing, variations in print, etc.) Since this plan refers to an imaginary text, the text may have any features that you wish.
5. Select one of the SWBATs that you wrote in question 2 and plan an activity for a class of students of your choice. Be sure to specify what level of language proficiency the students have and if this is in an L2 or FL setting. Use any one of the Classroom Plans as a guide on how to structure your plan.
6. Write objectives and SWBATs for each of the activities in Classroom 4D.

Chapter highlights

Teachers of L2/FL reading need to be sure that students consciously understand how and why to use the three main prereading strategies, and they need to carefully plan lessons to achieve the desired results.

1. *Establishing a purpose for reading.* Students should establish a purpose for reading a particular text, be it for thorough comprehension, to identify the main idea, or to find a particular detail. Having a purpose helps them adjust their reading strategies and expectations accordingly. Establishing a purpose also compels the teacher to identify reasons for reading that are appropriate for the difference that exists between the students' L2 proficiency and the language level of the text to be read.

2. *Activating and building background knowledge.* If students have prior knowledge of the topic or the style of text to be read, they should recall that knowledge and use it to help them predict what might be in the text. This information might also be of help later as they read. Students' knowledge of the text topic will depend on their individual content schemata. Their knowledge of text types will depend on their formal schemata. These will vary from individual to individual and from culture to culture.

3. *Previewing the text to build expectations.* Students should know that they can use the title, the introduction, the conclusion, and a variety of other visual text features to help them predict or anticipate the content of the text. Such previewing activities help to build realistic expectations.

4. *Prereading activities for lower levels of language proficiency.* Prereading work is also valuable at lower levels of L2/FL proficiency to activate schemata and build language. Activities differ in that students' nascent knowledge of L2/FL vocabulary and grammar shapes the strategies that teachers can use with this level of student (e.g., provide L2 for the students to use, rely more heavily on visual input, use the students' L1).

5. *As you plan.* L2/FL lessons should be planned according to several overarching concepts. Goals are statements of general objectives for a course; SWBATs are specific, behavior-oriented statements that guide teachers when they select activities to include in classroom plans. Activities need to be varied in terms of the senses, or modes, they involve: oral, aural, visual, tactile.

Appendix A   "The Neighbor's Kitchen"

From *Picture Stories: Language and Literacy Activities for Beginners,* by Fred Ligon and Elizabeth Tannenbaum. Copyright © 1990 by Longman Publishers. Reprinted with permission.

B. Number the pictures in order. Then tell the story.

C. Match the picture with the word. Match the word with the sentence.

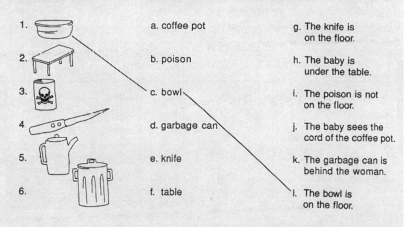

1.

2.

3.

4.

5.

6.

a. coffee pot

b. poison

c. bowl

d. garbage can

e. knife

f. table

g. The knife is on the floor.

h. The baby is under the table.

i. The poison is not on the floor.

j. The baby sees the cord of the coffee pot.

k. The garbage can is behind the woman.

l. The bowl is on the floor.

D. What is wrong in the neighbor's kitchen? Circle the problems.

E. Where's the poison? Listen. Write the number in the box.

F. Where's the knife? Listen. Write the number in the box.

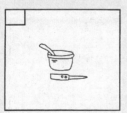 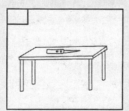 

G. Circle T for True or F for False.

1. The baby is under the table. T F

2. There's water on the kitchen table. T F

3. The woman is drinking coffee with three T F
   neighbors.

H. Fill in the blanks.

The woman goes to visit her neighbor.
Look at the picture in Exercise D. What does she see?

1. The spoon is _____ the bowl.
   1

2. The knife is _____ the floor.
   2

3. The curtains are _____ the stove.
   3

I. Write the story.
   Look at these words from the story.

neighbor	poison	water
kitchen	knife	baby
coffee	garbage	

Work with your teacher or a partner. Write other words you remember from the story.

_____

_____

Appendix B Foreign language textbook exercises

VAMOS A VER

The following activities accompany the reading "¿Funcionas mejor de día o de noche?" You may think that the reading is long and beyond your abilities, but don't jump to conclusions! You will find that you can understand more of it than you think. Don't worry: You won't be asked to do more than what you can reasonably be expected to be able to do at this point.

By following the step-by-step activities in this section, you will read parts of the reading closely and scan other parts of it for general information. Follow the **pasos**, and do not try to read the entire passage on your own.

You will use some of the information you learn from the reading to find out information about your classmates and instructor.

Anticipación

Paso 1. The reading on page 46 comes from a pop culture magazine. Look at the title; what question does it ask the reader? From the title, you should be able to make a good guess at the reading's content. Which of these two summary statements seems more appropriate?

☐ El artículo habla de los hábitos de dormir. En otras palabras, habla de los horarios de dormir.

☐ El artículo contiene información de los resultados de las investigaciones sobre las pesadillas (*nightmares*).

Compare your choice with that of a partner.

Paso 2. According to your answer in **Paso 1**, which words are most likely to appear in the article?

☐ sueño (*sleep*)
☐ energía
☐ apagar (*to turn off*)
☐ ritmo
☐ novio (*boyfriend*)
☐ sincronizar (*to synchronize*)

☐ psicoanálisis
☐ patrón (*pattern*)
☐ ir a fiestas (*parties*)
☐ sonámbulo (*sleepwalker*)
☐ levantarse

Paso 3. Read the introductory paragraph above the article. For now, skip over any words you do not know. Have you confirmed the article's topic? Did any of the words from **Paso 2** appear there?

From *Sabias Que? Beginning Spanish* by B. Van Patten, J. F. Lee, T. Ballman, and T. Dvorak, © 1992. Reproduced with permission of McGraw-Hill, Inc.

Paso 4. Before reading, do a quick survey of five or six class members (include your instructor) to see how they answer the question posed in the title. Save this information for later. (Remember to use **tú** with your classmates but **Ud.** with your instructor unless told otherwise.)

	FUNCIONA MEJOR	...DE DÍA	...DE NOCHE
Persona 1	_____	☐	☐
Persona 2	_____	☐	☐
Persona 3	_____	☐	☐
Persona 4	_____	☐	☐
Persona 5	_____	☐	☐

L E C T U R A

¿Funcionas mejor de día o de noche?

¿Te levantas de la cama llena de energía en cuanto sale el sol? O... ¿eres de las que apenas logran apagar el despertador a las 7 de la mañana, te levantas y andas como una sonámbula hasta que dan las 12 del día? Aquí te decimos cómo funciona tu reloj biológico y cómo puedes adaptar su ritmo, para que te "sincronices".

Un día, leyendo un estudio realizado por el Dr. Robert M. Witting, del Departamento de Desórdenes del Sueño, del Hospital Henry Ford, en Detroit (EE.UU.), supe lo siguiente: "En la mayoría de los casos", decía el Dr. Witting, "el horario de sueño es más una cuestión de preferencia personal que de biología. Sin embargo, cuando una persona prefiere estar levantada hasta tarde y mantiene este hábito, es difícil que pueda cambiar su horario de sueño". En otras palabras, el hecho de querer permanecer levantado hasta tarde en la noche,

como mis ex novios y mis hermanos, era una cuestión de gusto que, después de practicada por mucho tiempo, se convertía en un hábito difícil de romper.

Al seguir informándome sobre el asunto, leí que los especialistas afirmaban que nuestro cuerpo responde a nuestros deseos. Es decir, una persona que acostumbra acostarse tarde, puede levantarse con toda la energía del mundo al día siguiente a las 7 de la mañana, si se va de vacaciones en un crucero o quiere ver un super-programa de TV, por ejemplo. Asimismo, una persona que acostumbre a acostarse temprano, se sentirá motivada a estar despierta hasta la madrugada si QUIERE ir esa noche a una fiesta con un chico guapísimo, que le fascina.

Hay bases biológicas en el patrón del sueño

El Dr. Michael Thorpy, del Centro Médico Montefiore, en New York, explica: "Hemos descubierto que en cuestiones de sueño hay muchas individualidades y que cada persona tiene cierto patrón que la hace ir a dormir tarde o temprano, y para cada una de ellas ese patrón es normal". Según explican los médicos, nuestro "reloj" está localizado en el hipotálamo, en la parte central del cerebro, directamente detrás del nervio óptico, manteniendo nuestros sistemas internos sincronizados unos con otros y con lo que nos rodea. Durante la niñez, nuestro "reloj" va más apresurado, y ésa es la razón por la cual los niños se van a dormir temprano.

En la adolescencia, el reloj va más lento y uno se va a la cama más tarde. Por este motivo, muchos adolescentes se acuestan tarde, aunque al día siguiente tengan un examen en la escuela a las 8 de la mañana. Luego, a medida que vamos creciendo, necesitamos acostarnos más tarde, porque los períodos de sueño se hacen más cortos, a pesar de que las horas de sueño reglamentarias son importantes. Sin embargo, hasta esas horas de sueño varían de una persona a otra, porque hay quien sólo necesita dormir 6 horas para sentirse fabulosamente al día siguiente, mientras que otras necesitan 8 ó 9.

En conclusión: nuestro horario o "ritmo" de sueño es muy personal. Sin embargo, nosotros podemos hacer algo por cambiarlo un poco. Pero esto requiere práctica y tiempo, según afirman los expertos. En otras palabras, si tú te acuestas temprano, lo ideal para "cambiar" un poco tu horario es tratar de mantenerte despierta un poco más tarde de lo usual (digamos una hora más), para que tu "reloj" interno se vaya acostumbrando al nuevo horario.

En cuanto a las personas que se acuestan tarde, éstas pueden tratar de ir a la cama una hora antes de la habitual, para tratar de sincronizar su "reloj" y poder levantarse temprano. Lógicamente, esto no es tan sencillo, porque requiere dedicación y esfuerzo.

Tanto las personas que se acuestan tarde, como las que se acuestan temprano, pueden modificar su horario de sueño. Puedo dar una buena noticia: después de leer tanto y estudiar mi problema, he logrado cambiar mi horario de sueño. ¡Ya puedo irme a la cama más tarde!

¿Sabes en qué consiste la clave de mi triunfo? En que continúo durmiendo la misma cantidad de horas de siempre. Por ejemplo, si antes me acostaba a las 10 de la noche y me levantaba a las 6 de la mañana (lo cual suma 8 horas de sueño), ahora me acuesto a las 11 y me levanto a las 7... y esto no interfiere con mi horario de estudios. ¡Tú también puedes lograrlo! ¡Ánimo!

¡conoce tu reloj biológico!

Exploración

You are now ready to dig into the text. Read only the parts to which you are directed in each **paso**; the **pasos** divide the passage into manageable parts.

Paso 1. Read the first sentence of the article ("**Un día...**"). It will help you to know that **leyendo** is a form of **leer**. In this context, it means *while reading*. It is also useful to know that **supe** is a form of **saber** (*to know*). In this context, it means *I found out*.

Paso 2. Now that you have read the first sentence and understand it more fully, what can you say about the rest of the article? Is it written in the first person? Is the author a scientist?

Now skim the article and make note of who you think the author is. How do you know?

Paso 3. Since this reading discusses sleeping patterns, you will probably find references to experts or scientists. Scan the reading to locate any such references. Underline the names every time they are mentioned. Have you and a partner underlined the same items?

Paso 4. Now skim the reference to Dr. Witting. You will not understand everything, but you should be able to get the main idea. Which of the following would Dr. Witting agree with?

☐ El ritmo de tu sueño tiene una base genética. Si tus padres (*parents*) se acuestan tarde, probablemente tú también te acuestas tarde.

☐ El ritmo de tu sueño es simplemente un hábito. Si de niño (*child*) te acuestas tarde, de adulto también te acuestas tarde.

☐ Cambiar (*To change*) tu horario de dormir no es problemático.

Paso 5. Read the last two paragraphs of the article. Knowing that **me acostaba** and **me levantaba** mean *I used to go to bed* and *I used to get up*, which of the following would you say is true about the author?

☐ Ofrece un ejemplo personal de cómo es posible cambiar el horario de sueño.

☐ Ahora la autora continúa con los mismos (*same*) hábitos de dormir que antes.

Congratulate yourself! You have just gotten some basic but important information from a long passage without having to read it word by word.

5 Reading the text

Automatic processes are learned following the earlier use of controlled processes.
                                    – Barry McLaughlin (1978: 319)

Because the reading process is such an individual process that takes place inside readers' minds, moving it into the public arena of the classroom in order to monitor, analyze, discuss, and modify it is difficult. This public discussion is the most important activity that occurs in the reading classroom. Recent research indicates that becoming more aware of what readers do when they read, becoming conscious of their own reading processes, is a powerful tool for improving reading efficiency (Carrell 1989; Carson et al. 1990; Shih 1992). Basing our approach on that research, we start by exploring what happens when readers read – that is, when they consciously control and monitor their reading (i.e., become conscious of, pay close attention to, think about the elements in, or identify the interactions taking place in the reading process.)

To become better readers, students need to become aware of how they are reading and what they could do to improve comprehension. They need to develop their level of metacognitive awareness. The term *metacognitive* comes from the field of cognitive psychology and is increasingly used in language teaching and learning. **Meta** means after or behind, and **cognition** means the act or process of knowing or perception. Thus, **metacognition** is understanding what is behind, what supports or informs, readers' knowledge and perception. In the simplest terms it means understanding the processes of knowing, or how (not just what) readers know and perceive. Reading teachers are responsible for helping their students use every possible strategy and ability available to them during the act of reading. In order to do that, teachers need to understand reading behavior as thoroughly as possible.

This chapter begins with exercises to help you develop a conscious awareness of your own reading processes, enabling you to understand more fully the issues involved. Then it focuses on activities that help students develop during-reading strategies to build their comprehension of the text, to monitor their comprehension as they read, and to adjust their strategies as needed. Finally, the chapter turns to during-reading activities that can be used with students at the beginning and low levels of language proficiency.

Since the reading processes that L1 readers use are automatic and unconscious, it is virtually impossible to examine them. The only time that such automated processes may become visible in the L1 is when readers are given a text that is at or beyond their upper limit.

Exercise 5.1   Building your knowledge

Turn to Appendix A at the end of this chapter and read the passage once; take no more than 6 minutes for this reading. As you read, try to monitor your own processes. When you find yourself trying another strategy in order to comprehend the text, write a quick note about what you are doing. You may also annotate the text and take any notes you need to help you make sense of it. When the time limit is up, stop and write a list of the various things you did while reading this text (e.g., rereading words or phrases, trying to guess definitions of words, using organizational clues to follow the argument, using syntax to help understand grammar or meaning, etc.). Then, working in pairs or small groups of 3–4, discuss and compare your strategies and processes with others in the class.

Exercise 5.1 should cause you to think in detail about what happens when the reading process breaks down, thus giving you a glimpse of what happens to students when they try to read passages or texts in the L2/FL that are difficult for them. This activity requires that you monitor your own reading processes. You probably used a variety of reading strategies as you read.

The reading process

Teachers can help students build predictions and expectations for the text they are going to read by doing various prereading activities (see Chapter 4); teachers can also help students while they are reading. During reading, readers' minds repeatedly engage in a variety of processes, seemingly all at once. Using top-down and bottom-up strategies, readers use prereading information to make some predictions about the text. Using bottom-up strategies, readers start by processing information at the sentence level. As they process the information that each new sentence gives them, they check to see if and how that information fits, again using both bottom-up and top-down strategies. They are checking their comprehension of this text to see if what they just read fits with what they already know about this topic or what they expected to read. They are predicting what information they expect to read in the next few sentences. They read on, repeating this process until they come to the end of the paragraph.

At this point they are usually formulating the main idea of the paragraph. If they thought they recognized a main idea sentence at the beginning of the paragraph, they will now be checking to see if that early prediction is still a valid one. They may mark it in some physical way: highlight it in the text, make a note in the margin of the text, or write notes on a separate piece of paper. If they are unsure, they may decide to wait until they have read the next paragraph. If there is not a stated main idea in the paragraph, they may compose one. They read on in this manner until the end of the text or until comprehension breaks down, necessitating the use of different strategies.

This brief (and incomplete) description sketches the very complex process that occurs in the reader's mind during reading according to the interactive model. Very skilled readers carry out these processes automatically. Less skilled readers need to understand and learn the processes, then practice them consciously before their reading improves and the process becomes automatic, as the epigraph highlights. The teacher's job is to make these processes conscious for students so that if they are not already doing these things as they read in their L2/FL, they begin to consciously practice them and develop their ability to read more effectively. In order for this to happen, teachers need to work with students *while they are reading,* using activities that will require them to participate overtly in these processes. Doing such activities slows down the reading process and injects outside control into the readers' private worlds. In this regard, these activities are intrusive. However, the end result of engaging in such activities outweighs their inconvenient aspects.

Some actions aid readers' comprehension of the written text, some actions monitor readers' comprehension, and some actions help readers evaluate the information they get from the text and adjust their reading strategies if needed. All of these actions occur instantaneously and perhaps concurrently while readers read, but for purposes of examination they are separated here into distinct categories.

Building comprehension of the text

Readers use both top-down and bottom-up strategies to comprehend a text, and the mixing of those types of strategies constitutes the interactive process described in Chapter 1. The bottom-up strategies provide a linear or sentence-by-sentence building of comprehension. Top-down approaches, such as discourse-level strategies, aid readers' comprehension of larger pieces of text, such as a paragraph or section. They help readers see how an individual sentence or a group of sentences contribute to that larger meaning (a top-down approach). Efficient readers employ both types, moving from one to the other as they read (the interactive model).

Exercise 5.2   Building your knowledge

Look at each of the reading strategies you listed for Exercise 5.1 and determine if it is more bottom-up or top-down. Write BU or TD beside each one. Which are used most – top-down or bottom-up strategies? Compare your list with those of other classmates.

The following list includes several specific reading strategies, some of which you probably identified as you were doing Exercise 5.1.

- Note the key words in the first sentences of the paragraph or text
- Decide which word announces the main topic of the paragraph or text
- Decide which words announce the specific aspect of this topic of the paragraph
- Note if there is a sentence that states a probable main idea
- Note the most important words from each sentence as you read
- Ask yourself how this information relates to the information that came before it
- Look for examples that illustrate the ideas stated before
- Look for details that provide more specific information on the topic
- Look for a sentence that concludes this particular aspect of this topic
- Look for words that indicate a change in the kind of information
- Look for a sentence that provides information about a new aspect of this topic

Each of these strategies may be used several times while you are reading a text.

Several recent studies have emphasized the importance of providing explicit training in when, where, and how to use various reading strategies (Carrell 1989; Shih 1992). Given the importance of using strategies, teachers need to be able to introduce them into the classroom while students are reading. Classroom 5A is an example of such a plan, using Reading Textbook Sample 3, "Modern Fathers Have Pleasures and Problems." An examination of this plan and its implementation in the classroom provides further insights into the teaching act.

While planning this lesson, the teacher read the entire text and parsed it into comprehensible sections. Paragraphs 1–3 make a cohesive section; they discuss James Hogan's thoughts about his role as the father of a baby. In fact, from these paragraphs alone, readers could expect that the entire text will discuss only James Hogan's experience.

CLASSROOM 5A   LOW-INTERMEDIATE LANGUAGE PROFICIENCY (PART 1)

Objectives for this lesson
- Increase Ss' conscious awareness of during-reading strategies to build comprehension

SWBATs
1. Identify key words of a section of a text
2. State a main idea of a section
3. Predict what the next paragraph might contain based on text already read

Barb's class

Step 1 (6 min.)
T has Ss cover all of the text with a sheet of paper except the first three paragraphs. T instructs Ss to read those paragraphs and look up when they are finished. When all Ss have finished, T tells them to take a piece of paper and quickly answer these questions *without looking back* at the text: (1) What are two or three of the most important words in this section? (2) What is the main idea of this section? Write a complete sentence.

Step 2 (4–5 min.)
T calls on several Ss to report their important words and writes them on the board (putting checkmarks for each additional mention of the same word). When finished, T asks Ss why they chose those words. T repeats the reasons as Ss give them.

Step 3 (4 min.)
T has several Ss read their main idea sentence aloud to the class. T repeats each sentence so that others can hear it again.

Step 4 (5 min.)
T asks Ss what they think they will read in the next paragraph. T calls on several Ss to answer, repeating their answers as necessary for general comprehension. T then has Ss uncover and read paragraph 4.

Step 1 asks students to work individually to answer the two questions. Steps 2 and 3 review their answers. The great majority of students should be able to come up with generally the same key words and main idea. As the teacher listens to student responses, she will not make evaluative comments but merely act as the microphone, repeating answers so that all can hear and follow the discussion. She will use the majority response to guide her as she continues the lesson. If the majority response is the appropriate one, she will immediately focus students' attention on the discussion of how they got those answers (the second part of steps 2 and 3). If most students did not supply the appropriate answer, the teacher will then use questions to guide them to discover the answers. Guiding questions might focus on sentence-level information to see if there was a problem with literal comprehension: Who is James Hogan? What did he do when his daughter was born? Why did he do that? What problems has he had? Alternatively, questions might focus on the reading strategy of determining the main idea: All of these paragraphs talk about James Hogan; do they talk about *all* parts of his life or just one part? How many sentences talk about quitting his job? How many about his being a father? Which idea is more important here – James Hogan's role as a father or the issue that he has given up a job in order to care for his daughter? How many sentences are about problems of being a father? The teacher will decide which type of questions to use and how many to use based on her assessment of how well the class is accomplishing the objectives of the activity. The sentence-level set of questions focuses more on language, whereas the discourse-level set focuses on a particular reading strategy to build whole-text comprehension. If students are reading a text that is pushing the limits of their language proficiency, language questions will be helpful. If they are reading within their proficiency range, such questions are not as useful and will perhaps bore them. In these instances discourse-level strategies are more challenging and, ultimately, more rewarding.

Step 4 is actually a prereading strategy, but since the answer is based on information gained from previous text paragraphs, we also include it here as a skill for building reading comprehension. Given that all the sentences in paragraph 3 talk about problems, it is likely and appropriate that students will predict that the upcoming text will also talk about problems. Even though the teacher knows that the text proceeds in a different direction, she will accept all possible predictions and encourage students to keep all of them in mind as they continue to read.

The use of guided questions enables students to hear the kinds of questions that they should be asking themselves if they did not select the appropriate answer. This activity makes the process visible to students and is more instructive than the teacher simply acknowledging that one answer is correct and another is wrong. Frequently, the discussion among students in answering the teacher's "Why . . .?" question in steps 2 and 3 will bring out the same information without the teacher having to ask guiding questions. Therefore, the teacher should listen carefully to such discussions and emphasize (and sometimes elaborate on) the helpful ideas that students themselves identify. If the students can teach each other (with a little help from the teacher), everyone benefits: The students who already know how to determine a main idea are actively engaged in reviewing the strategy, and the students who are having trouble are getting the help they need from peers. Most important, the focus of the discussion is on how the process works – not on whose answer is right and whose is wrong.

TEACHER NARRATIVE

While teaching step 4 of the plan for Classroom 5A (part 1), I asked students to predict what they were going to read in paragraph 4, given what they had read in the first three. Most students said that it would contain more of James Hogan's experiences as a father. One student narrowed that to more examples of his problems. I pointed out that was a more specific prediction and asked why he thought that. A couple of other students provided other similar answers. Then one student said it might talk about some of the fun things. Again, I asked why. He answered that a parent has good and bad things happen. Quickly another student added that she agreed because of the title, which said "pleasures and problems." I asked her to read the title out loud. She did and then another student said, "Maybe it will talk about other fathers. The title says 'Modern Fathers.'" Without my guidance, the last student had introduced another valuable source of information on which to base predictions, another strategy. I congratulated the class for using a variety of reading strategies to predict. I then repeated the three strategies they had used: the use of previous text, the use of their own knowledge of the topic, and the use of the title.

– Jo Ann Aebersold, U.S.A.

The decision about how much of the class to base on sentence-level language and how much on reading skills can be definitively made only as the class begins to unfold. Even though teachers can predict how the class will go based on their knowledge of the text and the students, they need to be prepared to adjust their plans as they teach. Students' performance should direct the implementation of a lesson plan. If the great majority of students have the appropriate answers, there is no need for the teacher to ask guiding questions of either a language or reading skills nature; the class can simply progress at its own speed and practice what the students already know.

Classroom 5A (part 1) presents and practices building comprehension skills by having students write ideas on paper. Students can use other means as well. One of the most common is marking the text in some way, either by highlighting language or writing comments in the margin. Obviously, these means are possible only if the text belongs to the students. Yet another possibility is the use of overhead transparencies (OHTs) and OHT pens, as Classroom 5B exhibits. This Classroom Plan presents a more language-oriented strategy to build comprehension, using Reading Textbook Sample 4, "Our Future Stock."

CLASSROOM 5B   ADVANCED LANGUAGE PROFICIENCY

Objectives for this class
- Increase Ss' conscious awareness of strategies to build comprehension
- Show Ss the connectedness of text through vocabulary

SWBATs
1. Recognize words that all refer to the same idea
2. List clues that indicate reference to previous ideas
3. State how this ability increases reading comprehension

Giorgio's class

Step 1 (6–8 min.)
T puts an enlarged copy of the first three paragraphs of the text on the OHT and tells Ss that authors use many techniques to connect sentences within a text. One of those is the use of different words that refer to the same idea. T directs Ss' attention to the text on the OHT and reads the first sentence aloud to Ss. He asks what the key phrase is ("an incredible array of new technologies") and circles it with an OHT pen. He reads on, circling the words or phrases that refer back to the key idea. He then draws lines between them. He reads paragraph 2 in this manner.

Before he reads paragraph 3, he tells Ss to find a partner to work with. As he reads paragraph 3 aloud, he stops at the end of each sentence to ask Ss if there were any words referring to already mentioned ideas. T circles words that Ss tell him to.

When the paragraph is finished, T reviews Ss' choices with them, asking them if they agree with all the circled words. After class discussion (T asking guided Qs, as needed), T can make any changes Ss direct him to.

Step 2 (15 min.)
T instructs Ss to read paragraphs 4–5 individually and circle words in the same manner. Then T has Ss form small groups of 4 or 5 to compare and discuss the words they marked.

Step 3 (3 min.)
T hands one S in each group a paper copy of the enlarged text for paragraphs 4–5, a blank OHT, and a different color OHT pen, if possible. T instructs each group to put the OHT over the enlarged copy of the text and circle the words that their group agreed upon in those paragraphs.

Step 4 (8–10 min.)
T collects all OHTs and piles them one on top of the other on the corresponding text on the OHT to see where the discrepancies are. Ss then discuss the differences (T guiding with Qs).

Homework: T instructs Ss to read the rest of the text at home and continue to mark such connected words.

Exercise 5.3   Building your knowledge

Look at the text for Classroom 5B and circle all the words that refer to the key idea, "an incredible array of technology." Compare answers with two or three classmates.

Another strategy that builds comprehension asks students to look at the relationships between sentences in any one paragraph. Sentences can relate to previous sentences by providing a restatement or paraphrase of that sentence, by providing support (an example, statistical evidence, authority sources, etc.), by stating a reason, result, cause, or an explanation. Focusing students' attention on any words that announce these relationships helps students to look for them when they read. If such words are not present, this type of activity requires students to think about such relationships in a conscious way and make connections between the ideas even when the text does not.

Other strategies for building comprehension that can be emphasized in the classroom are recognizing transition sentences and recognizing a change in topic when transition sentences are not present. At the whole-text level, students need to be able to see how ideas have been organized in order to make the author's point, and they need to be able to distinguish major section ideas from paragraph main ideas from details. Various activities can be used to present and practice any one skill. For example, teachers can provide a partial outline and have students fill it in as they read a text from beginning to end. Or, teachers can instruct students to write a main idea for each paragraph. Then students look at which paragraphs cluster together to form a section and draw a bracket or box around them. One activity provides more guidance than the other, but both have the same purpose: to make students consciously evaluate the importance of different pieces of information. This list of strategies to build comprehension, although incomplete, points up the importance of focusing on building comprehension skills from time to time in class. Other strategies can be gleaned from different L2/FL textbooks that teachers use.

Exercise 5.4   Building your knowledge

Look at all the reading exercises in Reading Textbook Samples 1–5. What kinds of during-reading exercises can you find? What strategies do they promote? Is that purpose explained? Be prepared to discuss a during-reading exercise. Use other L2/FL books, too.

Your investigation of the various reading texts in Exercise 5.4 may have revealed that during-reading activities are (1) infrequent, (2) not always well explained, and (3) not integrated into the reading textbook as thoroughly as they might be. More than any other skill, during-reading activities are almost totally the work of teachers.

Monitoring text comprehension

Monitoring comprehension means that readers are constantly checking to see if the strategies they are using are furthering their comprehension of the text. It is difficult to distinguish strategies to build comprehension and strategies to monitor comprehension since they are interactive and thus occur simultaneously. Strategies that build comprehension focus on how the text progresses and the meaning of the text as it builds sentence by sentence and paragraph by paragraph. Strategies to monitor text comprehension focus on assessing from time to time what the text has stated as compared to what readers thought it was going to say. For example, examining the first sentences of a paragraph for a statement of a main idea that foreshadows the rest of the paragraph is a strategy for building comprehension. Stopping at the end of each paragraph and asking if the main idea predicted at the beginning of the paragraph is supported by the other information in the paragraph is a strategy for monitoring comprehension. In other words, if the reader's strategies for identifying the main idea of this paragraph did not work, other strategies are needed. If the strategies worked, the reader continues.

Classroom 5A (part 2) is a continuation of part 1 and demonstrates how strategies for monitoring comprehension are used with Reading Sample Text 3.

CLASSROOM 5A (PART 2)

Objectives for this lesson
- Improve Ss' ability to monitor their comprehension
- Help Ss see how text is connected

SWBATs
1. Confirm Ss' prediction of the main idea for this paragraph
2. Confirm Ss' proposed main idea of this paragraph using previous text
3. Identify the words that refer the reader back to previous parts of text

---

Barb's class

Step 5 (4 min.)
After Ss have read paragraph 4, T asks them which predictions were supported by the information in that paragraph. (Show of hands). T affirms that frequently predictions are not supported; the important part is to check. When they are not confirmed, T asks Ss what they should do. (Review the

CLASSROOM 5A (PART 2) *continued*

text carefully.) In this case, T tells Ss to look at paragraph 4 again to see (1) what its most important words are and (2) what the main idea is. (Ss answer.) T then asks Ss to check to see if the main idea of this paragraph (change) was mentioned in the first three paragraphs.

Step 6 (10 min.)
T reads the first sentence of paragraph 4 aloud to Ss. T writes "this change" on the board and points to "this." T tells Ss that "this" refers to an idea mentioned before. T repeats "this change" and asks, "What change is the author talking about? Where can we look to find the answer?" (Ss discuss and arrive at the answer: the paragraphs before.) T should affirm that answer and write "role" on the board to help Ss express the change of the fathers' role from a traditional style to a modern style: Fathers do more for their children now than before. T has Ss scan previous text to see if the word "change" occurred (no) and then later text to see if it occurs again (yes, in paragraphs 6–9).

Step 7 (6 min.)
T asks Ss to pick out the most important word(s) in the first sentence of paragraph 5. (Ss answer.) If Ss answer "reasons," T has them read the paragraph to see if their prediction is confirmed. If Ss can't identify "reasons" as the most important word, T points out that one of the two key words simply repeats the topic of the reading as a whole ("change") while the other ("reasons") introduces new information that will add to that topic. T tells Ss to scan the paragraph to check and see if "reason" or a synonym occurs.

Continuation
T directs Ss to read the rest of the text in the following way: Read the first sentence of the paragraph and answer Q1; then read the rest of the paragraph and answer Qs 2 and 3.
1. Does the first sentence of the paragraph contain the main idea for the paragraph? (before they read on)
2. Do the rest of the sentences in the paragraph affirm your prediction or not? (after they have read the paragraph)
3. How does the main idea relate to the topic "change of father's role"?

In steps 5 and 7, the teacher directs students to check the accuracy of their prediction by comparing it with the main idea that they came up with after reading the paragraph. In both steps, the teacher is prepared to guide the students to the appropriate answer if need be. Teachers should use students as the source of the information that needs to be taught or reviewed as much as possible; it not only promotes student investment in the class, it also helps teachers foreshadow or review other reading objectives. Another way that students can become a source of information that helps others in the class learn is to have them record short verbal reports (also called think-aloud protocols) to be played for the whole group. This technique for enhancing students awareness of and use of a variety of reading strategies is an increasingly popular tool in the reading class (N. J. Anderson 1991; Davey 1983; Devine 1987; MacLean & d'Anglejan 1986). Tape-recorded reports give teachers insight into the reading processes of individual students; they also allow students to hear how their peers use various strategies when processing a text.

The activities devised by the teachers in Classroom 5C teach strategies for monitoring comprehension in different ways.

CLASSROOM 5C   INTERMEDIATE (KELLY) AND ADVANCED (SASHA) LANGUAGE PROFICIENCY

Objectives for this class
- Establish habits for monitoring comprehension
- Make explicit the need for monitoring comprehension

SWBATs
1. State their own habits for monitoring comprehension (asking questions, checking back with statements in the introduction)
2. Use more than one habit for monitoring comprehension (hypothesis checking, knowledge checks, strategy changes)

Kelly's class	*Sasha's class*
Before this class begins, the teacher needs to have a student complete a verbal report tape that gives his reflections and thoughts as he is reading a text. If the student records several minutes of reflections, the teacher can select a portion that is particularly useful or use the tape in several classes.	
Step 1 (10 min.)	*Step 1 (5 min.)*
T puts one page of a reading text on a transparency and shows it on the OHP. T has Ss read the first three paragraphs. Then T puts a transcript on the OHP of an audiotape that was made by a person reading the same paragraphs and has Ss read it as T plays the tape. T tells Ss that this is a think-aloud protocol. T gives Ss time to read it carefully.	After Ss have read and discussed a text, T asks them *how* they tried to understand it. Did they ask any questions as they read? Did they look ahead to confirm what they guessed might be important? As the Ss give ideas, T writes them on the board. Once they have developed a list, T assigns another text for homework and asks Ss to put a check beside the strategies they used and which part of the text they used them in.

CLASSROOM 5C   INTERMEDIATE (KELLY) AND ADVANCED
(SASHA) LANGUAGE PROFICIENCY *continued*

Step 2 (10 min.)	*Step 2 (5 min.)*
Whole class discusses the reading strategies that this reader used.	In the next class T puts Ss in small groups to discuss the strategies they used. T asks Ss where in the text they had problems and what adjustments they made.

Step 3 (3 min.)
T assigns a different text for Ss to read aloud at home into a tape recorder. As Ss read the text for the first time, they should talk aloud about what they are thinking as they read. Then they should listen to their own tapes and make a list of the strategies they used. (During the next class, Ss are put into small groups to discuss the strategies they used while reading the same text.)

Exercise 5.5   Building your knowledge

Examine both classes in Classroom 5C to see how they are alike and how they differ. Consider how the differences may affect students' learning of the strategies being taught. Discuss your answers with classmates and note any new issues that are brought up for consideration.

Both of the plans in Classroom 5C could effectively make students aware of strategies for monitoring comprehension. One difference between them is that Kelly's plan helps the students develop a list of strategies for monitoring comprehension by recognizing them in the example she provided. In Sasha's class, students are asked to come up with strategies by recalling their own reading experience. The unknown factors in evaluating any plan are, of course, the abilities of the students with whom the plan will be used and the teacher using it. Regardless of the plan or the students, teachers need to remember to discuss the nature and the value of monitoring comprehension while reading, because few L2/FL reading textbooks do.

Here is a list of useful questions for readers to keep in mind when monitoring comprehension:

- Did I accurately identify the main idea of this paragraph?
- Does the information in this paragraph makes sense according to the information given in earlier paragraphs?

- Did I correctly identify possible transition sentences at the end of the previous paragraph or section?
- Does the information in this section fit with the overall focus that was stated in the introduction or the title? If not, why not? How is it different?
- Does this information make sense given what I have read in this text? given what I know of the topic from my own personal knowledge?
- Did I ask questions as I read?
- Did I make guesses? Did I check to see if they were confirmed or not?
- Did I recognize problems quickly?

Monitoring comprehension of the text is a vital and ongoing activity. It is like a gyroscope on a ship; it enables readers to adjust their strategies so that they do not veer too far off course. Students who do not monitor their comprehension as they read invent their own versions of the information in the text and frequently land at destinations other than those charted by the author.

Adjusting reading strategies

When comprehension is monitored but not adjusted, reader expectations may not be met. For example, the student in the Teacher Narrative at the beginning of Chapter 4 started reading *The Proud Tower* with the belief that it would tell him about the battles of World War I, but he found no mention of battles in the entire book. He had formulated expectations based on the title (excluding the subtitle). When he realized that the text did not provide any accounts of warfare, he did not question or adjust his initial expectations in order to align his comprehension and his predictions. In other words, he failed to try other strategies. If, as readers monitor their strategies, they sense that their expectations are not being met, then they need to adjust what they are doing. **Adjusting strategies** means changing the strategies readers are using based on the answers to monitoring questions.

Although Kelly's plan in Classroom 5C focuses attention on the use of monitoring strategies, it does not foster the use of adjusting strategies. In order to include this skill in the plan, Kelly could tell the students to listen again to their think-aloud tapes and identify three types of problems they encountered as they read the text and at least three different strategies that they could use to solve or avoid each problem. This simple addition would require no more than 5 minutes on the part of the students and would maximize the use of this activity. Classroom 5D provides an example of a plan to teach adjusting strategies.

CLASSROOM 5D   INTERMEDIATE LANGUAGE PROFICIENCY

Objectives for this class
- Make Ss aware of the value of using different reading strategies
- Prepare Ss to deal with reading problems

SWBATs
1. Note a reading problem and state what it is
2. Identify other strategies that Ss can try in response to a specific problem

Lucienne's class

Step 1 (5 min.)
T tells Ss that the purpose of this activity is to *monitor* and *adjust* their use of reading strategies. After a discussion of the meaning of those two words, T passes out a generic worksheet and tells Ss to stop after each paragraph and answer the Qs. The worksheet repeats the following sequence many times:
   Main Idea (MI) of paragraph (after reading it):
   Prediction for next paragraph:
   Confirmed?   *Yes   No*
   Questions I have at this point:

Step 2 (time depends on the length of the text read)
Next day: T puts Ss in small groups of 4–5 and has them compare the MI statements that they wrote for each paragraph (without looking at the text). T tells them to mark any MI statements that were very different from the rest of the group.

Step 3 (12–18 min.)
T tells Ss to note if they wrote any Qs by the MI statements that were different from the rest of the group. Then T tells Ss to review those paragraphs in the text as a group to see what they now understand to be the main idea.

Step 4 (10–12 min.)
T asks class as a whole how they did. This gives individual Ss a chance to talk if they want to. Or T can ask about a specific paragraph that she thinks will be problematic: How many of you had problems with paragraph X? What kind of problems? When did you become aware of a problem? What did you do? What else could you have done? What other strategies might have helped?

Step 5 (2 min.)
T tells Ss to look over their worksheets again now that they know the places in the text they didn't understand and think about what happened in those parts. Then they should write an entry in their Reading Journals that discusses what they learned about their reading comprehension.

Reading researchers have amassed clear evidence that poor readers are less likely than good readers to question their guesses about the meaning of a reading, and are less likely to recognize evidence that contradicts their guesses (see Kletzien 1991; Pressley et al. 1990). Even though these studies were conducted in L1 reading, the implications for L2 reading are important. Making students aware of explicit monitoring strategies and the need to adjust strategies is an important part of the reading class. Such activities are especially appropriate for academic work and higher reading proficiency levels, since they focus on organizational patterns of texts, language issues, and ways to respond to academic materials. They are also useful at lower levels to raise awareness of text types, to make explicit the purposes for reading various types of texts, and to emphasize strategies appropriate for different texts. Chapter 6 will take up the issue of evaluating the information comprehended from a text, a process that takes place after reading.

Reading activities for lower levels of language proficiency

In this section we limit our discussion to issues and activities related to the reading of modified language texts written specifically for students with lower levels of language proficiency, since reading an entire authentic text is rarely within the range of beginning students (see Chapter 4). Because reading texts for students at this level are usually quite short, most teachers and textbooks do not do during-reading activities. Rather, they concentrate on prereading preparation and postreading exercises to facilitate comprehension. The fact that few during-reading activities are usually done does not mean, however, that they cannot or should not be done. Even a short text should be augmented with short, during-reading activities from time to time.

In many modified texts the information is presented in a standard format: A main idea is given, and details that support the main idea follow. Occasionally, information is presented in a different way. For example, the author starts by presenting one view of a topic and then suddenly changes and presents the other. Students, expecting a standard progression of presentation, frequently lose the thread of information when the text does not develop as they expected. Some L1 readers may do likewise in these cases. Unlike the L1 readers, who stop and ask themselves what the author is doing, L2/FL readers automatically assume it is their own lack of language that is causing their lack of comprehension. In such cases, teachers should inject a short during-reading activity. The quickest, least intrusive way to do this is to have students read to a certain point and then stop. The teacher asks one or two questions about that particular part of the text – specific questions about the ideas or events described. Then the teacher asks students what they think will come next. If the students answer in a way that indicates that they still have not grasped the significance of the change announced in that part of the text, the teacher may encourage them to keep an open mind. The first *detailed* questions provided a check of the students' comprehension of the text they had read so far and also allowed students who had not understood it to hear the information they needed. This process strengthens the comprehension of all students. By asking the students to predict the next action, the teacher takes their thoughts forward to the text that is to come. The teacher's final comment reminds students that they should be flexible in their expectations. The teacher might also ask them to consider the idea that the author is changing his order of presentation. After they have finished reading the text, the class should discuss what happened in the text and look again at the crucial parts where the change occurred.

As you plan

During-reading activities are best introduced, modeled, explained, and re-inforced while students are actually reading during the class time. Students need careful work and discussion in class to be clear about the benefits of stopping while they are reading to examine the processes they are using. These strategies are easier to introduce, explain, and use when the text the students are reading is familiar and well within their proficiency range. However, it is when the text is particularly challenging that these strategies can be the most helpful; therefore, during-reading strategies should be used from time to time with more difficult texts as well. Because all of the activities suggested in this section constitute an interruption to readers' interaction with their texts, these activities should be the exception rather than a regular practice. During-reading activities are generally more useful for readers at the intermediate and advanced levels and are not as produc-tive for students at lower levels of language proficiency, who are probably interrupting their own reading quite a bit anyway.

The reading comprehension processes discussed in this chapter are inter-twined. When readers ask themselves a monitoring-comprehension ques-tion and they find that their predictions, hypotheses, assumptions, and understanding were correct, the process is transformed into building comprehension. Teachers need to be able to separate the processes in order to present and discuss them with students. In this way, students who are not using these strategies when they read in the L1 or L2 can begin to consciously employ them, with the ultimate goal of using them automatically.

McLaughlin describes the process by which a consciously monitored or controlled strategy evolves into an automatic one:

> In L2 learning, for example, the initial stage will require moment-to-moment decisions, and controlled processes will be adopted and used to perform accurately, though slowly. As the situation becomes more familiar, always requiring the same sequence of processing operations, automatic processes will develop, attention demands will be eased and other controlled operations can be carried out in parallel with the automatic processes as performance improves. (1978: 319)

During-reading activities may be the most challenging for teachers to put into practice. Teachers with a refined understanding of the many reading processes and strategies readers use will be more effective in the classroom.

Expanding your knowledge

1. Classroom 5A, part 2, contains activities that practice reading skills beyond those mentioned in the SWBATs. Examine each step carefully and identify what objectives and SWBATs are appropriate for those activities.
2. (a) Examine Reading Textbook Sample 4, "Our Future Stock," and identify the relationships that exist between sentences. Pick any two paragraphs; read each sentence in those paragraphs and answer the question "How does the information in this sentence relate to the previous sentence(s)?"
   (b) Write a multistep plan that would teach this skill to advanced-level students.
3. Read Reading Textbook Sample 5, "Theoretical Perspectives on Societies," and write a description of what a teacher could do with this text to teach students to monitor their comprehension.
4. Using Reading Textbook Sample 6, "More Men Infiltrating Professions Historically Dominated by Women," select a strategy for building comprehension and write an activity that lasts no more than 20 minutes to teach that strategy. Your activity may focus on the whole text or on a part of the text. Be sure to include objectives and SWBATs.

Chapter highlights

1. *The reading process.* Teaching reading means understanding the reading process – how it works and what happens when it breaks down. During-reading strategies and processes can be taught explicitly (1) through teacher modeling and (2) through activities, both top-down and bottom-up, that illustrate the various processes effective readers use.

2. *Building comprehension of the text.* Building comprehension of the text is the process through which readers construct their own understanding of the meaning of the text. Students can become conscious of their use of such strategies and can learn to use those strategies more effectively.

3. *Monitoring text comprehension.* Monitoring text comprehension is the process through which readers check back to see if their comprehension building is progressing smoothly. Such strategies include using verbal reports, stopping to verify main ideas and confirm hypotheses, recognizing and fitting in new or unfamiliar knowledge, and asking questions throughout the reading process.

4. *Adjusting reading strategies.* When reading comprehension and the monitoring of comprehension begin to break down, students need to know how to check and perhaps to adjust the strategies they are using – quickly and, eventually, automatically.

5. *As you plan.* Activities that interrupt reading should be used sparingly. A cycle of teaching how to monitor comprehension and how to use reading strategies should always lead to a review of those new skills, so that each new cycle builds upon an improved foundation and becomes a part of the students' learning spiral.

Appendix A   Reading text for monitoring strategies and processes

THE BACKGROUND AND COLLABORATIVE HISTORY OF THE STUDY

The roots of this inquiry are in the still young but highly diverse tradition of cognitive studies. Sketching these roots may be the best way to explain this study's theoretical foundations and its particular vision of how cognition, context, critical literacy, and classroom research can affect each other. The work in cognitive studies that has influenced us has explored thinking in a variety of situations. It includes studies of "everyday cognition," such as Scribner's observation of men setting up the delivery orders in a milk plant (1984), Chase's look at how cab drivers succeed with incomplete mental maps and visually triggered knowledge (1982), Hayes' discovery of the "ten-year" phenomenon in the musical development of major Western composers (1981), and Larkin's comparative studies of how physicists and freshmen represent and solve physics problems (1983). In the field of reading and writing we have drawn on work such as Brown and Palincsar's demonstration of the dramatic gains poor readers make as they develop the "metaknowledge" to control their own reading process (1989), Scardamalia and Bereiter's descriptive model of young writers' knowledge-telling strategy (1987), Rose's cognitive analysis of students with writing blocks (1980), and my own work with John R. Hayes and our colleagues tracking the shifting structure of the writing plans people make as they compose (Flower & Hayes, 1981c; Flower, Schriver, Carey, Haas, & Hayes, in press). Cognitive studies often use multiple methods that range from naturalistic observation to collecting clinical, structured, and cued recall interviews, to process tracing with think-aloud protocols, to posing experimental tasks, to building computer simulations. (These simulations, as in the Larkin study, are used to test how well the researcher's theory of what people do matches the procedures real people actually use when the simulation or the descriptive theory is used to solve a genuine physics problem.) In its still brief history, this diverse body of work seems characterized by its curiosity about real-world cognition and by the flexible, often inventive research methods it brings to its investigations.

   Working in this cognitive tradition, we set the additional goal of conducting *exploratory* empirical research – of understanding the phenomenon

From Introduction by L. Flower in *Reading to Write: Exploring a Cognitive and Social Process* by L. Flower, V. Stein, J. Ackerman, M. J. Kantz, K. McCormick, and W. Peck, © 1990, Oxford University Press.

itself in greater depth rather than conducting an *experimental* test of a theory about it. This has important implications for both the process of research and the nature and limits of our observations. In the mythos of experimental research (i.e., in the cartoon version) one begins in the morning with a clear-cut hypothesis – a potential answer to a well-defined question. By noon that hypothesis is expressed in an experimental manipulation and set of pre-/posttests. A large pool of subjects known only by number are "run," and once the results come in, the meaning of the study swiftly emerges, expressed as an Anova, or, better yet, a more powerful stepwise regression, in which a set of clear main effects can speak for themselves with little need for interpretation. This caricature of an experimental study would wring a rueful smile from any experimentalist who has wrestled with the imponderable problems of forming a testable hypothesis and the intractable nature of a good design. Nevertheless, these ideals of initial clarity, rigor, and falsifiable hypotheses are central to that mode of discovery and its particular virtues. In contrast to that procedure, the process of much research in composition shows an alternative picture of how knowledge can be developed. The exploratory investigations that go on, particularly in cognitive research, can give us a glimpse into what is possible when rhetoric and composition reclaim the tool of controlled empirical observation and put it to work in the service of their own educational questions about complicated human and rhetorical events.

Like many research projects launched by a surprise, this particular study had its beginnings in a classroom. To encourage the students in an advanced writing class to understand their own cognition and look more closely at their reading and writing processes, I had asked them to take the role of researchers, using observations of themselves as a tool for self-analysis and reflection. As they read a short text, they were to think aloud with a tape recorder, collecting whatever thoughts went through their minds during the process of comprehending the text and writing their own statement on the issue it posed. The transcript or "think-aloud protocol" they created would be only a partial record of their constructive processes, focused on the reader/writer's conscious play of mind. However, this record can be astonishingly rich, and unlike normal retrospection, it makes the surprising and evanescent flow of the writer's thinking available for later reflection.

6 Reviewing reading

> . . . discussions and question-and-answer sessions after
> the reading stimulate high-level thinking, which in turn
> whets the students' appetite to learn more.
> – Robin Scarcella and Rebecca Oxford (1992: 97)

In the world of ideal L2/FL reading classes, the students would all finish their reading and promptly begin to talk to each other about what they understood from the reading. Of course, they would all ask questions about the parts they were unsure of and give personal reactions to the parts that they found surprising, unexpected, comical, unbelievable. They would review the structure of the text. The conversation would then expand to other texts that they have read on the same subject and evolve into an evaluative discussion of how the information in those texts relates to the information in the text they just read and to life experiences they have had. They might even comment on the effectiveness of the organization of the information in the text and the writer's choice of language (vocabulary, grammar, transitions, etc.).

In the world of real L2/FL reading classes, however, such behavior rarely happens spontaneously. Students are unsure of what they have read; they feel that they do not have sufficient language to say what they want to say. They hesitate to admit that they are not sure what they just read. They are apprehensive about being evaluated by the teacher and their peers. They elect to sit silently and wait for the teacher to ask questions or for other students to speak.

Therefore, teachers need to devise ways of reviewing reading so that they can observe reading and work with it. In this chapter we examine different strategies that students can use to (1) review the information in the text, (2) discuss information not in the text, and (3) evaluate the information in the text. Then we look at postreading issues and activities for students at the beginning and low levels of language proficiency.

Reviewing information from the text

Even though exchanges among students do not occur spontaneously as described in the ideal reading class at the beginning of this chapter, teachers

116

can use planned activities to get students thinking about the text, reacting to it, and evaluating it. In order for students to reach these goals in this way, teachers need to be aware of the objectives of postreading activities:

- Identify the topic of the reading
- Have a general idea of what the text says about its topic
- Understand the main ideas put forth in the text
- Discern the relationships among the main ideas
- Understand the details given in the text to support the main ideas
- Recognize the information the text implies but does not state
- Recognize the structure of the information in the text
- Identify the language used to show the organization of ideas
- Assess the value of the information presented in the text
- Recognize language use, such as irony or satire

If teachers keep these in mind as they look at chapters from reading textbooks and as they plan and teach reading classes, they will continue to discover not only new subtleties of the objectives stated here but new objectives as well. It is this continuing inquiry into the process of reading and of teaching reading that propels teachers to develop their own appreciation and understanding of this very complex skill.

Comprehension questions

One of the most frequent and time-honored activities is the use of comprehension questions. Comprehension questions can be composed by teachers, book authors, or students. They can be presented in writing or orally. Questions can be asked before students read, while they read, or after they read. They can be answered individually or in groups. Students can write the answers or state the answers. Regardless of where questions come from or how they are used, comprehension questions in and of themselves can differ greatly in what they ask of the students.

A text comprehension question can cover various aspects of content: the thesis and main ideas of the text, various specific details, the difficult parts, and so on. It can also focus on language: particular rhetorical structures, grammar patterns, vocabulary. A set of reading comprehension questions found at the end of a reading text can focus on one type of question or it can combine types of questions. Questions that focus on language are usually found in vocabulary or grammar exercises (see Chapter 7). In this chapter, we limit the discussion to questions covering text content.

Reading comprehension questions in the L1 have been categorized over the years in various ways. Much of the work that has been done in this regard since the 1960s has been inspired by the work of Benjamin Bloom, presented in the *Taxonomy of Educational Objectives, Handbook 1: Cognitive Domain* (1956). The taxonomy, a hierarchically structured classification of the skills and abilities of the mind, consists of six levels, each successive level including and building upon the previous ones:

Knowledge: The ability to recall specific information and universal concepts, methods, and processes
Comprehension: A type of understanding such that the individual knows what is being communicated
Application: The transfer of information or concepts discussed in one context to another context
Analysis: The ability to see the organization of a communication and the relationships between ideas
Synthesis: The ability to put together pieces in order to see a structure that was not obvious before
Evaluation: The ability to consider and judge the value of the materials in a given context for a specific purpose

(adapted from Bloom 1956: 201–7)

Each level is further broken down into subcategories. Thus, when students recall factual information, they are using the thought processes of knowledge. When students recall information and paraphrase it in some way, in addition to knowledge, they are using the process of translation, a subcategory of comprehension. Bloom's complete discussion of these levels gives teachers a tool for distinguishing the cognitive processes that students can use in the classroom when answering reading comprehension questions.

Later works by others (Aebersold 1984; J. C. Barrett 1976; Bormuth 1969; Davies & Widdowson 1973; Pearson & Johnson 1978) attempted to connect Bloom's categories to the processes students use to answer different types of questions. In other words, in order to determine what thought processes readers must go through to answer questions, teachers need to know what information is provided to them in the text and how that information is provided. For example, a question eliciting the main idea of a paragraph requires different cognitive processing depending on whether the idea is explicitly stated in a sentence in the text, usually at the beginning of the paragraph, or whether it is not stated in any one sentence in the paragraph and must be constructed by synthesizing the information throughout the paragraph. In the first case, locating the information to correctly answer the text question is more, although not completely, a matter of literal-level comprehension; in the second, it is a process involving other levels of cognitive behavior.

Research examining categories of reading questions and some L2/FL textbooks frequently uses terms like *literal-level questions* and *inferential-level questions* to distinguish between information that is in the text and information that is not. Regardless of what term is given to different levels of questions, it is clear that some questions require more thinking and text comprehension than others.

Exercise 6.1   Building your knowledge

1. Read the text in Reading Textbook Sample 3, "Modern Fathers Have Pleasures and Problems," and then answer the postreading questions in exercise 3, "Finding the Facts," which follows. Note the part of the text that you needed to answer each question completely.
2. Compare your text notes with those of a few other classmates. How much of the text was absolutely necessary to answer each question adequately? (a sentence? a few sentences? a paragraph? a few paragraphs?) What level of reading questions are these?
3. Now repeat these steps with "Reviewing the Story" in the Comprehension Activities for Reading Textbook Sample 1, "Who's Calling?"

Even questions in low-level texts can be mentally engaging if they ask questions that require higher-level mental processes.

Classroom 6A describes a class plan in which the teacher uses questions as his main tool to build reading comprehension. It is based on Reading Textbook Sample 1, "Who's Calling?"

CLASSROOM 6A   BEGINNING LANGUAGE PROFICIENCY

Objectives for this class
- Discuss the story from the text
- Use the text to make inferences
- Understand the culturally shaped parent–child interactions depicted in the text
- Learn phrases to use when talking on the phone

SWBATs
1. Tell the story to a partner with a few prompts
2. Infer how Frank and Sarah know each other and identify clues in the text
3. State how direct or indirect American children are with their mothers in this situation
4. Use appropriate language to request to speak to a person when Ss call someone

CLASSROOM 6A   BEGINNING LANGUAGE PROFICIENCY *continued*

Kazem's class

Step 1 (12 min.)

(*Ss have read the text once and done the Comprehension Activities that follow.*)

T tells Ss that the title of this text is "Who's Calling?" (T writes it on the board) and states that the title is a question. T asks (on the board), "Who is calling? What's the answer?" When he gets an answer, he continues with the following questions: "Who is Frank Standish? Who does he want to speak to? Why is he calling? Why is he asking her out to dinner?" After Ss give possible answers, T asks, "Do we know for sure? Are we certain?" If Ss say yes, then T asks them to show him where the text says that.

At this point T makes a point about what we know for sure and what we think we know, but we are not sure = inferences. T asks Ss, "How does Frank Standish know Sara? Do we know for sure? Can we guess? What information in the text helps us to guess?" T asks, "Are there any questions about Sarah or Frank Standish?" T waits for Ss to answer and uses their answers to continue the discussion.

Step 2 (4 min.)

T puts Ss in pairs and identifies one S in each pair to restate the information that we know for sure about Sarah and Frank Standish. T tells the other S in the pair to listen carefully and help if necessary.

Step 3 (6 min.)

T tells Ss to work together with their partners to decide what we know for sure about Ben, Tina, and Carol and what we can understand. T circulates while Ss work.

Step 4 (4 min.)

T puts the pairs into groups of 4 people, or two pairs. T identifies one person from each pair to state first what we know and what we can infer. Each pair should check the other pair's information.

Step 5 (6 min.)

T has Ss in each group number off from 1 to 4 and assigns parts by number (1 = Sarah, 2 = Frank, 3 = Tina and Carol, 4 = Ben). Ss read the dialogue as a small group activity.

Step 6 (2 min.)

T tells Ss to close their books; then the Frank characters should call the Ben characters by phone and ask for Sarah. T tells other Ss in group that they may help (with their books closed). After 2 min. or so T calls on one or two groups to perform for the whole class, commenting on how polite the people are, etc.

CLASSROOM 6A   BEGINNING LANGUAGE PROFICIENCY *continued*

Step 7 (2 min.)
T tells Ss to take a sheet of paper and write the beginning of the phone conversation between Ben and Mr. Standish. When Ss are finished, T asks: "What is an inference?" T collects papers.

This sequence of activities allows for a lot of individual student talk time as the students review the information in the text, mostly from memory but sometimes by referring to the text. At the same time, the teacher is presenting and reinforcing the difference between stated information and inferred information. This distinction is seen again as the students do the exercises that follow the reading. While the distinction is the same, the focus presented in the exercises in the textbook sends the students back to the text to review specific bits of conversational language that convey meaning and feeling. After students have worked with the reading in class, as described in Classroom 6A, they should be assigned to read it a second time, go over any exercises that they have already done to check their answers, and complete the rest of the exercises in this chapter. A variation on step 7 would be for the teacher to have a handout ready with several statements about the information from the text and have the students individually mark each sentence as either stated or inferred. The teacher would then collect the papers and check to see if everyone had understood the concept and was able to apply it appropriately to the information in this text. Another variation would be to take the idea of inferences one step further and talk about probable inferences versus possible but not probable inferences; this refined distinction is always useful at all levels of reading.

Questions asked by teachers can be used to build comprehension of higher-level texts as well. In addition to vocabulary, and perhaps because of it, one of the most challenging tasks facing L2/FL readers at the advanced level of proficiency is establishing the main idea of an individual paragraph in order to later see how that paragraph might fit into the reading as a whole. Such an analysis activity is illustrated in Classroom 6B, based on the text in Reading Textbook Sample 4, "Our Future Stock." You may wish to read paragraph 3 of that text before you turn to Classroom 6B to see one way in which a teacher might work with her class to establish the main idea of a paragraph if they have had a problem comprehending it.

Such activities take a fair amount of time and thus cannot be done with each paragraph. This process should be done only when (1) that paragraph is of major importance to the overall development of the argument of the text as a whole, or (2) it has been ascertained that a particular paragraph has not been understood by a majority of the class. Working through this

CLASSROOM 6B   ADVANCED LANGUAGE PROFICIENCY

Betsy's class

Step 1 (4–6 min.)

T asks Ss if the main idea of a paragraph can frequently be found in the first or second sentence of the paragraph. T tells Ss to read just the first sentence and pick out 2 or 3 words they consider to be key words. T puts those words (*revolution, jobs, nonexistent*) on the board and asks Ss what they mean. T tells Ss to assume, for the moment, that these words are the main idea and to look and see if they can find any other words in the paragraph that mean almost the same thing. T puts the words from the Ss on the board. T asks Ss if their assumption that these words are important to the main idea is a good one. Should they continue with this assumption or try a new one?

Step 2 (3–5 min.)

T directs the Ss' attention to sentences. T asks if there are any sentences that are less important than other sentences because they are restatements, examples, or more details. T takes Ss' attention back to the most important sentences (1 and 2) and asks Ss to look at how these sentences are different and how they are the same. Then T asks Ss what the main idea of the paragraph is.

thinking and comprehending process with students from time to time allows them to see how others come up with main ideas of paragraphs and reminds them that these are strategies that they can and should use when they are unable to comprehend automatically. (It is also important to let students know that sometimes it is hard to understand the main idea of the paragraph because the writer of that paragraph did not construct it well.) This main idea activity works with almost all levels of students, even low intermediate. Sometimes just counting the number of words with similar meanings in a paragraph, or counting the number of sentences that have information on the same topic, helps students see which idea is prevalent.

At the beginning of this section, we mentioned several considerations that teachers must keep in mind when using comprehension questions. In addition to the kind of questions to be used, teachers must decide how to use them. Should questions be answered in class or for homework? Should they be done individually or in groups? Should they be used after the first reading but before the second reading of the text? Who should write the comprehension questions? The following are some general guidelines.

Questions that focus on language or low-level cognitive skills might best be done individually and at home and before any subsequent rereadings of the text. They help students build literal comprehension of the text. They are less cognitively demanding and text-bound, are easier to answer, and benefit other higher levels of mental processes. Questions that deal with analysis, synthesis, and evaluation are more demanding and less text bound. Since these higher-level questions can be frustrating for some students, teachers should plan their use carefully. Students benefit greatly from the thoughts, experience, and knowledge of their classmates, and small group discussions of higher-level questions may be the least threatening and most helpful way to introduce this level of work. A first assignment that asks students to engage in small group, oral discussion of higher-level questions is a low-risk alternative to having a whole-class discussion where only the bravest or best will risk giving answers. A subsequent assignment would be to write the answers to these, or other, higher-level questions. The advantage of the small group assignment is that students will learn from their peers before they must produce individual answers. The disadvantage of too frequent use of the small group format is that weaker students may become dependent on stronger students for answers.

The consideration of using oral questions as opposed to having students write questions is also important. Oral questions, whether high-level or low-level, are usually answered immediately and always provide the advantage of allowing students to learn from peers. On the other hand, students have less control over the language and content of the answers when they answer quickly in class. Written responses give slower students time to work, and they allow students more control over the language. Similar advantages and disadvantages accompany the choice between using questions in class or as homework assignments. In-class discussion generates enthusiasm and knowledge, but it allows some students to opt out of the activity. Responses to written questions are usually checked by the teacher, or by other classmates, and demand the participation of all. Variety, balance, and matching the task to the mode and type of question are all elements of a good class plan.

In the beginning of the course, teachers should assume responsibility for seeing that all levels of comprehension questions are included, writing them as necessary. As students learn about the different kinds of questions, they, too, should be involved in writing and categorizing questions.

Summaries

Another postreading activity to review reading is to have students write a quick, closed-book summary in class. Asking students to spend 10 or 15 minutes writing down what they just read is an informal and fairly unstructured way to get them to review mentally the information in an overt manner. If the teacher collects these summaries and reads them at home or in a spare moment in class, she gets a general idea of the class's reading comprehension as a whole and of how individual students compare with one another. In this way the summary writing activity is primarily an informal assessment tool of students' comprehension. However, if the teacher writes comments about each students' comprehension on the summaries and returns them to the students, the activity becomes a formal assessment. The value of writing a quick, in-class summary in order to cement, and perhaps augment, one's comprehension has a long history in L2/FL teaching. Teachers may use summaries for in-class learning-oriented activities as well, as shown in Classroom 6C.

CLASSROOM 6C   ADVANCED LANGUAGE PROFICIENCY

Johanna's class	*Ted's class*
Step 1 (12 min.) T tells Ss to write summaries of the text read with their books closed. T collects the summaries, reads them at home.	*Step 1 (12 min.)* T tells Ss to write summaries of the text read with their books closed.
Step 2 (Ss do other planned postreading activities that develop their comprehension of the particular text.)	*Step 2 (8–10 min.)* T tells Ss to sit in small circles of 3–4. T tells Ss to reread their own summary silently and then pass it to the person to the right to read. They should continue in this fashion until each one has read all the summaries in the group.
Step 3 (12 min.) (*In a later class after all the activities in step 2 have been completed*) T has Ss write another quick, in-class summary of the same reading.	*Step 3 (5 min.)* T tells Ss to discuss which summary in their group they like best and why. They should be prepared to report to the class as a whole.
Step 4 (10 min.) T passes back the first summaries to Ss and asks them to compare the quantity of main ideas and supporting details to their second summary. T then calls on various Ss to report on their findings.	*Step 4 (5 min.)* T calls on each group to report to the class on the positive aspects of the summaries that they liked.

Exercise 6.2   Building your knowledge

1. Consider the students' understanding of the purpose of the summary writing in each of the two classes in Classroom 6C. Who is doing the assessing? Where is the students' focus? What will the students understand as a result of the activity? How expansive is that focus?
2. Compare your answers with those of your classmates and discuss the thoughts behind each of them.

In both of the classes in Classroom 6C, the job of assessing students' summaries is squarely in the hands of the students. This contrasts with the initial summary activity described in this section, in which the teacher is the assessor, and raises the question of how effective learning relates to the issue of assessment being in the hands of the students or in the hands of the teacher.

When the teacher makes a formal assessment, the students are left out of the assessment process. They receive the final assessment, usually in the form of a grade, after the teacher has applied her own criteria. When the students make informal assessments, they are in the center of the activity and are greatly engaged in the process. They are learning what makes one summary more effective than another, and they evaluate their work by those criteria. When the students make informal assessments, however, is the teacher left out?

In a student-centered approach, the teacher plays a more discrete role in assessing. To keep track of what each student is learning, the teacher can have students write a journal entry or can give a quick quiz to see if their perception of their abilities to write summaries is somewhat close to the teacher's perception. As long as student and teacher perceptions are synchronized, the teacher need not put a grade on every summary. When students assess, they are actively engaged in finding out what makes one person's summary better than another's; they are not only building their comprehension of a particular text, but they are building their ability to comprehend reading texts that they will encounter in the future, leading to a transfer of skills. Thus, depending on how this particular technique is used, it can be primarily an assessment tool or a comprehension tool. Most of the time teachers are more interested in promoting comprehension strategies and skills in their students than in assessing those skills, and thus they devote more class time to building comprehension.

Discussing information not in the text

The ability to understand or posit information that is not overtly stated in the text is a higher-level reading comprehension ability. Many reading textbooks deal with making inferences. Some of those exercises are based directly on sentences in the text, and some are based solely on readers' knowledge and personal experience.

Exercise 6.3　Building your knowledge

Locate the exercises in Reading Textbook Samples 1–3 that require students to make inferences. Are those inferences tied to the text in any way or are they based on the student's own extra-text knowledge? (*Hint:* Consider all exercises, not just those labeled inferences.) After you've done this, state the difference between an inference and a prediction.

Inferencing and predicting are but two skills that require readers to posit information not stated directly in the text. In Classroom 6A, Kazem taught the skill of inferencing at a low level of language proficiency. Presenting the skill is only one part of teaching it. Helping students when they falter is the other. When students cannot make appropriate inferences, teachers need to be prepared to use text excerpts to guide students' thinking toward reasonable inferences (see Chapter 5 for examples of questions that can be used).

Exercise 6.4　Building your knowledge

Look at Reading Textbook Sample 3, and find the "Making Inferences" questions in part 2, "Comprehension." Write questions you could use if several students in your class were unable to answer question 3 in "Making Inferences." Compare your questions with those of your classmates. Be sure that the questions lead step by step without giving the answer directly.

Another useful inferencing activity is to determine how probable an inference is given text information and clues. Once inferences have been made, the teacher asks students to rate each inference as probable, not very probable, not possible, or in between. This type of exercise forces students to relate their inferences to the text and support their answers. Variations include activities that examine the truth quotient of an inference (probably true, possibly true, possibly not true, probably not true) and activities that ask students to mark inferences as either "can be supported" or "insufficient evidence to support."

Another type of activity dealing with information beyond what is stated in the text asks students to analyze the structure of the text or parts thereof. In Reading Textbook Sample 3, "Modern Fathers Have Pleasures and Problems," we noted that paragraphs 1–3 could be grouped together into a section because they all concerned James Hogan's experiences as a father.

Paragraph 4 could be included as well since it broadened the theme of the text to include all fathers, thus illustrating the title. This is the type of reasoning that readers need to learn to do on their own. Many textbooks provide exercises that call upon students to analyze the text, although they may not be labeled as such.

Exercise 6.5   Building your knowledge

1. Read Reading Textbook Sample 5, "Theoretical Perspectives on Societies," and complete the second postreading exercise, "Reading Worksheet."
2. Return to each question on the worksheet and determine the following. (1) Is it an analysis of text questions or not? That is, in order to answer the question, do students need to analyze various parts of the text? (2) What level of mental processing did it take for you to answer the questions? Was the information given in a sentence in the text (knowledge/ comprehension level) or did you have to look at various parts of the text in order to answer (synthesis)?

Activities that encourage students to distinguish main ideas from details by giving lists of sentences taken from the text and asking students to decide if each is a main idea or a minor idea are a first step toward analyzing text. Outlining activities are the ultimate step. Activities that ask students to outline the whole text are usually overwhelming, so teachers do not start with this type of activity; instead they have students do a variety of different kinds of activities with several different texts over time to build up to outlining. Classroom 6D shows two plans in which teachers break down the structure of a text for students.

Exercise 6.6   Building your knowledge

1. Decide if each plan in Classroom 6D will enable the students to do the SWBATs. Are there any other SWBATs that the students will achieve while participating in either or both of these classes? If so, add them to the list.
2. Tina's and Santiago's classroom activity sequences could be used sequentially if the idea of outlining was relatively new to the students and

CLASSROOM 6D   INTERMEDIATE LANGUAGE PROFICIENCY

Objectives for this lesson
- Increase students' ability to consciously analyze the structure of an academic text

SWBATs
1. Identify the paragraphs that comprise the introduction, parts of the body, and the conclusion
2. Identify the thesis statement in the introduction
3. Separate the main ideas of the body from the details that support them
4. Others?

Tina's class	*Santiago's class*
Step 1 (4 min.) T divides Ss into groups of 4–5. Each person in the group gets a different color of card. T then tells Ss what part of the text their color represents (e.g., pink = intro. & concl., green = 1st main idea and details, etc.). T explains what information each part should include on OHT.	*Step 1 (6 min.)* T puts Ss in pairs and tells them that they are going to outline the article that they have just read. T puts skeletal outline on OHT for a quick, general discussion of how an outline looks and what the different numbers and letters mean. T also points out the use of indentation to show the importance of a piece of information. T then gives Ss a handout customized to the text they are outlining (one number or letter for each point to be noted, and lines to show the appropriate place to start writing that piece of information).
Step 2 (6–8 min.) T tells Ss to work individually and to identify and take notes on the ideas in their parts so that they can present them to their group orally at the end of the time limit.	*Step 2 (15 min.)* Ss work together in pairs to fill in one outline. T circulates to see if help is needed.
Step 3 (10 min.) T calls the time and groups Ss to present the review of their part to the members of their small group. T should tell Ss to listen carefully and follow along in the text as each person speaks to see if the information is correct.	*Step 3 (5–10 min.)* T asks if there are any Qs. If so, whole class discusses. If not, T can either collect the outlines or do a whole-class check on the OHT.

therefore needed more presentation and practice, or if the text was above their level of language proficiency. Decide which class sequence you would do first and which you would do second. Be prepared to explain why.

Outlining activities, as in Santiago's class, or quasi-outlining activities, as in Tina's class, help students review the text in a structured way, paying attention to the differing values of pieces of information and the relationships among them. Outlining, like summaries, requires students to address their comprehension of the whole text and can be challenging. Unlike summary writing, outlining requires students to include all the information and display its hierarchical position in the text. Outlining places greater focus on the structure than does a summary, which is more meaning-oriented.

Exercise 6.7   Building your knowledge

Look at the outlining postreading exercise in Reading Textbook Sample 5, "Theoretical Perspectives on Societies," to see how it aids students in outlining a whole text. Then construct a similar handout for an exercise on Reading Textbook Sample 4.

Other visually oriented activities that require students to analyze and organize information without the use of questions are charts and lists. Examples of this type of activity may instruct students (1) to list all of the reasons for action 1 on the left side of the page and all of the reasons for action 2 on the right side of the page or (2) to fill in a chart for which the major parameters are already constructed. Although these are not as challenging as outlining a text without aids, they do build the types of analytical skills that students can later employ in outlining activities.

Classroom 6D also serves to illustrate the teaching issue of finalizing activities. When teachers finish teaching a reading strategy, it is useful to conclude that section by reinforcing that reading strategy or objective so that students will remember it. When students work with the content of a text and its meaning, it is easy for them to place the content in the foreground of their minds and the strategy in the recesses. Being reminded of the strategy and its value to the reading process helps students build their metacognition. One way to do this is, of course, for the teacher to simply tell them. Another way is illustrated in step 7 of Classroom 6A.

Exercise 6.8   Building your knowledge

Neither of the classes in Classroom 6D has a finalizing step in the plans. Suppose that the idea of outlining was new to students, or that the format that is used in the L2/FL is unfamiliar to them. What final step might the teacher do if she really wanted to emphasize the format to the whole class? Write a final step for each class; it need not be long or involved, but it should reinforce the strategy of outlining.

Finalizing activities are a small but important step in a lesson, because they review the main purpose for a reading activity and thus focus students' attention on it.

Evaluating information in the text

As students read, their comprehension of the text is shaped by their previous learning and experience. They understand the ideas, they make inferences, they question information as they compare it with their own prior experience or knowledge of that topic. These responses to the text are the first step toward evaluative reading. Other strategies that readers should use to read a text evaluatively include:

- Identify the author's purpose in writing the text
- Examine how the author establishes her or his perspective
- Recognize persuasion in writing
- Distinguish fact from opinion
- Check the logic of the development of the author's perspective
- Establish the assumptions underlying the text
- Recognize the influence of the author's personal beliefs and attitudes
- Note the author's use of language to set tone and register

Dagostino and Carifio (1994: 91), in a highly academic book on evaluative reading, list nine instruction goals on the path to evaluative reading, each with multiple strategies, and Silberstein (1994: 85–6) lists five in her teacher-oriented reading techniques book. Both agree that a certain amount of evaluation occurs as readers infuse their own schemata to help them comprehend the text. However, a good deal of evaluation also goes on after the text has been read, as readers consciously think about the text and apply the evaluative reading strategies in a systematic manner.

In addition to focusing students' attention on the fact that they should consciously compare and contrast the content of reading texts with their own knowledge, teachers need to help students apply evaluative reading strategies to specific texts. The purpose for doing so is not to reject or accept the information provided by the text but simply to understand its source, its techinques, and its bias. Students should be encouraged to keep an open mind about what they have read and to take stock of the differences from and similarities to their own knowledge and bias. "The goal in mature reading is incorporating a healthy skepticism into one's reading, perhaps slowing down to reflect given the guidance of analysis and questioning" (Dagostino and Carifio 1994: 84).

Frequently, students know little or nothing about the topic that they read about in texts. In these cases especially they need to be able to evaluate the text. Some of the information they can use to evaluate a text can usually be found in the text itself.

- Does the text present its information in an organized way?
- Are the arguments structured in a step-by-step manner?
- Are there any gaps that are not addressed?
- Does the text present opposing perspectives?
- Does the text confirm any opposing perspectives?
- Does the text use objective, nonemotional language?
- Does the text offer verifiable support for the argument, such as statistics or data collected by others not associated with the author?
- Does the author cite reputable, well-known authorities as sources of information?

A second source of evaluative information is to consider what the reader knows about the author.

- Is the author well known in this field?
- What bias, if any, is the author known to have?
- What affiliations does the author have to particular groups, and what are the views of those groups on the topic?
- What background, experience, education does the author have in this particular area?
- What are the author's views on this topic?

Unfortunately, information about the author is seldom found in the text. Readers often do not know whether the author is a generally respected expert on the topic or not. Even without knowing the status or bias of the author, readers can apply several strategies and begin to develop their evaluative reading abilities.

Silberstein aptly points out that evaluative reading can be done at varying levels of proficiency, but that teachers should beware that engaging in this type of reading may "initially prove an uncomfortable activity. Some students will come from educational and political systems where this would be a dangerous and/or foolish activity" (1994: 86). Students will vary in their ability and interest in developing evaluative reading skills.

Reviewing activities for lower levels of language proficiency

At lower levels of language proficiency, there is a tendency to work with students' comprehension after they have read the text rather than while they are reading. There are two main reasons for this. First, a lot of prereading work is done to prepare students to comprehend. Second, reading texts at this level are usually short, which means that teachers can frequently go over the whole text with the students in class, a luxury that teachers of advanced and superior levels can rarely allow themselves, if at all. A standard practice in low-level classes as well as low-level texts is to ask the students several sentence-level comprehension questions to see if they understood various pieces of information in each sentence. Although some sentence-level questions are useful and therefore appropriate, they should be limited in number because they focus on language and require little thought to answer. Overuse disengages the mind, with the result that students have neither noted the language nor maintained great interest in continuing their investigation of the content of the reading text. At low levels, students can participate in a coherent discussion of the main points of the reading if it is carefully orchestrated and conducted by the teacher. It is also important to build in many opportunities for meaningful practice and repetition. Review Classroom 6A to see these principles applied in a class and Reading Textbook Sample 1 to see them applied in a textbook. Besides questions, we also recommend the use of other activities that stimulate the students' minds by involving them in doing something with the content and the language of the text.

The possibilities that follow vary in what they do and how they do it. As you are reading them, think about what they ask the students to do, what they provide, and what they require students to provide. One activity type that can be done with students after reading is an organizing activity. **Organizing activities** involve giving students pieces of information from the text and then asking them to put those pieces of information in the order of presentation. If the text is a story told in pictures, not in text, like "The Neighbor's Kitchen" in Appendix A to Chapter 4, the teacher could make a worksheet containing several sentences that are in scrambled order and then ask the students to number them in the order that the text presented them – without looking at the pictures, of course. This is exactly what one of the exercises in this text did, except that it was done with pictures rather than sentences. When students have finished this, the teacher could have them read the summary to a partner in order and supply words that show order, such as *first, then,* and *next.* The teacher could either supply possible words on the board or leave it up to the students to come up with them, depending on the students' abilities. Another example of an organizing activity is to provide students with a scrambled sentence that contains one main idea in the reading. Students then have to unscramble the words and write the sentence. Although both activities focus on content and on language, one focuses more on content and the other more on language. Can you say which is which? What other reading objectives could be practiced using this type of activity?

Another possibility to promote comprehension among low-level students is to give students the key words from the text, mostly nouns and verbs with a few adjectives, and ask them to retell the story. This activity can be extremely structured, with each noun-verb combination being given so that students have to focus mostly on the grammar structure of the sentence; or it can be less structured, and thus more challenging, by merely presenting the list in an unordered way so that students have to read all the words and decide which they need as they construct sentences to retell the story.

There are many activities that can be done with low-level classes; the focus of these activities will be either more content-oriented or more language-oriented. Within any one activity, the level of difficulty can be raised or lowered by providing less or more structure or language to the activity. Teachers need to be careful when providing more structure to an activity so that they avoid an activity that fails to mentally engage the students. With these parameters in mind, teachers can explore the use of many activities. Their number is limited only by the teacher's ability to observe, collect, adapt, create, try out, and adjust them.

As you plan

In this chapter, as in previous methods chapters, we have elaborated on specific strategies (reviewing information in the text, discussing information not in the text, and evaluating the information in the text) and activities (using several levels of comprehension questions, using inferencing techniques, using evaluative questions, and creating summaries and outlines). Whatever postreading comprehension activities teachers plan for students, they need to engage all levels of the students' cognition, especially the higher levels, in order to build real and meaningful reading comprehension skills that students can call upon when they read on their own. Teachers who use only literal, sentence-level questions and statements are focusing only on vocabulary and grammar comprehension, and thus are not fully engaging students in reading comprehension.

L2/FL textbooks usually provide a wealth of materials in both reading texts and exercises for teachers to choose from. However, neither should be used blindly. Teachers need to consider and select in an informed manner. Teachers must look carefully to evaluate the purpose and value of each exercise in a book and each activity in a lesson plan. All reading activities are not equally helpful in reaching course goals. Teachers need to be sure of the purpose of the postreading activity: what it provides and what it expects students to provide, and, most important, if the way it asks students to use the strategy is relevant to the way in which students will actually apply the strategy when they read on their own. Whether the activity comes from an exercise in a textbook or from the teacher's plan, it should benefit students – not just occupy their time in class. Activities should build not only students' reading abilities but also their metacognition (discussed in Chapters 2 and 5). Identifying the reason for doing an activity is as important to the development of students' knowledge of reading as it is to teachers' knowledge of the teaching of reading.

Teachers also need to be observant and flexible in their use of materials and plans. No activity in and of itself is always appropriate for any given group of students. **Adapting** either materials or a plan means changing various aspects so that the resulting class activities are tailored to the needs and abilities of students as well as the objectives of the class and the goals of the course. Materials can be adapted in advance of the class in which they will be used, during the planning stage. Teachers can decide that they will use an exercise in a way different from the instructions, or they may wish to disregard a provided exercise completely and develop instead their own worksheet or handout. Although it may not always be possible to produce a large quantity of handouts in a given teaching situation due to a shortage of preparation time or a lack of the means to produce or reproduce them, their use greatly enhances student learning. If well constructed, handouts address the precise needs of the particular group for whom they were developed.

Teachers have yet another opportunity to adapt: At the time that a plan is implemented, teachers should be prepared to change and vary that plan as the class evolves. The teacher should be observant enough to recognize and identify special needs as they arise, and flexible enough to adjust plans on the spur of the moment to take advantage of meaningful teaching opportunities as they arise. At the same time, it is the teacher's responsibility to ensure that all necessary strategies are presented so that course goals can be achieved, that previously taught strategies are revisited from time to time so that students keep them in mind, and that the quantity and variety of exercises be balanced so that students' minds stay engaged in the activities.

There are two main reasons that teachers do postreading activities: to assess students' comprehension of the text *and* to continue to build their comprehension of it. In this chapter we have focused more on the use of postreading activities to build comprehension than on assessment, even though it is in their interaction that effective teaching resides. In actuality, teachers do continually assess informally to find out not only what their students understand of a particular text but also to discover what reading abilities their students employ and with what degree of mastery. Teachers then choose activities that will help students develop their understanding of the text. The details of formal assessment, in which teachers provide written evaluative feedback and determine final course grades, are discussed more fully in Chapter 9.

Comprehending a text is different from recalling it. Memory in an L2 can be significantly shorter than in the L1. When students are looking for answers to questions in the text, they are using both reading abilities as well as memory. However, when they are not allowed to refer back to the text, they are forced to rely solely on memory. When teachers are evaluating rather than building comprehension, students might benefit from being given a minute or two (no more) to look at the text again before receiving the questions; this allows them to jog their memories before doing the evaluative exercise. One minute is enough to take their memories back to the text, but it is not enough for the unprepared student to read the text and do well on the assessment.

Expanding your knowledge

1. (a) Using Reading Textbook Samples 1 and 2, identify the purpose of each postreading exercise. (*Hint:* Some exercises will clearly identify their purpose in their heading or in the instructions; some will not.)
   (b) Consult with your classmates about their findings. If you found any exercises that had purposes other than those mentioned in the reading strategy list in this chapter, add those to the list and share them with your classmates.
2. Classroom 6B has no objectives or SWBATs written in the plan. Reread Betsy's plans and then write appropriate objectives and SWBATs.
3. Notice that neither class plan in Classroom 6D uses questions to procure information for the outline, although they certainly could have. Choose one of the classes and write a list of questions that would elicit the same information from the students without the use of an outline form.
4. Form small groups of three or four persons and select an L2/FL reading text. Any text will do for this activity as long as each member of the group works on the same text. Each of you should individually write

several questions for that text. Try to write questions requiring various levels of cognitive processes as outlined in Bloom's (1956) taxonomy, but don't identify the level you intend each question to be.

5. Using the handout you made for Reading Textbook Sample 4 in Exercise 6.7, write a plan that uses your outlining exercise.
6. Examine Reading Textbook Sample 6 and identify what higher-level cognition purposes teachers could work on using this text. Then write a plan for that section of the lesson. Be sure to write objectives and SWBATs.
7. Interview one or two L2/FL reading teachers to see if they can add to the list of reading objectives on page 117. Also, ask them if they have any favorite postreading activities. Ask them to explain not only what they do and how they do it, but also why they do that activity.

Chapter highlights

Reviewing the reading of a text in the L2/FL classroom through the use of planned comprehension activities allows both teachers and students to observe readers' comprehension.

1. *Reviewing information from the text.* The reading strategies that teachers wish to develop in students so that they will use them while they are reading are usually addressed in postreading activities. The strategies become the objectives of the activities that teachers do in class. The completion of postreading activities promotes greater understanding of the information stated in the text. Asking reading comprehension questions is the most widely used activity to review information from the text. Answering these questions involves differing degrees of mental processing and thus provides different levels of challenge for readers. Writing summaries is another type of activity that can be used to promote comprehension.
2. *Discussing information not in the text.* The ability to understand or posit information that is not overtly stated in the text is a higher-level reading comprehension ability. Inferences, analysis of text structure, and synthesis of information in various parts of the text are all part of these abilities. Activities that ask students to infer, to make charts or outlines, and to extrapolate new information from the text as a whole deal with these levels of cognition.
3. *Evaluating information in the text.* The information that readers gather as they read should be questioned and evaluated by the readers to see if (1) it fits with their own personal knowledge of the subject, (2) it is

presented in a consistent, logical, and complete way, and (3) it is supported by sufficient details and by known and respected experts whose affiliations are noted in the text.

4. *Reviewing activities for lower levels of language proficiency.* At lower levels, teachers usually review the entire text with their students in order to promote both comprehension of content and the learning of the language used to present that content. Activities are usually carefully focused and structured so that students can follow and participate fully, and include comprehension questions and organizing activities.

5. *As you plan.* Postreading activities need to be balanced so as to include all levels of thinking abilities. Teachers need to make informed decisions about which activities to plan and which exercises to use from textbooks. In addition, teachers need to be flexible and observant in creating and using plans in the classroom; they need to adapt materials and meet the needs of the students and the objectives of the lesson and course. Reading comprehension activities can be used to assess or build readers' comprehension. The way a teacher sets up the activity determines whether the activity assesses or not.

7 *Vocabulary issues in teaching reading*

> . . . research evidence indicates that, for both word recognition and learning word meaning, direct teaching apart from context is a useful addition to contextual learning.
>
> – I. S. P. Nation (1990: 190)

Knowing vocabulary is important for getting meaning from a text. L2/FL readers frequently say that they need more vocabulary so that they can understand the meaning of the sentences. Understanding the basics of grammatical structure enables readers to understand the relationship between words, but it does not provide access to the meaning of the sentence. Knowing the meanings of the **content words** (nouns, verbs, adjectives, and adverbs) does. On the other hand, teachers cannot teach students all the words they need to know to read a text with ease – limited classroom time does not permit it – and the students cannot learn all necessary vocabulary in one class – memory does not allow it. Thus, teachers need to decide which words students need to know and how to bring words to the attention of students in meaningful and useful ways.

Teachers have long considered frequency of use to be an important factor in determining which words to focus students' attention on: The words that they will encounter most frequently in the language as a whole are the ones that they should learn. Over the years, several word lists have been produced of words that occur frequently in texts. Since word lists differ depending on the types of texts that are analyzed, any one list is of limited use to a particular group of students. Furthermore, individual students may have a need for words that are important to their areas of interest but are not used frequently. Thus, word frequency, although important, is not the only principle that guides teachers' selection of vocabulary to present in the classroom.

In this chapter, we discuss principles that inform teacher decisions about teaching vocabulary in the L2/FL reading classroom. The chapter is divided into three major categories of vocabulary issues, ordered by time: before reading, during reading, and after reading.

Vocabulary before reading

Once a text has been selected for use in class, teachers need to decide which vocabulary words to teach before students begin to read the text. In making this decision, they need to consider (1) what their students already know of the vocabulary in the text, (2) what vocabulary students need to recognize to make sense of the text, and (3) what vocabulary they will need to know to function in the L2/FL in the future – that is, the overall vocabulary goals of the course.

Words that appear frequently in a particular text because they are related to the topic of the text are known as **topic-specific** or **content-specific vocabulary.** For example, in a text on the topic of ice cream, the words *flavor, texture, cone, sundae, toppings,* and *carton* might appear frequently. Since some knowledge of these words would be helpful for this reading text, they should be presented before students read the text so that students will have a general understanding of these words and recognize them when they encounter them in the text. Although topic-specific vocabulary is quite useful for short-term comprehension, it may not be frequent enough in the overall L2/FL to be emphasized for students to learn. That is, students need to recognize it but may not need to learn it.

Vocabulary that readers recognize when they see it but do not use when they speak or write is known as **receptive vocabulary.** Readers have a general sense of a word's meaning but are not sure of its many meanings or nuances of meaning. **Productive vocabulary** is the vocabulary that people actually use to speak and write. Like L1 speakers, L2/FL speakers have a larger receptive than productive vocabulary. Not every word that L2/FL students encounter should become a part of their productive vocabulary.

Most students need to see a word many times in different contexts before it is learned, or entered into long-term memory. Although there is some indication that salient words in a particular text, whether high frequency in general English usage or not, may be learned from reading (C. Brown 1993: 278), presenting topic-specific words before reading does not necessarily result in students' learning those words. If teachers want students to learn vocabulary, they must emphasize those words in postreading activities. The **introduction of a word** and the **learning of a word** are different matters and require different strategies in the classroom.

Learning a word is a complex matter involving many types of knowledge. In *Teaching and Learning Vocabulary* (1990), Nation identifies the following categories of knowledge about a word:

> *Form:* Readers recognize the word in print and distinguish its various grammatical forms (noun, verb, adjective, adverb).

Position: Readers know the grammar patterns and structures in which a word can occur and the words that frequently appear before or after it, the collocations.

Function: Readers know how common or rare the word is and in what types of situations and texts it would most likely occur.

Meaning: Readers know the various meanings and nuances of a word as well as its synonyms.

(adapted from Nation 1990: 29–32)

This is a lot of information to learn about each word that students wish to add to their productive vocabulary. The vocabulary work that students do in their L2/FL classes is just a first step toward learning a word.

Teachers may use exercises presented in L2/FL reading textbooks to present vocabulary before reading, or they may come up with their own activities to present vocabulary before reading. As shown in Chapter 4, one way to preview topic-specific vocabulary is to preview the topic that students are going to read. By previewing the topic, teachers create the concept (or meaning) of the word even if the students do not have the word in their L2/FL vocabulary. With the concept in their minds, students have a need to see and hear the word, which the teacher can then provide if no one else in the class can. Huckin, Haynes, and Coady (1993: 284) suggest that learning is promoted by creating the need for vocabulary before presenting the words themselves.

Exercise 7.1   Building your knowledge

Examine the activities presented in Classroom 4A–D (Chapter 4). Determine if the vocabulary in those exercises is topic-specific or high-frequency in general English. How is it presented? What is provided for the students and what are they expected to come up with? Is the information provided in a visual or an aural way? What are the advantages and disadvantages of each way?

The activities that focus on the topic first and then on the word to express the ideas that come up while thinking about the topic exhibit a **context-to-vocabulary approach,** or a **meaning-to-progression approach.**

Introducing vocabulary in the context of the topic of the reading text, and not as lists of words separate from the topic or context, is vital to comprehension. Context provides a framework of meaning within which readers comprehend and remember words. That framework and all the associations that readers have of the word within that framework help them learn. This is an important issue in teaching vocabulary and is probably the reason, historically, the teaching of vocabulary has been associated with the teaching of reading. It is also the reason vocabulary should be presented, practiced, and reviewed within a context. The activities teachers use to teach vocabulary and the way they use them depend, of course, on what the text lends itself to, what resources teachers have available, and the needs, interests, and language abilities of students. Teachers may plan activities that (1) focus more on the context as a whole *or* on individual words, and (2) provide students with the vocabulary *or* ask students to generate it.

Whatever activities teachers plan to use to teach vocabulary before, during, or after reading, they should be clear about the answers to the following questions: (1) What kind of vocabulary is being taught? (2) What does the activity ask students to do? (3) What information is provided for students? (4) What do the students have to provide and where do they get it? The answers to these questions help teachers to plan useful vocabulary activities.

Vocabulary during reading

While reading in the L2/FL, students come across words that are unknown to them. The quantity of unknown words in a text will vary depending on how closely the language level of the text is matched to the students' level of language proficiency. The closer the match between the levels, the fewer unknown words they will encounter; the greater the disparity between levels, the greater the quantity of unknown words. Regardless of the match, readers need to know how to employ strategies to deal with the unknown words they encounter when reading. Therefore, teachers need to have knowledge of the strategies available to readers for use during reading, and they need to promote the understanding and use of these strategies in the L2/FL reading classroom.

Teachers have two primary ways to facilitate the learning and use of vocabulary strategies. The first and most powerful way is for the teacher to model the use of these strategies in reading class. When students are reading a text in class and ask, "What does _____ mean?", teachers can guide them to use their resources to answer their own question. To do this teachers need to be prepared to supply at a moment's notice the relevant questions to guide students through the use of a particular vocabulary strategy. Those questions are presented in this section. The second way is for teachers to plan and teach activities that develop students' knowledge of and use of individual vocabulary strategies. In this section we look at which strategies can be of use to students during reading, and when and how teachers can introduce strategies to students.

One of the most useful and overarching strategies for dealing with unknown words encountered while reading is for readers to determine whether or not the meaning of the unknown word is vitally important to their purpose for reading the text. If readers are reading to get a general idea of a text, then they can probably skip over a fair number of unknown words as long as those words are not key words. One strategy to determine if the meaning of a particular word is necessary to the overall meaning of the sentence is to read the sentence without that word and see if a general meaning is obtained. Another strategy is to examine the grammatical function of the word. If it is an adjective or an adverb, readers can probably get by without it.

If, on the other hand, an unknown word appears several times and seems to be key to the general idea, then that word needs to be dealt with. Nouns and verbs are usually important enough to the basic meaning that readers cannot get a general idea without knowing what they mean. In these cases there are three vocabulary strategies that can be helpful: (1) using the context surrounding the word to guess its general meaning, (2) analyzing the parts of the word to guess its probable meaning, and (3) using a dictionary to look up its exact meaning.

Guessing the meaning of a word from the other words around it, the **context,** is perhaps the most useful vocabulary skill that readers can have. The ability to use the words and information around an unknown word in order to guess, or infer, what that word means *in a general sense* will serve students well in almost every reading situation.

Clarke and Nation (1980, as summarized in Nation: 1990) outlined the following procedures for guessing meaning from context:

PROCEDURES FOR GUESSING MEANING FROM CONTEXT

1. Look at the unknown word and decide its part of speech.
   - Is it a noun, a verb, an adjective, or an adverb?
2. Look at the clause or sentence containing the unknown word.
   - If the unknown word is a noun, what adjectives describe it? What verb is it near? That is, what does this noun do and what is done to it?
   - If the unknown word is a verb, what noun does it go with? Is it modified by an adverb?
   - If the unknown word is an adjective, what noun does it modify?
   - If the unknown word is an adverb, what verb does it modify?
3. Look at the relationship between the clause or sentence containing the unknown word and other sentences or paragraphs. Sometimes this relationship will be signaled by a conjunction like *but, because, if,* or *when,* or by an adverb like *however* or *as a result.* Often there will be no signal.

Punctuation may also serve as a clue. Semicolons often signal a list of inclusion relationships; dashes may signal restatement. Reference words like *this, that,* and *such* also provide useful information.

4. Use the knowledge you have gained from steps 1–3 to guess the meaning of the word.
5. Check that your guess is correct.
   - See that the part of speech of your guess is the same as the part of speech of the unknown word. If it is not the same, then something is wrong with your guess.
   - Replace the unknown word with your guess. If the sentence makes sense, your guess is probably correct.
   - Break the unknown word into its prefix, root, and suffix, if possible. If the meanings of the prefix and root correspond to your guess, good. If not, look at your guess again, but do not change anything, if you feel reasonably certain about your guess using the context.

(adapted from Nation 1990: 162–3)

Each part of steps 1–3 is important; using any one of these steps by itself increases the probability of guessing correctly. Teachers may use any one of these steps in isolation simply by asking questions that relate to step 1: Is this word the action of the sentence (or the doer or receiver of the action)? Does this word tell us something about the action (or the doer or receiver of the action?). Once this type of information has been established, the teacher can then conclude by asking what grammar function this word has. Sometimes knowledge of the grammar function helps students to get meaning from text. It is certainly the basis for the next steps of guessing meaning; it helps them to look for possible synonyms in an appropriate grammatical category.

Questions that highlight any step of the guessing-from-context strategy can be practiced by teachers with the class (or individual member of the class) any time that they are discussing a piece of text. It is important not to overuse or underuse these types of questions. Every time teachers tell students the meaning of a word, they lose an opportunity to encourage and aid students in building their own strategies to cope with unknown vocabulary.

Part C.5 of Nation's (1990: 162–3) "Procedures for Guessing Meaning from Context" is actually a separate vocabulary strategy altogether: analyzing the parts of a word. The ability to look at a multisyllabic word and see its meaningful parts is very useful to students when they are trying to understand words they do not know. Multisyllabic words are not commonly used at beginning and low-intermediate levels of L2/FL proficiency, but they are commonly found in the types of texts that high-intermediate and advanced learners might be reading. Native speakers of English have a vast but usually unconscious knowledge of word parts. L2/FL students need to have this knowledge as well.

Every word has a **base,** also known as a **root** or **stem,** which is the smallest unit of meaning. A base can be a complete word, like *hand,* or a part of a word, like *-duce.* A base can occur in many words: *handy, to handle, handyman, to unhand,* and *reduce, introducing, productive.* **Prefixes** are word parts that precede the base and add meaning to it. Most native English speakers have a general idea of the meaning of individual prefixes. In contrast, many do not know the meanings of **suffixes,** the word parts that follow the base, although they can readily identify their grammatical functions. Those preparing to teach English need to have a conscious and accurate knowledge of both. Teachers should have a complete prefix and suffix reference on hand to consult, such as a dictionary or vocabulary development book.

Teaching the skill of analyzing word parts can be woven rather naturally into the class discussions that occur while reading a text. When the whole class is discussing certain lines of text or certain paragraphs containing a multisyllabic word, teachers can use the following procedures to help students.

PROCEDURES FOR ANALYZING PARTS OF WORDS

1. Ask students to look at a certain word and divide it into its parts. Tell them to look for familiar prefixes, bases, and suffixes.
2. Ask students what the base is and what it means. If they are uncertain about whether a part is the base or not, ask them to think of other words they know that have the same part.
3. If there is a prefix, ask what it means.
4. If there is a suffix, ask what its grammar function is. You might want to ask the meaning of the suffix or you might not.
5. Have students check the meaning they have come up with to see if it fits the context of the sentence(s) they are reading. Can they think of a synonym for the meaning?

Going through the steps with them quickly not only reminds them of the steps involved in this skill, but also of the fact that they can use this skill to answer their own questions and thus become independent readers. Teachers should remember to encourage students to check the meaning they come up with to see if that interpretation makes sense in the text as a whole. This final step is very important and is often overlooked.

A final vocabulary skill that is helpful but frequently overused by students when they are reading is using the dictionary. The most important step of this skill is teaching students when to use the dictionary and when not to use it. To be an efficient L2/FL reader, students need to be able to read *without* a dictionary as well as *with* one. There are some reading situations in which using a dictionary is inappropriate or impossible, such as when reading for pleasure or taking a test. As a rule, students should look up a word only (1) when they have already encountered it several times in the text and do not have a general sense of its meaning or (2) when they think that a word is vital to their *overall* comprehension of the text. Each word in a sentence is important in that it adds some further element of meaning to the message of the sentence. However, students need to learn to be satisfied with a general comprehension of all but the most important words, which are the ones students should take the time to look up in the dictionary.

There are many types of dictionaries for use in the L2/FL classroom. At early stages of L2/FL proficiency, students may rely on bilingual dictionaries. This is appropriate at beginning levels when students have too little vocabulary in the L2/FL to understand even simple L2/FL definitions. As their proficiency grows, teachers should require students to use an L2/FL learner's dictionary. There are many available on the market. Learner's dictionaries differ from regular L1 dictionaries in that they (1) include a limited number of words, (2) define a word by using simple, high-frequency words, (3) provide clear explanations of concepts and their relationships to other words, (4) give an example of the word used in a sentence, and (5) list and explain any idioms using that word.

As students progress to advanced levels of L2/FL proficiency, they should be required to use a regular native-speaker dictionary so that they can enlarge and refine their understanding of the vocabulary that they look up. Using monolingual dictionaries promotes the learning of the various nuances of the word as well as of the concepts of a word. An added benefit is that monolingual dictionaries facilitate the user's ability to paraphrase a word, that is, to associate that word with other words that have similar or partially overlapping meanings. In this way L2/FL learners build proficiency in the target language.

Dictionaries contain more than word entries. When students change to L2/FL monolingual dictionaries, they need to be introduced to the kind of information that a dictionary offers. Teachers should be sure that students preview the entire dictionary before focusing on its main function, providing the meaning of words.

In order to look up the appropriate meaning of a word, students need to know what information each word entry contains and how it is organized. A dictionary word entry can contain the following: the division of the word into syllables and accented syllable, the pronunciation, the most frequent meaning of the word, synonyms, other grammatical functions of the word, former meanings of the word that are no longer used, the most common grammatical function of the word, the older languages from which the word is derived, other meanings of the first grammatical function, and other meanings of the other grammatical functions. Dictionaries are brimming with information that is generally underutilized.

Since dictionaries differ in the kinds of information they contain and the ways in which they display it, it is important that every student use the same dictionary entry when teachers teach dictionary skills. This practice ensures that all students follow the same process at the same time. However, once the skills have been learned, the bulk of their dictionary practice should be with their own dictionaries, since ultimately, when students read, they need to skillfully use their own dictionaries.

The most common mistake that students make when using a dictionary is that they use the first meaning given, whether it fits the context or not. Students who practice the following procedures when using the dictionary will avoid this problem.

PROCEDURES FOR USING THE DICTIONARY

1. Look to see if the unknown word is a noun (N), verb (V), adjective (Adj), adverb (Adv), or preposition (Prep). If it is a verb, notice if there is a noun object after it. If there is, look for VT (transitive verb) in the word entry in the dictionary. If not, look for VI (intransitive verb).
2. Look up the word in the dictionary.
3. Look for the abbreviation of the grammatical function that corresponds to the unknown word.
4. Read the first meaning under that grammar function.
5. Go back to the sentence in the text; read it again substituting the meaning you found. Ask yourself if that meaning makes sense in the context of the reading. If it does, go to step 7.
6. If it doesn't, go back to the dictionary and read all the other meanings under that grammatical function. Ask yourself which one makes the most sense in the context of the reading.
7. Decide if you think this word is important enough to add to your vocabulary. If it is, do whatever you do to enter this word into your long-term memory. If it isn't, continue with your reading.

Prompting students with these steps, or parts thereof, from time to time in class reminds them that a dictionary needs to be used intelligently in order to be effective. How much teachers stress dictionary use will depend on their approach to teaching reading in general, their course goals, and their students' tendencies and needs. Some students need to be encouraged to use a dictionary while others need to be discouraged.

In previous paragraphs of this section we examined in detail the steps in various strategies that equip readers to cope with unknown vocabulary in a text. We stated that the most effective way to promote these strategies while students are actually reading a text in class is for teachers to ask questions that will remind students of the steps they can follow on their own to come up with meanings for words. Teachers can focus attention on during-reading vocabulary strategies by having students read a designated portion of the text. Teachers will then ask students which words they did not know the meanings of and conduct a class discussion of which strategies might be useful for a particular word. Using the agreed-upon strategy, the whole class will come up with a definition for that word. This activity is one that teachers can realistically do *while* students are reading. Other activities to teach these strategies need to be done either *after* students have read the text once or twice or *completely apart* from a text in a separate lesson, in which the sole focus is the vocabulary strategy. The approach of presenting during-reading vocabulary strategies in after-reading exercises is the most common approach used in textbooks. Only a few books present vocabulary strategies in separate chapters.

Exercise 7.2 Building your knowledge

Examine the vocabulary exercises presented after the texts in Reading Textbook Samples 3–5 to see if they present any during-reading vocabulary strategies. If so, note (1) which strategies, (2) if the strategy is labeled or not, (3) whether the steps involved in that strategy are explained or only practiced, and (4) if the exercises refer the students back to the text itself or if they provide other text samples for students to use in applying this strategy.

Even though students need to master a complete arsenal of vocabulary strategies, useful vocabulary strategies should be practiced rather than formally taught while the students are reading a text in class. Interrupting the reading process to present a vocabulary strategy lesson is counterproductive to facilitating reading comprehension. For vocabulary strategies to be fully understood and practiced, they should receive their own class time and attention – after a particular text has been read, as an appendage to that reading, or apart from a text – as a stand-alone vocabulary lesson. However, when the occasion arises naturally – as when a student asks "What does _____ mean?" during a class reading activity – teachers should not miss an opportunity to quickly guide students through the steps of the vocabulary strategies that they have already studied.

Vocabulary after reading

After students have read and discussed the text, they are ready to have a last look at the vocabulary. There are a variety of purposes for revisiting certain words from the text: to increase comprehension of the text, to promote vocabulary development, or to test knowledge of various words or vocabulary skills. If the main purpose for postreading vocabulary work is to promote vocabulary development, both teachers and students should focus on either (1) reinforcing vocabulary skills or (2) highlighting individual vocabulary words to be learned. Both of these are valid reasons for devoting time to vocabulary work after reading and discussing a text. Since each student's knowledge of vocabulary is individualized to a great degree, especially as language proficiency increases, the ideal situation is for students to take responsibility for selecting and learning vocabulary. In reality, students benefit from, and usually depend upon, the teacher to structure their vocabulary study. In this section we promote the ideal situation, while acknowledging and addressing the reality, by examining (1) the issues associated with reinforcing certain vocabulary words and skills and (2) an individualized system for students to develop their own vocabulary.

When selecting words to focus students' attention on, teachers should pick words that will further the students' general vocabulary level. For most students that will mean useful words: that is, words that are used across a variety of contexts. For example, whereas the words *cone, carton, sundae,* and *toppings* are topic-specific to ice cream, words such as *containers, product,* and *extras* frequently appear in other contexts as well. In addition, the number of highlighted words per text should be limited to a few so that students can concentrate on learning them. The benefit of teaching vocabulary after reading and discussing the text is that the students' comprehension of the text can be used as the starting point for building the associations for a word, which makes it easier to learn. Many textbooks have vocabulary exercises that refer readers back to the text to look for certain words that have the same meaning as a word given in the exercise. Such exercises take advantage of context and word associations. They also rely on recognition of a word rather than production, which is much more demanding on the students' resources. Exercises that require students to produce the words to be learned should follow recognition exercises so that students can have further contact with the word, perhaps using it first to produce paraphrases and then original sentences about the content of the reading and, finally, using it in a completely different context. Type of vocabulary, number of words to be learned, use of context, recognition before production, and progression from familiar context to other contexts are all issues that

teachers should keep in mind when planning after-reading vocabulary exercises to reinforce specific vocabulary words.

Examining the meaning of a text should always supersede examining the
language used to convey the meaning, except when teachers feel that the
language level of the text has been extremely challenging. In this case,
doing some vocabulary work after reading the text but before discussing it
might aid comprehension. Working on specific vocabulary allows – indeed,
directs – another examination of various parts of the text, thus providing
students yet another opportunity to develop their comprehension of those
portions of the text before any in-depth class discussion takes place. If,
however, adequate in-depth comprehension has occurred, then the most
relevant and pertinent issue at hand is to explore and share that comprehension. The real purpose of reading is to comprehend the text.

When reinforcing vocabulary skills, teachers need to be prepared to
carefully and thoroughly introduce, explain, demonstrate, and practice each
skill separately. Students need to be very clear about what the skill involves
and why it is useful to them. Some textbooks practice but do not teach the
vocabulary skills discussed in the previous section of this chapter. Others
present vocabulary strategies in separate chapters. (See the Table of Contents of *Reader's Choice* in Appendix 3B for an example of this kind of
textbook.) When using a textbook, teachers should examine it carefully to
see if it addresses all aspects of the vocabulary strategy being taught. If not,
teachers will need to fill in the missing aspects. When teaching a vocabulary skill without a book, teachers should prepare separate materials that
use the context of a reading text so that students see the connection of the
vocabulary skill to the process of reading.

Another issue that teachers must consider is whether to *practice* (not
present) a variety of these vocabulary strategies within one text or whether
to focus on practicing just one. The answer to this question depends totally
on the students and their grasp of the basics of the skill. If they know what
the skill comprises but have trouble using it (or simply do not use it),
teachers might want to focus on one skill at a time until students gain some
degree of mastery with it. This same approach is advisable if the students
do not seem to remember what the skill involves. If, however, the students
have metaknowledge of the skill and have had some success at using it in
the past, then teachers might decide to have them *practice* a variety of
vocabulary skills after reading the text.

How do teachers decide which approach to take with students? Since
teachers' decisions should be based on students' abilities and needs, they
need to know what students know about the particular skill. A quick way to
assess their knowledge of a vocabulary skill is to ask them. For example, if

teachers want to know about students' abilities to identify words that are defined in the text (a subskill of guessing meaning from context), they might ask: (1) If you want to check to see if a word is defined in the text, what clues can you look for? (2) What kinds of words do we expect to be defined in the text? If in response to the first question several students can quickly respond that they look to see first if there is a comma immediately after the unknown word and then another comma a few words later, or if there is a comma and the word *or* followed by a word or two and then another comma, teachers know that students have a general sense of the strategies to employ when checking to see if a word is defined in the text. Furthermore, if students respond to the second question with "technical or topic-specific words," teachers can be reasonably sure that they know the rudiments of this particular vocabulary skill.

This approach assesses the knowledge of the class on the basis of several students who answer the questions that teachers pose. When assessing the whole class on the basis of a few, it is important to check a variety of students in the class before deciding how best to proceed. Once this decision has been made (e.g., focus on one vocabulary skill or mix them, practice during or after discussing the text, work individually or in small groups), teachers need to select materials.

Exercise 7.3   Building your knowledge

1. Read the descriptions of these two exercises and then answer the questions in step 2.

   Book exercise

   The book exercise starts by instructing the students that they need to find which of the words listed below are defined in the text. It then gives the words and the paragraphs that the words can be found in. When students find the word in the paragraph, they are to copy the definition that they found in the text, if they found one. If they didn't find one, they are to write "not defined in the text" beside the word.

   Teacher's exercise

   The teacher's exercise asks the students to look at paragraph 2 and locate the words that they didn't know in that paragraph. She then asks the students if any of those words were overtly defined in the text. When students answer, she asks how they know that is a definition of the word they didn't know. Then they proceed to another teacher-picked paragraph and repeat the same procedure, as time and student interest permit.

2. Write "book" or "teacher" under top-down or bottom-up. Which exercise
 . . .

Top-down   Bottom-up

1. gives more direction to the students?
2. picks out the words the student will
   investigate?
3. provides more guidance in selecting
   answers?
4. focuses more on the process, or the
   vocabulary skill?
5. more resembles the type of activity students
   will do when they read on their own?
6. requires more from the student? In what
   ways?
7. must be done in class? Why?
8. is more suited to students' needs?

The teacher's exercise is more top-down than the book activity (although this is not axiomatic). However, not all parts of the teacher's activity are top-down; although the teacher does not choose the words, she does choose the paragraphs the students look at. This is less top-down and more bottom-up than having the students start at the beginning of the reading text, identify words that they think are defined in the text, and then look only at those. It is, however, less bottom-up than only scanning for the words that the book provides while knowing that some of them will be defined and some will not.

There are many variations that teachers can make in their plans that not only keep students alert but also shift the structure of the activity slightly and thus change the level of difficulty and utility for the students. As teachers gain experience, they recognize not only how to vary their plan but also the specific ways in which the variations increase or decrease the students' participation.

Individualizing vocabulary development

No matter how much structure and direction teachers provide to help students learn vocabulary in class, the final responsibility for learning new words rests with the students. This is particularly true as students begin to read more texts of their own choosing. Some students will write the meanings of new words in the margins of the texts they are reading; some will write a list of them and their meanings (sometimes in translation) on a separate sheet of paper. Notes in books and decontextualized lists are not as flexible to review as the card system we recommend here. This card system requires the student to find out a fair amount of information about each word and to write it on an index card in the following manner.

On the front of the card	*On the back of the card*
Write the word.	Copy the definition of the word.
Write its pronunciation.	If a verb, note the grammar structures that can follow it.
Copy any related family words.	Copy any synonyms.
Copy the sentence containing the word from the text.	Write your own sentence using the word.

Working with a word in this way increases students' chances of remembering it. However, establishing a card for each word takes time. Therefore, this system should be used only for a limited number of high-frequency words that the student is interested in learning. Teachers should encourage students to do this for no more than a few words (5–10) per reading text. Once a vocabulary file card system is established, students can then carry the cards with them and review them in the following manner on a daily basis in spare moments.

PROCEDURES FOR REVIEWING VOCABULARY WORD CARDS

Step 1. Students should look at the word, its pronunciation, and related family words on the front of the card to see if they can recall the definition.

Step 2. If they think they know the definition, they should turn the card over and check.

Step 3. If they cannot recall the definition, they should look at the sentence in which they found the word, on the bottom of the front of the card. If they can give a definition, they should turn the card over and check it.

Step 4. If they cannot come up with a definition at all, they should turn the card over and read the definition and the sentence they wrote themselves using the word. They can even add another sentence using the word.

Step 5. After they learn the word, the card can be removed from the "to learn" pile and put in the "to review from time to time" file.

When used regularly, this is an effective way of learning vocabulary. It is fluid and individualized, allowing students to be in charge of their own learning. Teacher intervention is needed only at the point when students are trying to decide if an unknown word they are considering entering into this system is high frequency or not. Occasionally, teachers might collect students' "to learn" file to see what they are studying or the "to review" file to see if they have mastered the words. Usually a quick verbal check in class is enough to see if they are making progress.

Although most reading textbooks provide several postreading vocabulary exercises, teachers need to be sure that such exercises promote the learning of words that are frequent and useful to the level of the students. These exercises may or may not promote the use of vocabulary skills that students will need in reading texts that are not part of L2/FL textbooks. Each and every vocabulary activity has a process behind the product that students are asked to produce. Teachers need to be aware of exactly what each activity asks students to do beyond what the directions ask (the product), and what student skills are called upon to produce those answers (the process). Moreover, teachers need to remember that the continued use of textbook exercises can set up the expectation that students need not be involved in searching for their own vocabulary words to learn. Students need to be reminded that ultimately they are responsible for the continued growth of their vocabulary and that part of that process is the selection of words they have encountered before but are not sure of. Teachers need to ensure that vocabulary skills are used in order to promote independence on the part of readers.

Expanding your knowledge

1. Look at Reading Textbook Samples 1–5 to see when they work with vocabulary (before, during, after students read the text?). Note which kind of vocabulary (topic-specific, high-frequency, or other) is the focus each time.
2. Using Reading Textbook Samples 1–5, answer each of the following questions: Does each exercise emphasize developing vocabulary skills or stressing individual word meanings? If it emphasizes vocabulary skills, does it focus on one or does it review many? If it emphasizes learning individual words, is each of the words in the exercise a useful high-frequency word for a student of that language proficiency level to learn?
3. Read Reading Textbook Sample 4. Make a list of topic-specific vocabulary and put a check in front of the words that are used frequently

enough in the text to be worth presenting to students before they read. Will students be able to guess any of their meanings by reading a few specific sentences in the text? If so, identify those sentences.

4. (a) Using Reading Textbook Sample 5, identify three to five words in the text that students at this level might not know and whose meaning can be derived by analyzing word parts. Write a set of questions that you might use in the classroom to guide students through the process for each of these words (*Hint:* Consult the steps in the list "Procedures for Analyzing Parts of Words" as needed.)

    (b) Pick three to five different words that this level of student might look up in the dictionary. Determine what information students will need to get from the text in order to use the dictionary successfully. Write a set of questions that you could use to guide students to select the appropriate definition from the many offered for that word in the dictionary.

5. Using Reading Textbook Sample 1 or 2, make up a worksheet to present the strategy of guessing meaning from context to low-level students. Remember that your worksheet needs to point students to the strategy without using too much language to explain the procedures.

6. Look again at the postreading vocabulary exercises in the Reading Textbook Samples that focus on vocabulary *strategies.* Answer these questions for each one: Does it explain the usefulness of this vocabulary skill? Does it give all the steps involved in this skill? Does it illustrate how to apply this skill?

7. Look at the vocabulary exercises (not the vocabulary skills exercises) in the Reading Textbook Samples to see what kinds of activities they use to define individual words. Describe what they ask the students to do, how they do it, and the value of the exercise to the students. For example, the first postreading vocabulary exercise in Sample 1 gives students a group of nine words and asks students to circle those that express generally the same idea. It is a like-word association exercise, paraphrasing at the word level; it helps students to build vocabulary in groups.

8. Look at three to five other L2/FL reading textbooks at varying levels to see what kind of vocabulary and vocabulary skills they teach before, during, and after reading and how they teach them.

Chapter highlights

Students state that knowledge of vocabulary is central to understanding reading texts; teachers need to prepare themselves to help students develop their skills to deal with unknown words.

1. *Vocabulary before reading.* Teachers present topic-specific vocabulary before having students read a text in order to aid student recognition of these words as they read and thereby increase their comprehension of the text. This practice promotes short-term memory of a word but not necessarily long-term learning, which requires several contacts with a word in various contexts before students know its various nuances of meaning. Context is crucial to working with vocabulary words.

2. *Vocabulary during reading.* Having students read a text together in class offers teachers the ideal opportunity to model the use of vocabulary strategies that students can use themselves to deal with unknown vocabulary: deciding whether the meaning of a word is vital to overall comprehension, using the context of surrounding words and phrases to guess its general meaning, and analyzing the parts of the word to get at its general meaning. Being able to use the dictionary properly is an important vocabulary skill to be used judiciously while reading. In addition to being modeled in class, all vocabulary skills need to be presented at a separate time so that students can fully understand the various procedures and their value to the reader.

3. *Vocabulary after reading.* Postreading vocabulary work is done to reinforce the learning of vocabulary strategies or the learning of particular words, or to have students revisit vocabulary in various parts of the text in order to increase their reading comprehension. Only high-frequency words at the students' level of language proficiency should be singled out for individual postreading work. In addition, students need to learn to take responsibility for their own vocabulary development.

8 *Using literature*

> . . . there has to be a distinction between the *study* of
> literature and the use of literature as a *resource*.
> – Ronald A. Carter and Michael N. Long (1991: 3)

Reading textbooks for L2/FL reading classes, and especially those for higher-level classes, frequently contain literary texts such as short stories, poems, and excerpts from longer works of fiction. This chapter is designed to alert you to the issues, problems, benefits, and adjustments that may arise when you use literature in the L2/FL reading classroom. If your personal preference or the teaching situation you are in leads you to select a substantial number of literary works for your classes, we recommend that you turn to the standard literature for using literature to teach language (see Carter & Long 1991; Collie & Slater 1987; Duff & Maley 1990; Gower & Pearson 1987; Short & Candlin 1989). On the other hand, if you find that your class textbook includes a few literary works, or you are thinking about using a piece of fiction in your classes, this chapter will serve as an initial guide.

Our approach to using literature in the L2/FL reading classroom includes four considerations: (1) the reasons for using short stories, novels, poetry, and other types of literary works to teach language, (2) some features of literary texts, (3) the adjustments in methods that teaching literature may demand, and (4) criteria for selecting suitable literary texts for our students. These considerations echo our purposes throughout the text, focusing on *why* we should teach literature and on *how* to teach literature.

Reasons for using literature

Fiction and poetry have been a part of language curricula for many years, fading in and out of popularity in response to new theories and methods. Reading textbooks continue to include literature, and a current emphasis on extensive reading opens up a wide range of possibilities for using literary texts. Still, if fiction is used in the language class, it must serve the functions of teaching language and engaging the students. The teacher's evaluation of the reasons for using literature must also be based on the elements introduced earlier: student needs, abilities, and interests. Matching students' abilities with the literary text is especially important. They may be interested in reading literature and want to become familiar with various aspects of a culture through its literature. However, difficult language, complex cultural issues, and the subtle conventions of various genres of fiction may leave students more frustrated than enlightened (see Field 1984).

Editors of reading textbooks sometimes make broad claims about what the study of literature will achieve, indicating that it will "improve your reading, speaking and discussion, vocabulary, knowledge of word forms, writing" (Draper 1993: iv) or at least "improve . . . language skills" (Gower & Pearson 1987, General Introduction, n.p.). Teacher trainers such as Duff and Maley (1990: 3) agree with Carter and Long (1991) that literary texts are to be used as "a language teaching resource rather than as an object of literary study." Collie and Slater (1987), who also address the why, what, and how of teaching literature, argue that literature offers valuable, authentic, and relevant materials that provide cultural enrichment, language enrichment, and personal involvement for the students.

The reasons for studying literature given by Carter and Long (1991: 2), rather similar to Collier and Slater's, imply a set of goals or objectives for the student:

The cultural model
The language model
The personal growth model

These three models are helpful in setting the parameters for course goals and objectives. The cultural model focuses on the value of literature as a window to culture, helping students appreciate and understand other cultures. The language model argues for developing language skills through the study of authentic literary texts; it has been dominant at several times in the history of L2/FL teaching and follows a long tradition of translation as the primary activity that students engaged in to learn an L2/FL. The personal growth model, as Carter and Long define it, helps students "achieve an *engagement*" with the text and develops the students' pleasure in reading while they grow as individuals (1991: 2–3). This individual growth results from a broadening of the reader's experience and from the thinking and reflecting that accompany careful reading. Skilled teachers, therefore, must recognize and articulate their goals and purposes, sometimes rejecting or modifying the suggestions of others. A general list of reasons to use literary texts would include the following:

- To promote cultural understanding
- To improve language proficiency
- To give students experience with various text types
- To provide lively, enjoyable, high-interest readings

- To personalize the classroom by focusing on human experiences and needs
- To provide an opportunity for reflection and personal growth

When any of these are included in the general course goals, literary texts may well be the best materials to use in that class.

Features of literary texts

Narratives from two of our students illustrate their different experiences reading informational texts and reading narrative texts.

STUDENT NARRATIVES

When reading a story the reader shares the writer's thoughts and feelings as the reader thinks and tries to predict about the future or the conclusion while he is attracted, but reading informational texts wouldn't attract the reader after he gets what's needed from the information written. Besides, that information doesn't move the reader's feelings and emotions, and doesn't motivate the reader towards thinking and predicting.

– Hani Halawa, Jordan

When I read a story, I will read it carefully. I want to know when and where the story happened. And I must understand the characteristics of every protagonist in the story. Then I can imagine the plot of this story and follow the development of this story. I think I will enjoy reading a story.

When I read an informational article, I will just read the main point of this informational article. I want to know what happened and what was the result. I just get some information from the article.

– Kuei-lan Lee, Taiwan

Since students find informative texts and literary texts to be different, the teacher must begin preparation by learning the technical differences between literary and expository works. Next the teacher should examine the differences between the various genres of literary works that will influence objectives and lesson plans for the reading class. The issues presented by literary texts may differ in degree and in nature from those presented by informational texts.

Specific examples illustrate several differences between informational and literary texts. Texts A and B, which follow, show two strongly contrasting genres of writing. What processes for monitoring comprehension does the reader employ when reading these texts? Which text seems easier to understand? Why?

Text A
A 39-year-old novelist presented [herself] in October complaining of increasing fatigue and severe "writer's block." For a month she had found it increasingly hard to wake up and get going in the morning. Her energy level was low; she was unable to concentrate on her writing and had trouble meeting deadlines. She had gained 2.25 kg and had difficulty avoiding desserts and high-calorie snacks. Whenever possible, she would nap at her desk or "vegetate" in front of the television. Bills went unpaid, and laundry piled up. She felt "disgusted" at her "incompetence" and pessimistic about the future.

Text B
There's a certain slant of light,
On winter afternoons,
That oppresses, like the heft
Of cathedral tunes.

Heavenly hurt it gives us;
We can find no scar,
But internal difference
Where the meanings are.

None may teach it anything,
'Tis the seal, despair, –
An imperial affliction
Sent us of the air.

Exercise 8.1   Building your knowledge

1. How did you feel about your comprehension as you read each text? What would you guess is the source of each? Do you have any ideas about the author of each text? Did either text have any effect on your emotional state at the time you read it?
2. Try to formulate the main idea of each text. Compare your statement with those of your classmates.
3. What do you believe is the *purpose* of text A? of text B? Is the purpose the same for both? If not, how would you contrast the purpose of each?

Text B[1] is crafted to produce in the reader the actual feeling of sadness and heaviness that a pale winter light, marking seasonal change, creates in many people. Text A (from Rosenthal 1993: 450), on the other hand, is a clinical description of a woman experiencing depression related to seasonal changes. On the surface the texts appear to be quite different, but the topic

1 From *The Complete Poems of Emily Dickinson,* edited by Thomas H. Johnson. 1929 by Martha Dickinson Bianchi; copyright © renewed 1957 by Mary L. Hampson. Published by Little, Brown & Company in association with Harvard University Press.

is the same: the effect of the "slant of light," or the deprivation of sunlight we experience in winter. The methods for teaching texts A and B would have to take into account the different techniques the writers use to present this topic. For instance, it is not useful to approach the poem with a scanning activity, nor to approach the case study with an introductory lecture on metaphors.

The broad differences in these texts illustrate a number of issues that teachers confront when teaching literature, and these issues are not confined to literary vocabulary or language difficulty. The features of literary texts – genre, plot, character, setting, and theme – are additional elements to address. Elements can be charted to make the distinctions between text types clearer:

Informative	*Literary*	*Poetry*
Main idea (MI)	Plot	Theme or MI
Organization of argument	Character development	Imagery
Credentials of author	Theme or MI	Special and general vocabulary
Points that support MI	Special and general vocabulary	Sentence structure
Use of graphs, charts, etc.	Important information about author	Tone
	Setting	Cultural knowledge
	Time sequences	
	Cultural knowledge	
	Tone	

Such a list highlights significant differences between informative and literary texts, but it does not indicate which elements will need the most explanation in class or which will be most foreign or difficult for the students.

Adjusting methods to literary texts

As long as the teacher plans carefully, it is unnecessary to deny students the enjoyment of reading literary texts. Although paying attention to genre, plot, character, theme, language, and setting may appear to complicate the reading process, knowing these elements and how they affect comprehension helps teachers guide their students successfully through the readings. The following basic definitions of literary terms should be a part of the teacher's knowledge base, but they need not be part of students' formal instruction.

Literary terminology

Genre: Just as informational texts may be organized and labeled as arguments, descriptions, or comparison and contrast, literary texts are organized by genres. Genres are types of writing, including the two broad categories of poetry (love poems, sonnets, epic poems, comic verse, verse dramas, odes, and various other types) and fiction (short stories, mysteries, romance novels, science fiction, horror, international thrillers, war stories, and historical novels). Since different genres have different aims and create different expectations, being able to identify the genre of a work will help the reading teacher focus a lesson on that text.

Plot: The sequence of events in a narrative that constitutes the action is the plot. Since the narration of events is common to all societies and a part of the oral traditions and cultural histories of nearly all (if not all) peoples on earth, the concept of plot is readily accessible to students. On the other hand, expectations for plot development are shaped by culture, especially issues of complication, suspense, revelation, and resolution. Some poetry may also include events and tell a story, but generally speaking, plot is less important in poetry.

Character: The characteristics of the people in the work – how they do or do not change, what conflicts they have – are central to most fiction. Character is revealed by what the people in the work say, what others say about them, what they do, what they think, and how others act toward them. Both poetry and fiction have characters, although generally speaking the characters in a work of fiction are drawn in more detail and have a larger role in the theme or meaning of the work than in poetry.

Theme: The message, main point, purpose, or central issue of the piece is the reason it was written. Whereas the expository text may be designed to argue, persuade, describe, or compare, the literary text may try to recreate a human situation (of events, of feelings, of conflict, of pain). The situation the author creates is designed to present some insight or knowledge about life or about human character that gives the reader a new or deeper understanding of some human experience. Theme may be stated explicitly or left implicit. There is often a close connection between the title of the work and the theme.

Setting: The details of location, surroundings, and place (including weather, geography, culture, and historical factors) constitute the setting of a literary work.

Plot, character, theme, and setting are not elements separate from the reading task. Classroom activities may isolate those elements in order to explain them, but eventually students must integrate them as they read.

Teachers also need to be conscious of their beliefs about different types of literature and to know how much their beliefs have been shaped by personal preference and by culture. Since everyone approaches a text with both individualized and culturally shaped expectations, the class should establish shared expectations for a given work *before* the reading begins.

STUDENT NARRATIVE

I like the detective stories, particularly Sherlock Holmes story. I like that point that he solve many difficult mysteries by using his sharp brain. So, this story is very interesting for me. Another good point of reading this story is that we can enjoy guessing what happen next.

– Tosh Oniya, Japan

Students like Tosh will be eager to guess and to formulate their expectations for a mystery story. However, a student who does not share those expectations may be confused and frustrated by the conventions of the detective story. Polling students about their preferences gives the teacher the information necessary for preparing students to use literary texts.

Criteria for selecting literary texts

When the teacher has some autonomy in the selection of literary texts for the L2/FL classroom, two criteria that will shape the selection are (1) the cultural content of the works and (2) the relevance of the works to the lives of the students in the class. Cultural content that is too implicit, as in the novels *A Catcher in the Rye* or *Huckleberry Finn,* may so complicate the students' access to comprehension that the reading becomes a chore rather than a pleasure. Since the cultural content is familiar to the teacher, she will need to be thoughtful and sensitive in assessing how difficult it will be for the students. Second, some degree of match between the students' lives and interests and the literature they read will increase their motivation and interest. Younger students usually respond well to stories about issues that are central to their own lives – relationships, work, cultural adjustment, music. Older students often have a broader range of interests. The teacher who knows her students' preferences will be able to make wiser choices. Whenever possible, a teacher-designed survey of preferences and interests will help in the selection process.

One additional consideration the reading teacher must address is the level of the language in the texts. Literary texts come in nearly all levels, either as authentic texts or as modified texts, and may be appropriate at the advanced level as well as at the beginning or low-intermediate level. In texts A and B, words like "concentrate" and "pessimistic" from the expository text are not much more familiar than the words "oppresses" and "affliction" from the literary text. A short story by O. Henry is not necessarily more difficult than an article from the local newspaper. In other words, it is impossible to make categorical statements about which is harder, more complex, more dependent on allusions, or more contextualized, because the level of language can override genre differences. Current reading textbooks include a wide variety of reading selections in modified English, and most major works of Western literature are available in a simplified form. The choice to use authentic or modified texts will mean weighing the advantages of a controlled level of vocabulary and grammar against the richness of authentic texts. The language proficiency of the students will be the major determining factor, for a text that is too difficult is hardly the right choice to promote enjoyment and growth through reading literary works.

If you decide to use literary texts in the L2/FL classroom, remember that the task is not to have students *study* literature; it is to plan lessons around works of literature, beginning with the shaping of goals and objectives that will focus their language learning. Students will not become great readers in the L2 from reading one novel in a course or a few short stories. Their abilities will strengthen as they read more, read a variety of texts, and internalize the reading habits that we are advocating here. Their abilities will also strengthen as they build one new strategy on the foundations of others until they have a scaffold of support. Likewise, teachers will build on the foundation of their previous knowledge about teaching informative texts (recall our learning spiral in the Introduction) to make the adjustments needed for using literary texts.

As you plan

Planning reading classes that use literary texts means paying close attention to the cultural assumptions and beliefs that influence the students' understanding of the text. The overarching issues that apply to teaching literature include (1) the criteria to use in selecting literary texts and (2) the appropriateness of the activities to the established objectives and SWBATs for the course. Various texts about teaching literature present sets of criteria to use in the process of selecting literature for the reading classroom. Carter and Long (1991) include availability and cultural connections among their criteria that address the need for cultural and background schemata; they also

Table 8.1 Comparison chart of prereading activities for expository and narrative texts

Prereading activity	*Informative or expository text*	*Narrative text*
Predicting content or theme from titles, subtitles, headings, preface, etc.	A useful strategy throughout the text	Only the title may be available for this strategy, since a story seldom has divisions. Chapter titles in a novel (when provided) may be helpful.
Learning topic-specific vocabulary before reading	Useful for key words in the text, important concepts	Useful if the subject is one with many unfamiliar words, e.g., a novel set on a farm or in a workplace
Activating background schema	Useful	Useful
Scanning for main idea	Useful	Main ideas are often deeply embedded and not easy to retrieve from scanning.
Skimming exercises	May provide Ss with a quick overview of the material	Often not useful because plot and character development are rarely retrieved from skimming
Conceptual mapping	May clarify a complex topic	Outlining main events will clarify plot and may be more appropriate; character descriptions will also help Ss recognize and identify main characters in the story.

emphasize other criteria like conceptual and linguistic ease or difficulty, relationship of the text to other texts in the course, and connections to the types of students in the class. Indeed, all of the issues that we raise in Chapter 3 on course design are applicable here – especially student needs, interests, and language levels. In selecting literature or reading books that include literature, it is necessary to review all of these criteria.

There are excellent resources that analyze potential materials for L2/FL reading classes. One is a column in *TESOL Matters* called "Briefcases," which provides brief descriptions of works, including novels and short stories, that other teachers have used in their ESL classes. Another resource is a pair of books that annotate works appropriate for the ESL reading classroom: *A World of Books: An Annotated Reading List for ESL/EFL Students* (D. S. Brown 1988) and *Books for a Small Planet: A Multicultural/Intercultural Bibliography for Young English Language Learners* (D. S. Brown 1994).

The type of text is the determining factor in the focus and development of classroom activities. As a review of how activities match texts, Table 8.1 lists types of prereading activities for both informational and literary texts.

Literary texts in the L2/FL reading classroom provide a refreshing and lively change from other kinds of work in the course. Our cautions about the need to adjust and adapt methods and goals are not meant as a deterrent to using literature. On the contrary, we find literary texts quite useful for improving students' language skills, helping them understand cultural differences, and opening opportunities for their personal growth and understanding. Using a variety of texts will challenge and enrich the teacher as well as the students. As long as the course goals and objectives match the classroom activities, both teacher and students stand to gain.

Expanding your knowledge

1. (a) Working in small groups, find a literary text (no longer than 5 pages) at any level and read it. Make notes on your recognition of genre, plot, character, and setting.
   (b) Compare your observations with those of other group members.
   (c) Determine which of these elements are more important to the main point of the text you have selected.
2. Develop a prereading activity for text A (in this chapter) that includes a recognition of and discussion about the source – the *Journal of the American Medical Association*. The discussion may include how a case study is presented in a medical journal and the introduction of technical words like "fatigue," "concentrate," and "pessimistic."

Chapter highlights

1. *Reasons for using literature.* Increasing the students' interest and motivation, providing variety, and encouraging cultural understanding, per-

sonal growth, and language development are all excellent reasons for using literary texts in the L2/FL reading classroom. The teacher must always remember, however, that the main reason for using any text is to improve the students' language skills. Thus, the teacher needs to set appropriate objectives for reading literature, objectives that focus on language development rather than on the study of literary forms.

2. *Features of literary texts.* In order to use literary texts to the fullest advantage, the reading teacher needs to understand the differences between literary texts and informational texts, and needs to have a general knowledge of the different genres of literature and of issues such as setting, theme, character, and plot.

3. *Adjusting methods to literary texts.* The use of literary texts demands adjustment in methods as well, one keyed to an assessment of students' attitudes toward literary texts. The teacher needs to learn about students' assumptions about literary texts and approach texts from the perspective of understanding the characters and issues, rather than analyzing topic statements and supporting examples, which would be more typical in the study of expository texts. On the other hand, the teacher will often find it useful to modify traditional reading activities that are successful with informational texts so that they work equally well with literary texts.

4. *Criteria for selecting literary texts.* Cultural content, relevance to students' lives, and language level are major considerations in selecting literary texts. Both authentic and modified literary texts are available for the L2/FL reading classroom; the students' language levels, motivation, needs, and interests will determine which type of text is most appropriate.

5. *As you plan.* Although planning reading classes that use literary texts is similar to planning classes that use informational texts, two areas demand special attention. First, the selection of the text will demand sensitive and thoughtful consideration. Second, the students' cultural backgrounds and assumptions about literary works may influence the success or failure of a given work. The more the teacher is able to make those assumptions a conscious part of the learning environment, the better the chances for good communication in class and enhanced learning.

9 *Assessing L2/FL reading*

> In every possible way our language tests should
> complement teacher efforts to create a positive student
> attitude toward the course.
> – J. Donald Bowen, Harold Madsen, and Ann Hilferty
> (1985: 357)

The teacher's role in the reading classroom as a facilitator of learning is inextricably mixed with the role of assessor. Teachers observe and encourage the process of students' learning as it occurs during class time, and teachers simultaneously evaluate the products of students' learning when students speak and respond. These assessments in the L2/FL reading class encompass a variety of measures, from the most informal, alternative, developmental, learning-based, student-centered types to the most formal, teacher-controlled, traditional, and standardized methods. They range from small forms, such as a quiz to recall knowledge or an exercise at the end of a reading, to much larger forms, such as a presentation of a project or a unit examination that measures learning throughout an entire course. Our discussion of assessment examines both the teacher's and the students' assessment needs and focuses on how reading teachers can become thoughtful, attentive, reliable assessors, able to use both alternative and traditional assessment measures that are beneficial to all.

Many people tend to equate *test* with assessment, but assessments are not always tests. **To assess** is to engage in an *ongoing process* that may include exams (periodic exams, midterms, finals), progress tests, quizzes, exercises worked in class or at home, or any other kind of testing or learning instrument. **To test,** in contrast, is to administer a single instrument that tests one or more aspects of a student's learning. Testing is a part of many assessment programs; assessment programs incorporate but do not depend totally upon individual test instruments. However, both tests and other kinds of assessment need to be as accurate, reliable, consistent, and valid as possible.

Various types of assessment activities provide structured feedback to students and become part of their public record or grade for the course. Informal activities serve to give teachers feedback on students' comprehension and mastery of skills, but do not become part of the students' grades. We begin with a survey of several alternative reading assessment methods, methods that provide ongoing, student-centered, learning-based ways of charting students' work in the course and that may be used either formally or informally. Then we describe various traditional methods of assessing reading, identify types of standardized language tests, and note some of the problems inherent in all types of tests and assessment. We conclude with guidelines for writing tests and for preparing a course-level assessment plan.

Alternative methods of assessing reading

Research on assessment and testing since the mid-1980s supports the need for alternatives to traditional tests. The epigraph for this chapter is one example of this shift away from using assessment as a way to "keep students in their place." Instead, assessment needs to help students understand just where they are situated in the quest for second language proficiency (Cohen 1994: 3).

We have selected six alternative activities to present. The teacher's use of these activities will determine their role in the final computing of students' grades, and it will be important for the teacher to inform the students about which activities are being used as part of the course evaluation. The following are the general qualities of alternative reading assessment methods: continual, ongoing, in the students' hands more than the teacher's, non-threatening, low-risk, progress oriented, focused on student's own development, often group generated rather than individual, providing an opportunity for students to learn (as well as be assessed).

Individual teaching preferences, the demands of the school or teaching situation, and the needs and abilities of the students should determine the particular mix of methods, activities, and instruments teachers use. The six more familiar alternative methods given here provide an introduction, a kind of tool kit for alternative assessment. Some of these methods focus on evaluating the products of the students' learning; others, by assessing how well students are participating in classroom activities, make learning processes observable.

Journals (audio and written)

Student journals are a superb way to keep learners involved in the processes of monitoring comprehension, making comprehension visible, fitting in new knowledge, applying knowledge, and gaining language proficiency. The journal can be an informal or a more structured assignment. Appendix A, "Keeping a Reading Journal," contains a description of Parry's (1992) journal system in an advanced class and provides a sample student entry. Reading journals may be assigned even at the beginning and low-intermediate levels. The instructions might be to respond to a simple question, like "What do you think about the reading?" At higher levels students may be asked to retell the story in their own words or be given key vocabulary words to prompt them to write a sentence or two about different aspects of the story. They may also be asked to describe a picture that appeared in the text. Journals are flexible and adaptable, and a number of authors provide clear illustrations of how they have successfully used journals in the reading classroom (Green & Green 1993; Peyton & Reed 1990).

Although reading journals may become time consuming for the teacher, there are techniques for easing that burden. Students may keep an audiotape journal (Foley 1993), or students may read each other's journals, using a checklist to see if their classmates have included all the items that were assigned over a period of time. Although teachers rarely assign grades to journals, they do monitor the student's ability to keep up with the writing in order to spot those who are having trouble, need encouragement, or are procrastinating.

Portfolios

An increasingly popular and well-regarded method of educational assessment during the past decade is to have students compile a portfolio of their work in the course. The portfolio may include the student's journal, but it also needs to include other items, such as drafts of writing assignments for the class, homework exercises, marked exams, summaries of articles or other reading assignments, and statements of goals for reading – either goals drawn up by the teacher or personal goals developed by the student. Zhang's (1993) specific application of the portfolio to the L2/FL reading classroom consists of a number of elements that could serve as a part of the evaluation of the student's work in the course.

Homework

Homework is probably the most familiar item in this list, and it can be used for alternative assessment in a number of ways. Homework should not be something dreaded, complex, and overwhelming for students. Its function is to let students learn what they do not know – what they need to ask questions about. It does not always need to be read by the teacher, since students can read each other's work for informal evaluations and fill in their self-assessment reports with the results. Nor does homework need to be corrected and graded. Sometimes the teacher checks it to see if students understand a concept or a process, but the teacher does not need to mark for accuracy on every point of grammar and usage. When students are assigned homework that demands that their comprehension of a text become visible to another, they are doing work that is a valuable part of an assessment plan.

Teacher assessment through observation

There are various times during a class period when the teacher has the opportunity to evaluate student comprehension and participation – for example, during group work, when students are reading, or during other planned activities. These observations range from formal grades to mental notes. Mental notes are often too fleeting; an intermediate solution is a chart, with activities labeled and dated. This is quick and easy to use, and may be as basic as that displayed in Table 9.1, which is filled in by the teacher with checks, minuses, or pluses to note the student's performance.

Table 9.1   Chart for teacher observation of students' in-class performance

Name of student	*Taking notes?*	*Participating in the small group?*	*Asking or answering questions?*	*Explaining to another?*
Abdoul				
Jose				
Sumi				

Exercise 9.1   Using your knowledge

Look at Classrooms 6A and 6B (Chapter 6). Which activities could you use to record your observations of students' participation by marking them with a plus, minus, or check?

Self-assessment

Although it is controversial, we include self-assessment in the reading classroom as one of our alternatives. Nunan (1988: 118), an advocate of self-assessment as part of the learner-centered classroom, says that "making the intentions of the educational endeavor explicit to learners, and, where feasible, training them to set their own learning outcomes, will make them better learners in the long run." Various types of self-assessment instruments have been developed. Cohen (1994: 205) has a checklist for self-rating of reading ability, and Peters (1978: 162) has a self-rating scale that is easily adapted for L2/FL readers. Another valuable resource on self-assessment is Gardner (1996), which is devoted to this topic. A task-based checklist allows students to rate their ability on specific tasks. It can be developed as a grid that includes a box for each task students are to complete; students then evaluate their performance of the task with a letter grade or a mark. The student's own perception of how much he has participated in the class may be more accurate than the teacher's; for example, a student who is present but daydreaming may assess his work lower than the student who is engaged mentally, if not verbally, by the task being done in the group. The students' abilities to reflect on their levels of engagement constitute a part of the metacognitive awareness they need concerning their own learning processes. The teacher may or may not collect and monitor each student self-assessment. When she does, she gets a new perspective on how the individual students perceive their levels of performance. Although self-assessment measures are useful as part of an overall assessment plan, they can seldom be used as the only measure. Moreover, external evaluators (school boards, supervisors, parents, etc.) may be skeptical of this kind of assessment. The advantage of self-assessment is that students become conscious of and involved in the assessment process.

Peer assessment

Peer assessment is yet another way to provide alternative methods of evaluating student work in reading classes. Students are quite capable of evaluating each other's levels of participation, attentiveness, and work produced in a given activity. Moreover, when they know that they will be evaluated by their peers, many students make an effort to be cooperative group workers and to stay fully engaged in the activity. Students must understand the criteria that they are being asked to use in the evaluation of their peers. Adopting a grid or chart like that in Table 9.1 is a quick way to provide structure to a peer evaluation activity. Each student circles his own name in the list and then marks others with pluses, checks, or minuses. Indeed, students could complete both self- and peer evaluations in the same activity.

Engaging students in the evaluation process encourages learning on a number of levels. Students may also be called on to participate in test writing, as we explain later in this chapter. What should be evident in the activities thus far are the principles of student-centered, ongoing, non-threatening, and learning-focused alternative assessment methods.

Exercise 9.2   Building your knowledge

Look at Classrooms 6C and 6D. Working in pairs, find three different places where you could employ the alternative assessment methods described here. In your Teaching Portfolio, write a brief explanation of how you would conduct each assessment. Compare your plan with the plan that another pair of students has produced.

These six alternative reading assessments provide information that students need about their own levels of reading comprehension and that teachers need about the reading comprehension levels of the students. The key to a successful integration of these methods with more traditional testing is to strive for balance in the mix. For other ideas on alternative assessment see the *TESOL Journal* (Faltis 1995).

Traditional methods of testing reading

The recurring theme in this book has been that true understanding begins with, and builds on, self-reflection; we believe that this philosophy holds for attitudes and beliefs about the testing process as well. Thoughtful, reliable testers need to be conscious of their own biases and beliefs about tests.

Exercise 9.3   Recalling your knowledge

1. Take about 5 minutes to recall and to jot down some notes in your Teaching Portfolio about (1) the best test experience (not necessarily an academic situation) you ever had and (2) the worst test experience you ever had.
2. Working in groups of three, describe your best and worst experiences to each other. Then write a list of the factors that made the worst test so terrible and the best test so satisfying.
3. Each group presents its list and the whole class constructs a master list of the most common elements.

Your group discussions of the worst test experience may have highlighted the tendency of tests to make students feel inadequate and insecure. Shohamy's study *The Power of Tests* (1993) reiterates Foucault's (1979) argument that tests are "the most powerful and efficient tool through which society imposes discipline" (Shohamy 1993: 2). Societies' tests, from driver's license tests to civil service examinations, wield that kind of power. Within the classroom teachers have a similar power. They can use tests to punish and to exclude, or they can develop tests that have the primary purpose of being teaching tools to enhance learning.

Classroom teachers must negotiate between the authority they exercise in giving a test and their responsibility as educators to provide a learning atmosphere in which students can achieve as much as possible without unproductive tension and anxiety. The best way to do that is to keep in mind the occasions when tests created positive experiences (Exercise 9.3). Were the best test experiences discussed in terms of feeling achievement, confidence, success, and the power of knowledge? Did they lead to further learning? These are the questions that can lead a classroom teacher to produce better assessments.

Many books about general language testing also include at least one chapter or major section on assessing reading (Cohen 1994; Heaton 1975; Hughes 1989; Madsen 1983). These books explain various kinds of test items, give instructions on how to construct test items, and make practical, reliable suggestions for classroom testing. The following six types of tests and test questions are commonly used in assessing reading.

Multiple-choice questions

The most familiar type of reading comprehension check is multiple-choice questions. They are the common currency of many standardized tests, including language assessment tests like the TOEFL. ESL reading textbooks frequently have multiple-choice questions following a reading passage. Multiple-choice questions, however, can be problematic. They can be used to trick the test taker by confusing or obscuring the meaning of a passage. The teacher's job when using any kind of test measure is to focus on measuring the student's reading ability instead of measuring the student's test-taking savvy. Certain techniques for dealing with multiple-choice questions, when taught explicitly, will *alone* improve students' scores. Nevo (1989: 212) argues that "it would appear useful to devote attention, time and effort to guiding and training students in coping effectively with a test format like [the multiple-choice test]."

The choices in a multiple-choice question consist of a correct answer and a variety of responses called **distractors.** These distractors need to be carefully formulated. Heaton (1975) points out that distractors that are silly or outrageous are useless; those that have subtle turns of phrase may be unfair. A choice that is close to the correct answer, with elements in it that are correct, may also be unfair. In addition, students will sometimes guess the correct answer, but the teacher has no way of knowing when the student has guessed. Constructing multiple-choice questions demands considerable time, thought, and skill. Although multiple-choice questions are quick to complete and score, they have these disadvantages: They are difficult to construct, they focus on texts out of context, and they are not really *teaching* devices.

Exercise 9.4   Building your knowledge

1. Using Reading Textbook sample 6, "More Men Infiltrating Professions," write three multiple-choice test questions to test students' comprehension.
2. Compare your three questions with those of another classmate, checking to see if the distractors are carefully formulated and suggesting revisions when you think it is appropriate.

Vocabulary tests

Vocabulary needs to be taught and assessed, but testing vocabulary is not the same as testing reading comprehension. Textbooks often provide vocabulary checks that consist of lists of words to define. Such checks focus more on testing the students' recall of what the words mean than on assessing what the text as a whole means. Vocabulary tests may help the teacher identify general problems with understanding key words, but they do not test comprehension, and they lead students to think that learning words is the only key to good reading. We believe that reading comprehension should be assessed using more holistic measures than testing memory.

Cloze tests

Another popular type of assessment measure used to test reading is the **cloze test,** in which students are asked to supply words that have been deleted from a reading text. Strictly speaking, a cloze test demands the deletion of words according to a set system with no variation. Since deleting too many or too few words can cause problems with the validity of the test, the fifth, sixth, or seventh words are usually deleted. Thus, a cloze test differs significantly from a fill-in-the-blank or completion exercise in which the teacher determines the key words that students are to recall.

Several variations on the cloze test have been developed to make it more useful and flexible. A slightly modified version of the cloze test is the **C-test,** which is similar to the cloze but includes one or more of the letters of the correct answer at the beginning of each blank. More distant variations include changing the cloze to a test of grammatical items by asking students to delete only verbs or prepositions. These later instruments may serve to test some discrete element of a student's language performance, but the teacher who uses them needs a thorough understanding of the nature and validity of such tests.

Cloze tests have proved useful and valid in making whole language assessments, and they are especially useful for determining the difficulty of a reading passage. In the L2/FL reading classroom, however, Hughes (1989) argues that the cloze does not give a dependable, valid assessment of reading comprehension, especially when students need to be taught appropriate test-taking strategies in order to perform well.

Completion tasks

Completion of sentences is another form of comprehension testing that demands recall and writing as well as comprehension. Usually a reading passage is supplied, followed by a set of statements to be completed by the student. In the simplest versions of this type of test the student may use the words from the original passage to complete the sentence; in more complex versions the student must interpret or analyze the text before completing the sentence. Another type of completion is the fill-in-the-blank exercise. The teacher selects a passage or constructs one, then deletes words from it in order to test memory of the passage, use of grammatical structures, or some other element. The completion test is useful because it demands production of language and may reveal a good deal about the student's comprehension of the full text.

Short answer and open-ended questions

Short answer and open-ended questions are as much a test of writing as they are of reading. In this format the student is given a passage to read, then asked to write a few sentences or a paragraph in answer to a question about the reading. Alternatively, the student may be asked to write a summary of the passage – a task that is demanding even in one's L1. Although the task requires a good deal of recall and production of language, it also complicates the testing procedure. Is the student being tested on writing ability? Is the student's general and cultural knowledge of the topic producing skewed results? Are other factors at work that may create variation in test scores? The difficulties of the short answer and open-ended question are balanced, however, by a number of advantages: They demand production of language, they reinforce writing skills, they can elicit inferential responses, and they provide a more holistic and authentic task.

Contextualized or authentic tasks

Recent trends in language teaching have emphasized the use of authentic tasks (sometimes referred to as contextualized tasks) and authentic assessment of language performance. This emphasis on authenticity is based on the belief that the more students sense that the language they are learning is language that they can use in real situations, the more motivation there is for learning. It follows that testing must also come directly from the context of the teaching, which in turn comes from the context of the students' language needs. For example, rather than having students take a multiple-choice exam on an essay they have read, the teacher could have pairs of students discuss the main points of the article, either before the teacher or on tape. In an academic setting the discussion may be closer to what students will be required to do in their other classes.

Authentic tests aim to give the closest and most accurate evaluation of actual language ability. While that sounds like a simple and obvious objective, putting authentic language testing into practice has its challenges and has been the impetus for a great deal of research, writing, and debate (see Bachman 1991; Omaggio 1986; Shohamy & Reves 1985; Spolsky 1985). Test situations are by nature artificial, and making them truly authentic is no easy task. In an overview of communicative testing methods for assessing reading comprehension, Cohen (1994: 227–9) mentions writing letters, telephone requests, telephone responses, and announcements for others, all based on an earlier reading assignment. Putting the reading assessment task into a real-life setting or context gives it more authenticity and helps motivate students' participation. But some techniques in authentic testing – for instance, getting students to respond to global issues – raise another problem: whether one is testing intelligence or reading comprehension (Omaggio 1983: 36). Authentic testing provides a fuller context for the reading task and can be designed to match course goals and materials very closely; however, the tasks take time to construct and are difficult to score precisely.

These traditional assessment methods appear in most L2/FL reading textbooks. Reading teachers need to be able to analyze the usefulness of each type and be able to use them when constructing their own tests.

Exercise 9.5   Building your knowledge

1. Draw up a list of the pros and cons of each of the traditional assessment methods described in this chapter. Add any other advantages or disadvantages that you have thought of or experienced personally.
2. Compare your list with those of two other classmates in a group discussion.

Writing tests for the classroom

Teachers eventually need to write their own assessment instruments, alternative or traditional. Four general guidelines are helpful for that process:

1. *Keep the course objectives clearly in mind at every step.* A wonderful test that fails to assess the skills or language proficiency addressed by the reading class is not really a wonderful test. For example, in an extensive reading course it would be inappropriate to present students with a final test requiring recall of specific details of minor points. Such a test would not only lack validity but would be of questionable authenticity, since defining lists of words is not a common language task outside the classroom.

2. *Carefully match the test to what is to be tested.* Tests can veer off the mark rather easily; construct and content validity are always concerns. For example, after five classes devoted to an intensive development of prereading strategies and when and how to use them, an appropriate test would assess the students' ability to use various strategies and to switch strategies when it is useful to do so. A test of students' comprehension of a lengthy academic essay would tell the teacher little about their prereading strategy use.

3. *Recognize the potential for bias and variation.* In order to anticipate potential bias arising from cultural differences in the ways students think about and practice reading, it is the teacher's responsibility to investigate students' attitudes and beliefs about reading (Steffensen & Joag-Dev 1984). Another way to reduce bias or variation is to use as many types of assessment tasks as possible. N. J. Anderson et al. (1991: 61) argue that "more than one source of data needs to be used in determining the success of reading comprehension test items."

4. *Design the test to assess what the students know.* Construct tests that focus on the specific tasks that were covered in class and that assess students' ability to participate in the reading strategies and processes that were taught. Never assume that students are familiar with techniques that may be common only in certain cultures (e.g., making inferences, asking questions, analyzing structure).

Teachers may also need to prepare students to perform well on different types of test questions. Cohen (1994: 136–7) lists eighteen different test-taking strategies for improving performance on multiple-choice tests, including tips about budgeting time, postponing and coming back to a question, and trying to answer the question before looking at the options given in the test. Making these strategies explicit to students will help them achieve scores on multiple-choice tests that are more consistent with their reading comprehension.

The guidelines for writing tests presented in Kirschner, Wexler, and Spector-Cohen (1992) highlight several ways to eliminate the problems that students may have with comprehension of test questions. The authors emphasize the need to match the point distribution in the test to the importance of the ideas in the text, to balance the types of questions in the test, and to label each question or task with the points it carries in the total test score. They provide a detailed checklist for writing specific test questions that cautions against including vocabulary that is too difficult, giving vague directions, and using syntax that may interfere with the students' comprehension of the question (1992: 556). Cohen (1994) and Shohamy and Reves (1985) also include guidelines and lists of important factors to help in the test-writing process.

One other important technique for constructing tests is to involve students. Basing his work on the premise that "learning is more important than judging," Murphy (1994–5) discusses the advantages of having students generate questions, develop vocabulary lists, identify grammar points, and work interactively with the teacher to create tests that not only assess current levels of work but that can be reused to check later progress. Murphy has developed a "More Complex Interactive Grading Example" to illustrate a variety of techniques as alternatives to the traditional patterns of test writing and test administering.

Planning course-level assessment

An overall assessment plan for the reading course should be explicit, systematic, as unbiased as possible, reliable, consistent, and integral to the course. In addition, the assessment plan needs to be clear to the students and to external agents who may examine it. The more the assessment tasks match the kinds of tasks that students have been engaged in during the class, the more the assessment will be fair and valid.

Assessment plans, like lesson plans, should begin with a set of objectives and SWBATs. If the class has been designed to improve students' speed and comprehension in reading academic texts, the assessment instrument needs to measure those abilities. If the class has been focused on extensive reading, then assessment of general ideas is in order (see Cohen 1994; Heaton 1990; Hughes 1989). We offer the following steps as a guide:

1. *Review course goals and objectives.* (a) Has this course focused on extensive reading, academic reading, survival skills for immigrants,

beginning reading proficiency, others? (b) What kinds of reading tasks have students been asked to do in the course? (c) What kinds of tasks should they be able to do at the end of this course?

2. *Know which aspects of reading are to be assessed.* Cohen (1994: 216–23) advocates considering types of reading, types of meaning, and types of comprehension skills.

3. *Know the important variables that exist in the class.* What ethnic groups are represented in the class? How do their different beliefs and learning styles affect their response to assessment measures? What types of assessment are these students familiar with? Do they need to be taught some test-taking strategies?

4. *Decide upon the elements that will constitute the assessment plan.* Determine the frequency of homework, tests, quizzes, alternative assessment measures. Regular, carefully constructed quizzes as a part of the whole plan may reduce the need for several longer, formal tests (Cohen 1994). Balance the types of measurements and methods used in the plan.

5. *Write out the plan.* Even experienced teachers need to write out the plan and evaluate it more than once; the first evaluation should be after a day or two, the other(s) later during the term. Teachers also need to be able to explain the course assessment plan to others – to students, to colleagues, to administrators, to school boards, to parents.

Practice in preparing this kind of plan will make it an increasingly familiar and manageable task. Articulating and, if necessary, defending the plan are integral to teaching the course. Experience is the best teacher for constructing assessment plans, and regular evaluation of the plan is the best critic. The best assessment, whether alternative or traditional, is integrated into the course and becomes an important part of the instructional process. The assessment thus becomes "systemic" and provides the feedback that every teacher needs in the classroom (Shohamy 1993: 18).

Expanding your knowledge

1. Dedicate one or two pages in your Teaching Portfolio to a summary list (or a chart) of the alternative and traditional methods of assessment that are presented in this chapter. The traditional methods are discussed in terms of their pros and cons. Develop pros and cons for the alternative methods.

2. Using Reading Textbook Sample 6, "More Men Infiltrating Professions," develop one alternative and one traditional method for assessing

a high-intermediate class's comprehension of the text. Write the plans in your Teaching Portfolio.
3. Obtain a copy of a syllabus for a reading course and analyze what it reveals about assessing and testing.

Chapter highlights

A wide range of alternative and traditional methods of assessing reading are available to the L2/FL reading teacher. Learning to mix these types, to test throughout the students' learning process, and to develop lesson and course-level assessment measures are all major responsibilities for the classroom teacher.

1. *Alternative methods of assessing reading.* Alternative methods of assessment are characterized by their ongoing, student-centered, learning-centered, nonthreatening nature. They include having students keep journals, assemble portfolios, complete homework, and do self- or peer assessments. They also include having the teacher assess through observation.
2. *Traditional methods of testing reading.* Traditional methods include multiple-choice questions, cloze tests, vocabulary tests, completion exercises, open-ended and short-answer questions, and contextualized or authentic tasks. Each method has pros and cons that affect the use of that type of testing in a given classroom.
3. *Writing tests for the classroom.* In the process of writing tests, it is important to keep course objectives in mind, know exactly what is being tested, and understand which types of tests best match that material. Including students in the process of developing assessment measures, even formal tests, is recommended as a productive way to enhance learning and to accomplish assessment.
4. *Planning course-level assessment.* Course-level assessment plans, especially, need to take into account course objectives, specific reading skills that were targeted, and other important variables within a given class.

Appendix A   Keeping a reading journal

Keeping a Reading Journal

Your instructor may ask you to keep a record of what you read, and to make comments on it. Even if you are not asked to, you may want to do so for your own interest, for it can help you keep track of your thoughts and deepen your appreciation of your reading. Here are some suggestions for keeping a reading journal:

1. Buy a small notebook, which will keep all the entries together and be easy to carry around.
2. Write the date at the beginning of every entry you make in the journal.
3. Before you write anything about a new book, be sure that you write the name of the author and the title. You may also want to record the name of the publisher.
4. You may find it helpful to identify the book in terms of one of the categories identified above, and you should certainly make a brief statement of what the book is about and give a summary of the story. Depending on what your instructor asks you to do, you may write a single entry when you finish a book, or you may write a series of entries as you go through it. For a longer book, which may take a week or more to read, it is probably better to write several entries.
5. In addition to summarizing the story, it is particularly interesting to record your own reactions to the book. You may want to do this by making comments as you tell the story, or by writing a paragraph of comments after your summary. Alternatively, you can write the account of the story on the right-hand pages of your notebook, and then express your reactions to the various episodes on the opposite left-hand page.
6. If your instructor is going to read your journal, be sure to leave plenty of space for his or her comments: doublespace your handwriting, leave the left-hand pages free, and/or leave very wide margins.

Obviously, different individuals vary a good deal as to what they want to record in a reading journal, just as they vary in what they choose to read. So there is no model of journal-writing that you must follow, but you may find the following students' reactions to books they have read interesting. (The entries are given exactly as they were written, except that a few spelling and punctuation mistakes have been corrected; you should understand that in this kind of work the emphasis is not on writing correctly or elegantly.)

Mehmet   5/13

The Story of a Shipwrecked Sailor, by Gabriel García Márquez

February 28 brought news that eight crew members of the destroyer Caldes, of the Colombian Navy, had fallen overboard and disappeared during a storm in the Caribbean Sea. The ship was traveling from Mobile, Alabama, in the United States, where it had docked for repairs, to the Colombian port of Cartagena, where it arrived two hours after the tragedy. A search for the seamen began immediately, with the cooperation of the US Panama Canal Authority. After four days, the search stopped and the lost sailors were declared dead. A week later, one of them turned up. His name was Luis Alejandro Velasco. Velasco struggled to survive and made it, becoming a hero.

This story was wonderful to read. When my cousin interrupted me reading it I almost hit him. I was upset that I had to stop reading the book. It is like watching a movie and the best part is about to happen then the screen goes blank. I would recommend anyone to read this book because man's struggle against the sea is breathtaking to read.

Sandra   2/24

The book I read this week is entitled *First You Cry* by Betty Rollin. This book tells a story which all women can relate to. The author is the principal character of the book. Betty Rollin, an NBC news reporter, has always been a winner. But something unpredictable would turn upside down her confidence in herself, in her successful career and love life. Betty, for a year now, knew she had a lump in her left breast. Her internist told her that it was nothing to worry about since a lot of women have them. But to be more cautious he ordered a mammogram. The diagnosis of the internist after the test did not show anything alarming. Although she did not worry about the lump, she could not forget it. In 1974, a year later, she went to see Dr. Ellby about the lump. He himself did the mammogram and recommended a surgeon. In the meantime she had to wait for the mammogram results. She describes her trust in life since she was a little girl. Everything always seemed to work out just fine for her. She had a golden life with her husband. She had a fine job at NBC. So she thought everything will always work out. The day came when she went back to see Dr. Sengeiman, the surgeon recommended by Dr. Ellby. She was devastated by the news that she had cancer. Then she realized how lucky she has been to be married to David, a wonderful man who helped her survive these hard times with his love and patience. At first, she had felt resentment toward her internist who led her to believe that the cyst in her breast was not cancerous. But after, she said she could not blame him for not recommending the removal of the lump, since in his best judgment it was not cancer. After the removal of her left breast, she stayed for a week in the hospital. She dreaded the day when she would have to leave to face the world out there. But remarkably after stages of depression, anger, and hate, she regained her sense of orientation in life. In the last sentence of the book she said it so well: "If I don't have a recurrence of cancer and die soon, all I've lost is a breast, and that's not so bad."

10 Planning the reading lesson

> To plan lessons that will appeal to students'
> interests and needs, teachers need to ask students
> for their input and involve them in shaping
> instruction.
>
> — Alice Omaggio (1986: 422)

Whatever the degree of detail a lesson plan has and whether or not it is written on paper, it serves the purpose of providing teachers with a guide to how they would like the lesson to unfold in the classroom. No matter the length of a class, whether 15–20 minutes in an elementary school L2/FL class or 2–3 hours in an adult education class, teachers need to plan the lesson ahead of time. A lesson plan can be brief, as is frequently the case with experienced teachers who have taught reading for many years, or it can be painstakingly long, as it is for the novice teacher who has little or no experience in the L2/FL classroom.

Planning a lesson involves considering (1) what is to be learned, (2) how to teach that, (3) what materials to use, (4) how much time each activity will require, and (5) how to assess the students' abilities during and at the end of the lesson. Objectives, SWBATs, activities, materials, and assessment methods all interact to shape the plan that a teacher constructs for a given class period. Each of these factors in turn demands other considerations. For example, the objectives and SWBATs for a given lesson are determined by the overall course goals that were established for the course and by the objectives and SWBATs for preceding lessons. The objectives for an individual plan are further shaped by the materials that the class has at its disposal. Teachers may choose some objectives and SWBATs over others for a particular lesson because the text available lends itself more readily to them. The objectives of a particular plan are also modified to some extent by what the students already know. When teachers know that students have a reasonable mastery of some of the SWBATs for a particular lesson, they may delete some steps or cover them quickly to spend more time on the aspects that students do not know or that have given them problems in the past. Each of the other factors involved in a lesson plan can be examined individually as well. The resulting matrix is a complex grid of intersecting factors, all contributing to the decisions teachers make when they plan a reading lesson for the L2/FL classroom.

Components of a lesson plan

In order to analyze the specific components of a lesson plan, we use Reading Textbook Sample 3, "Modern Fathers Have Pleasures and Problems," and construct a 45-minute class period during which students work with the information in the text, which they read at home before coming to class (Table 10.1). We assume that adequate prereading work has been done during the previous class. Notice that although this plan covers a complete class period, it does not cover a complete chapter in the reading textbook. This is typical; it may take parts of two or three class periods to deal with all the before-, during-, and postreading activities.

Lesson plans include a number of components. We discuss each of them separately in the section that follows, but all are necessary in order for the plan to serve as a useful tool for the teacher. As you read our description of these components, keep the lesson plan clearly in mind; Exercise 10.1 (on page 188) will ask you to make a careful analysis of each point.

Objectives and SWBATs

The foundation of any lesson plan is its objectives and SWBATs. The stated objectives for each lesson plan should be consistent with the goals established for the course; the SWBATs are aimed toward fulfilling the objectives. The Classroom Plans in this book give examples of objectives and SWBATs for the activities in it. In addition, several exercises focus on what SWBAT statements are and how they turn objectives into more specific, measurable targets. D. S. Brown (1994: 396–7) distinguishes between terminal and enabling objectives, with the latter being the "interim steps that build upon each other and lead to a terminal objective." If the objectives or the SWBATs are weak, unclear, too general, or not well articulated, formulating the other components will be difficult.

Activities

Activities are the tools for achieving objectives and SWBATs (see Chapter 4 and Richards 1990). In reviewing possible activities, consider what mode the activities emphasize, how recently, if ever, the students have done activities like that, and most important, if the activity promotes the targeted objectives and SWBATs. Fanselow's *Contrasting Conversations* (1992) is devoted to the objective of developing teachers' abilities to think of alternatives or variations of activities so that teachers become more flexible and open to new ways of perceiving and operating. The use of a variety of activities in the classroom expands students' opportunities to learn while maintaining their interest. It "refreshes the students" as a Taiwanese EFL teacher once put it.

Table 10.1　Reading lesson plan: intermediate language proficiency

---

Objectives
- Recall some of the content of the reading
- Categorize information from the text
- Listen and take notes on new information
- Determine if information is text-based or not
- Bring students' world knowledge to the topic of the text

SWBATs
1. Write the main ideas of the reading by categories
2. Listen to others, pick out and add new ideas to Ss' notes
3. Scan to find specific information in the text
4. List other ideas, not from the text but still within the category

---

Step 1 10:00–10:06 a.m. (6 min.)
T groups Ss by fives and tells them to close their books. T hands a different color sheet of paper to each 5 Ss in the group. Each person writes his/her name on the sheet. One paper has the heading "What is a modern father?" (green paper); another, "What are the pleasures of a modern father?" (pink paper); the third, "What are the problems of a modern father?" (yellow paper). At the top of each paper are the instructions: "Write an idea that you remember from the text. Be sure that it answers the question. Be quick, don't worry about grammar. Then pass this paper to the person to your right." Ss write and pass until the papers return to the first writer.

Step 2 10:06–10:15 a.m. (9 min.)
T instructs whole class to listen as other Ss read their ideas and to add any ideas they don't have to their list. T calls on 3 or 4 different Ss with green papers to read their list of ideas, then 3 or 4 Ss with pink, and finally, yellow. *T: Remember to repeat ideas as they are given and praise Ss for new ideas.*

Step 3 10:15–10:19 a.m. (4 min.)
T tells Ss to open their books to the text and scan for the number of the line that mentions each idea that they have on the paper in front of them and to write that line number beside the idea (individual activity). When they are finished, T asks if someone found ideas on their paper that were not in the text. Ss answer and other Ss have a chance to say if they found that idea in the text or not. This is also an opportunity for Ss who had ideas other than the ones that were mentioned earlier to bring them up. Everyone can look at these ideas in the text as they are being discussed. *T: Remember to call out the line numbers so that everyone will follow in their text. Also, remember to praise Ss as they respond!*

Step 4 10:19–10:27 a.m. (8 min.)
Tell Ss, in their small groups, to think of ideas not mentioned in the text and to add them to each list. T collects all papers and arranges them by color. (Quantity of text ideas to be assessed silently by T.) *Homework:* Read the text again and write the answers to exercises 1–4 on paper.

Step 5 10:27–10:32 a.m. (5 min.)
T asks Ss why it is important to be clear about what information is in the text and what information is in the reader's mind. When you write a summary, which information should you include? Should you include your own ideas? Why not? T calls on different Ss and notes the accuracy of their responses.

Step 6 10:32–10:45 (13 min.)
This part of the lesson will be used to introduce the next reading, or to teach a reading or vocabulary skill, or to review something that was taught earlier. For example:

T hands back Ss' summaries of a reading text from 3 classes ago and asks them to number the ideas they wrote about in their summaries and then check to see if each idea is mentioned in the text. Are there any ideas in your summary that are not in the reading text?
or
T asks Ss to open to the text "Modern Fathers Have Pleasures and Problems" and find all the words and phrases that deal with time (full-time, to spend more time, free time, 30 hours per week, more time, enjoy every minute, never have enough time to). T writes them on board as Ss speak. Then with books closed, T asks Ss to make sentences using these phrases and combining the ideas of time, parents, and babies. If there is enough time, T asks Ss to make sentences using these same words and phrases, regarding time and their own studies.
or
T says, "We are going to start a new reading text. It's about . . ."

Materials

A lesson plan identifies the materials and special equipment needed to teach a particular class. In the rush to get from one classroom to another or in the nervousness of facing a class or trying a new activity for the first time, it is easy to forget some items. A materials checklist is useful for new teachers and for teachers who move from one classroom to another. Teachers in new situations or who are teaching in a new culture especially need to be aware of materials needs; materials that were easily available and commonly used in the classroom in the teacher's past experience may not be as accessible in the new culture.

Homework

Homework assignments need to be part of a lesson plan and integrated into the activity or the part of the lesson that is most connected to the work being assigned. The assignment needs to highlight special instructions, reminders, or cautions to the students. It should also indicate how the homework will be used – for example, for in-class discussion, for a recorded grade, for part of a following assignment.

Assessment methods

Assessment measures also belong in the lesson plan. They may be formal or informal, traditional, or alternative. They must, however, assess whether or not students are indeed able to do the SWBATs. An informal, unobtrusive assessment could be to note how many students are answering correctly when they are working in small groups; a more formal, traditional assessment could be a short, written quiz at the end of the class period. The assessment of each class influences the lesson plans for subsequent lessons.

Exercise 10.1   Building your knowledge

Analyze each component in the Reading Lesson Plan (Table 10.1):

Objectives and SWBATs: Examine the objectives and SWBATs and match activities with them.

Activities: How many activities are completed in the 45-minute period? Which activities are student centered? Which are teacher centered?

Materials: Make a list of the materials necessary for this class. Could any of them be a problem to obtain in another country?

Homework: Why was the homework assignment given at the end of step 4? What instructions need to be given with the assignment? Does the teacher indicate how the homework will be marked or recorded?

Assessment methods: Is any assessment indicated in this lesson plan? What alternative or traditional assessments could be included? Are there places where informal assessment or peer assessment would be appropriate?

Factors that influence planning

How a teacher structures classroom activities depends on the students in the class and the teacher's philosophy about teaching. In all cases, however, a number of factors will influence the shape of a given lesson plan. The following brief review of those factors provides the basis for more detailed analysis in the next exercise.

Time

Time is a pervasive factor in teaching; there never seems to be enough of it – from the teacher's point of view. In constructing the lesson plan, the teacher estimates how long it will take students to complete each activity. Some steps must be completed in one class period in order to have maximum effect or in order to prepare the students for the work they will do on their own before the next meeting. Therefore, it is essential to guess as accurately as possible how much time each step will take. Teacher-centered activities are relatively easy to estimate, but student-centered or group activities are less predictable. Usually, breaking activities into steps makes it easier to make those guesses, but having students work in groups makes timing harder to judge, even for experienced teachers. During the actual class the teacher should note the time that each step took as compared to the time allotted for it. When an activity turns out to be difficult and consumes more time than planned, the teacher must readjust the time allotted to the subsequent activities or decide to omit an activity or carry it to the next class.

Progression

Progression, or sequencing, is the order of the activities or parts of activities. It deserves special attention because skillful sequencing facilitates students' learning. If the steps of an activity are ordered progressively, perhaps from known to unknown, or from easy to difficult, or from small parts to larger parts, students will have a learning experience comparable to going up a staircase one step at a time. Each step will follow logically from the preceding one and the effort expended in getting up the stairs will be natural. If activities are not sequenced logically, students will have the sense of having gone up the steps two or three at a time, perhaps stumbling along the way. The learning spiral (see Introduction) depends on each step forming a foundation, a support for the movement to the next step.

Student groups and cooperative learning

Throughout this book we ask that readers work in small groups or pairs to discuss concepts, compare experiences, and develop ideas. We encourage cooperation and collaboration. Teaching methodology since the time of

Plato has emphasized the need for interaction among learners, and there is currently a strong focus on group work, learner interaction, and student collaboration. It is through reading, talking, sharing, arguing, and trying to put into writing their ideas that students truly learn. L2/FL classes function best in this way. Students who have tasks to complete – using the second language to complete them – are safer, better supported, and more likely to learn in a group. Students who have tasks to complete in small groups in the L2 risk less, have access to expanded resources, and experience increased motivation to learn.

Closely related to student grouping is a methodology of learning and teaching named **cooperative learning,** which has gained some popularity in recent years. Its main premise is to have students work together to learn.

> In cooperative learning there is an *interdependence* established among the students in each group as they strive for the achievement of group or individual objectives. This technique draws from both behaviorism and humanism. On the one hand, it frequently offers groups rewards (in the form of points or grades) as its prime motivation; on the other, it urges students to develop more fully their own individual identities while respecting those of others. (Richard-Amato 1988: 193)

To some extent, the group takes pressure off the individual learner and places responsibility on the collective. By working through the problem in the less threatening environment of the group, individual learners gain confidence and use the L2/FL more than they would dare to in front of the whole class. For a detailed description of cooperative learning techniques, consult Richard-Amato (1988).

Working with student groups and using collaborative learning activities is time consuming, takes meticulous planning, and demands thoughtful objectives and SWBATs. Yet, despite these apparent drawbacks, responses to these methods indicate that students learn well and enjoy learning in these situations.

Variety

Teachers want to repeat the sequence of activities enough so that students feel secure about how things are going to happen and what is expected of them in the process. Repetition is especially valuable at lower levels of language proficiency when the language being taught is also the language of instruction. However, there is value in variety as well. Changing how objectives are taught as the course progresses not only maintains interest, but it also frequently creates opportunities for learning by addressing different learning styles (see Reid 1995). Other ways to create variety include using various modes (oral, aural, visual, tactile), the use of free, open-ended activities versus highly structured activities, and the use of student groups and collaborative learning. Variety in reading classes is virtually unlimited. The secret to using variety in activities is to balance the old and the new, or the known and the unknown, in order to keep students mentally working toward the objectives of the class.

Students' needs, interests, and abilities

Finally, we reiterate our position that students need to be involved in the planning process, not only of course goals (see Chapter 3) but of specific lessons. The students' reception of activities and their comments about activities serve as a guide to their needs and interests. The teacher may also solicit students' opinions about what was helpful, what was not helpful, and which skills they want to work on more. Teachers can share the responsibility for learning and the power of planning with their students. For example, students could decide what strategies they want the class to explore with certain reading texts. Students need to develop not only their knowledge of how to approach a text in the L2/FL but also their confidence in doing so. They need to know that they can read effectively on their own, without a teacher there to make all the decisions for them. That confidence comes only from the experience of having tried it on their own and having been successful most of the time. If students can do that before they leave the classroom, the reading teacher has succeeded.

As you use the lesson plan

A carefully constructed, well-articulated lesson plan is useless if it is not *used* in class. Using the plan involves the following:

- Look at the plan just before going into class.
- Review the objectives and activities.
- Be sure to have all the necessary materials and equipment.
- Once in class, put the plan in a prominent place, separate from other papers (perhaps use colored paper so it stands out from the other papers on the desk).
- Glance at the plan at each change from step to step to remember *what* was planned and *how* it was planned.
- Tell students the purpose of the activities as they are doing them (this type of teacher-to-student communication focuses students' attention and builds metacognition).

- Provide transitions for students at each shift from one activity to another (announcing the end of one activity before moving to another, or doing a culminating activity – e.g., having students explain why categorizing is an important reading and thinking skill, or summarizing the content of the text one more time, or giving a quiz).
- Have alternatives in mind for omitting steps or filling in when the time estimates in the lesson plan prove to be inaccurate (it is more important that the students *understand* what they have done in class than that the teacher have the satisfaction of having finished the lesson plan).
- Note the time it took to complete the steps in the plan.

A plan is just a plan. It serves as a guide rather than a rigid program. The key to success with lesson plans is the ability to evaluate what happened in class and then to use that information to adjust future lesson plans.

Classes have a life of their own. When unplanned events happen in the classroom, teachers need to be flexible and to adjust. Frequently, wonderful opportunities to teach in meaningful ways occur during these unplanned events. Sometimes a student will ask a pertinent question that is at the heart of the matter under discussion and captures the thoughts and attention of the whole class. A teacher should be aware of these "teachable moments" and take full advantage of them by stepping away from the plan and engaging students in the opportunity of the moment. Teachers become more skilled at recognizing and taking advantage of teachable moments as they become more experienced and secure in their teaching.

From plan to syllabus to curriculum

Just as each lesson should fit the objectives and goals of the course plan or syllabus, each course syllabus should fit within the objectives and goals of the school's or program's overall reading curriculum. A reading curriculum is a written plan for the entire instructional program of reading. It enables the teacher to see the goals and objectives of each individual course in the perspective of the whole program. The establishment of a reading curriculum focuses teachers' attention on what abilities the students need to attain and simultaneously provides teachers with criteria for evaluating students' progress. Thus, in its most general definition, a reading curriculum includes the reading abilities to be developed, the methods to be used in developing those abilities, and, perhaps, the methods to be used to check if students are indeed developing those reading abilities. In short, a reading curriculum promotes quality in a reading program: quality teaching, quality learning, and quality administration.

Since beginning teachers are not usually involved in the development of a reading curriculum but instead are handed a curriculum when they start a new job, we will not deal with the particulars of curriculum design, curriculum review and alignment, and curriculum evaluation here (see J. D. Brown 1995; Richards 1990). However, a teacher who accepts a new teaching position should request a copy of the reading curriculum so that she can orient herself to the expectations of that reading program and determine the relevance of the reading courses she will be teaching in order to meet those expectations. Appendix A to this chapter illustrates a sample ESL reading curriculum.

Curricula differ in how detailed they are. A basic reading curriculum usually includes:

- A clear statement of the mission of the reading program as a whole
- A statement of the program's philosophy of how students develop their ability to read in an L2/FL and, therefore,
- How teachers should teach reading
- An analysis of the students and their needs
- A schedule for the reading program and an assessment of student progress within the program
- A program design that reflects the goals and resources available
- A statement of the goals of each course within the program
- A statement on assessment of student progress within the course

A more detailed curriculum might include a scope and sequence section in which not only the goals but the objectives and materials for each course are delineated, as well as an assessment schedule and a plan for each part of the course. A curriculum guide can be quite complete and helpful, but also quite confining if applied too rigorously.

> Curriculum in schools will always be in a state of tension between those requirements that are aimed at ensuring some sort of common content for all and those requirements that demand differences in approach, methods, and materials to attain the common outcomes. (English 1992: 17)

Whether a curriculum is handed to the teacher or the teacher participates in developing it, it should leave room for the individual teacher to interpret its methodology while striving to help students meet the overall goals and objectives of the courses and the program. Learners do not come in standardized forms, nor do teachers. Each must make his or her own way toward the desired outcomes in student learning.

Expanding your knowledge

1. Match the exercises to the SWBATs and objectives in the Reading Lesson Plan (Table 10.1).
2. Write a partial lesson plan for the reading class period that might precede the class described in the Reading Lesson Plan. It should detail how to introduce the reading text "Modern Fathers Have Pleasures" (Reading Textbook Sample 3).
3. In step 4 of the Reading Lesson Plan, the teacher collects the students' papers and organizes them by color. What might the teacher do with these in the next reading class to further promote any of the SWBATs of this plan? Come up with as many different ideas as you can. Be able to state an objective for each idea. Compare your ideas with those of your classmates.
4. Plan how you would "correct" the exercises that the students were assigned for homework in step 4 of the Reading Lesson Plan for the following day. Think of at least two different ways. Analyze them for (1) teacher centeredness versus student centeredness, (2) modes used, and (3) time needed.
5. Using Reading Textbook Sample 6, "More Men Infiltrating Professions," decide what objectives you could teach. Then write complete lesson plans for as many class periods as you would need to teach those objectives. Your plans should be as specific as the Classroom Plans have been.

Chapter highlights

Planning a reading lesson entails not only the writing of a plan but also an awareness of the necessary elements in the plan, factors that influence the plan, how to use the plan, and the relationship of the daily lesson to the course goals and the reading curriculum of the school or program.

1. *Components of a lesson plan.* Lesson plans contain standard information, starting with the objectives and SWBATs, and detail activities to be done and materials to be used, note assessment methods to be used, and describe homework to be assigned.
2. *Factors that influence planning.* The factors that influence the shape of a lesson plan include (1) the objectives that have been established in accordance with the overall course goals (which consider the students' needs, interests, and abilities), (2) the sequence of activities that will be used so that the students will be able to progress smoothly from one

activity to the next, (3) plans for grouping students and the time allotted to each part of each activity, and (4) some conscious attempts to include variety in modes and types of activities.

3. *As you use the lesson plan.* The plan should be placed in a strategic position and referred to while teaching. Teachers should state the objectives of each activity and make clear transitions from one activity to the next so that students understand what they are doing and why. Teachers should note actual teaching times on the plan to use later when they review the class. Finally, teachers need to be flexible enough to adapt their plans as the need arises and to take full advantage of "teachable moments" as they occur.

4. *From plan to syllabus to curriculum.* A lesson plan is one step on the road to meeting the course objectives. The course, in turn, is one part of the curriculum. A curriculum lays out, in varying degrees of detail, the plan of the entire program, indicating how courses fit together to achieve the program goals.

Appendix A   A sample L2/FL reading curriculum

Reading goals by level

LOW LEVEL

- To read modified L2 texts at Ss' level with good comprehension of stated information
- To use appropriate strategies to preview the text and predict content
- To identify the main idea of each paragraph during reading or after reading

- To be familiar with the formats of useful authentic materials (menus, schedules, the phone book, local maps, the local newspaper – especially the weather, movies, events, and sport sections, etc.)

- To develop strategies to build vocabulary

LOW-INTERMEDIATE LEVEL (INCLUDING THE ABOVE ABILITIES)

- To read longer, modified L2 texts at Ss' level with good comprehension of stated information
- To exhibit increased use of before-reading strategies with longer texts
- To comprehend the thought relationships between supporting ideas in modified L2 texts
- To begin to use during-reading monitoring strategies

- To comprehend titles of authentic materials
- To preview authentic prose texts to glean the topic and some details

- To understand and use learners' L2 dictionaries
- To begin to apply vocabulary-guessing strategies when reading
- To be familiar with the physical layout of and resources available in the local L2 library

HIGH-INTERMEDIATE LEVEL (INCLUDING THE ABOVE ABILITIES)

- To identity types of supporting information in modified L2 texts
- To evaluate the author's point of view and compare it with Ss' own

- To read authentic materials with good comprehension of topic and some comprehension of interrelationship of supporting ideas
- To begin to transfer skills and strategies learned with modified materials to authentic ones

- To transfer vocabulary skills used with modified texts to authentic ones

- To use library indices to search for newspaper and popular magazine articles on a specified topic
- To use other library resources such as encyclopedias, reference books, etc.

ADVANCED LEVEL (INCLUDING THE ABOVE ABILITIES)

- To have good comprehension of most types of nontechnical, authentic materials
- To exhibit moderate comprehension of authentic materials in the reader's specialization
- To be aware of the cultural background of current issues in authentic materials

- To competently use a variety of vocabulary strategies to address unknown words
- To fully use the resources of the library to conduct research

11 The learning spiral and the reading teacher

> . . . the exploration of classroom issues and
> problems should lead teachers from practice to
> theory and back to practice again as a sort of on-
> going professional growth spiral
> — David Nunan (1989: 16)

The classroom reading teacher, whether new or experienced, continues to need the skills of observation, comparison, integration, and expanding her knowledge base; the learning spiral continues to operate. If it flattens out, the teacher ceases to observe, reflect, inquire, and incorporate new information. The teacher who abandons the learning spiral and becomes a "manager" in the classroom will have a tedious, flat, and deadening experience, as will the students.

TEACHER NARRATIVE

In 1974, when I became a teacher, the work was not real. I was the classic teacher-technician, and my work was classroom management. I managed the kids, the programs, and the paperwork. I viewed academics as the experts who were going to manage me, and I looked to them to be the "someone elses" who would tell me what to do with my students in my classroom. When the methods didn't work, or didn't work with everyone, I blamed the experts. Or worse — I blamed the kids.

> — Nancie Atwell, U.S.A. (quoted in Patterson et al. 1993: vii–viii)

All the methods we have presented in this book are, in fact, worthless if they lead only to classroom management and fail to create for the teacher and the students a satisfying environment for learning and teaching. Or, to return to the cooking image used in the Introduction, dependence on a few methods can result in a repetition of recipes rather than a mastery of the art of teaching reading.

A teacher's growth and development depend on a variety of conditions and variables. Since the mid-1980s there has been a groundswell of activity based on the belief that classroom research is an important factor in teacher satisfaction. The power of classroom research to identify and address problems, to give teachers confidence, to engage students, and to create positive results in student learning, teacher satisfaction, and classroom atmosphere has been remarkable. The traditional model of research was conducted by experts outside of the classroom who were trained as researchers; they studied teachers and their methods and made recommendations about classroom practices. Cochran-Smith and Lytle (1993: 6) argue that "this approach emphasizes the actions of teachers rather than their professional judgments and attempts to capture the activity of teaching by identifying sets of discrete behaviors reproducible from one teacher and one classroom to the next." Teacher research, on the other hand, is conducted by teachers in their own classrooms who are addressing real problems and trying to find ways to solve those problems. It is the kind of inquiry that results from experiences in the classroom. In the field of composition it is called **practitioner inquiry;** others refer to it as **action research, classroom research,** or **teacher inquiry.**

This kind of research is based on the assumption that teachers are in the best position to analyze, evaluate, solve problems, and formulate plans for teaching since they are inside the classroom rather than observing from the outside. Moreover, it fosters an integration of practice and theory, as the epigraph from Nunan describes (see also van Lier 1994). The differences between "research on teaching" and "teacher research" are succinctly presented in Table 11.1, from Cochran-Smith and Lytle (1993). They are emphatic about the four conditions that promote successful teacher research: (1) The teachers themselves must ask the research questions, (2) the teachers must be central to the process of expanding their own knowledge bases, (3) the results of the teacher research must be worth the effort – for teachers, students, school systems, and communities, and (4) the teachers must have some authority for decision making in the research and in the actions the research generates (Cochran-Smith & Lytle 1993: 13).

Classroom research begins with simple inquiries about, or a nagging dissatisfaction with, some aspect of what is going on in the classroom. These inquiries may range from wondering about what teachers actually do in their classroom to what the learners are doing to solving a specific problem. Even a suspicion that something in the classroom could be improved is an impetus for engaging in this kind of inquiry.

A number of books and articles provide detailed lists of ways to begin classroom research, including journals, observations, tape or video recording of classes, and oral reports. Nunan (1989) gives meticulous instructions for several methods of data gathering, including diary studies, interviews, questionnaires and checklists, protocol analysis and stimulated recall, case studies, classroom observation schemes, and classroom ethnography. Kebir

Table 11.1   Research on teaching and teacher research

	Research on teaching	*Teacher research*
Ownership	Professional researchers: university-based or R&D center-based	Teachers: K–12 school-based, college/university-based, or adult program-based
Supportive structures	Academic community organized to provide formal/informal support for research: monetary, work load, scheduling, and institutional support, as well as local and national forums for dissemination and publication	Teaching organizations (school or university) lack formal/informal support for research: inflexible work loads and teaching schedules, little monetary support or release time, and few local or national forums for dissemination/publication
Research questions	Generally emerging from study in a discipline (or multiple disciplines) and/or analysis of theoretical and empirical literatures; referenced to the major work in some area(s) of the field	Generally emerging from problems of practice: felt discrepancies between intention and reality, theory/research and practice; reflexive and referenced to the immediate context

Source: M. Cochran-Smith and S. Lytle, *Inside/Outside: Teacher Research and Knowledge,* Figure 1.1, pp. 12–13. Copyright © 1993 by Teachers College Press. Reprinted by permission.

(1994) and Clennell (1994) give samples of transcripts and data collected in classroom studies they conducted. Samway (1994) acknowledges the difficulties of keeping field notes while conducting a class and illustrates a system to make the process easier. Handscombe (1993a,b) outlines a program for research linked to practice and gives steps to follow in setting up an investigation.

As an introduction to teacher research, keeping a detailed diary of what happens in class for two weeks or making a video- or audiotape of several classes will provide sufficient data for a useful investigation. Several authors have outlined instructions to guide teachers through the steps in this kind of research. Richards and Lockhart (1994) include four excellent tools: enumerated guidelines for doing classroom research (pp. 27–8), a list of questions that constitutes a guide to making journal entries (pp. 16–17), a lesson report form (p. 137), and guidelines for peer evaluation (pp. 24–6). Patterson et al. (1993: 163) provide an exhaustive set of categories for identifying the types of comments recorded in a diary and journal. While these and other sources help refine and sharpen inquiries (see also J. D. Brown 1988; Burton & Agor 1994; Carroll 1994; Cumming 1994; Nunan 1992), the central element in teacher research is that it belongs to the teacher and does not have to conform to the constraints or conventions of more formal systems.

We encourage teachers to assume the perspective of action researchers. That perspective allows teachers to monitor and adjust the validity of classroom methods and practices, to try new approaches, and to recognize the theoretical underpinnings of practice (Handscombe 1993a: 2). By keeping inquiry alive and healthy, teachers nourish their teaching, their students, and their own self-confidence.

Since the reading process is complex and not fully understood, most people have an implicit or unconscious model of it. The reading teacher, however, needs to have an explicit and conscious model of reading. The concept of making understanding more explicit that we raised in the Introduction bears reiteration:

> Many personal theories are implicit; that is, they lie outside awareness, and they are divorced from the more structured knowledge contained in formal theories. . . .
>
> Implicit theories are our individual submerged rationales about events in the world and about our own behavior in the world.
>
> (Rando & Menges 1991: 7)

Teachers must understand their own reading processes, the theoretical frameworks for those processes, and how those process have been shaped by training, culture, and individual factors. Transforming the implicit into the explicit constitutes understanding. The growth spiral of learning and understanding provides the excitement, engagement, and fulfillment that creates a healthy environment for teaching and for learning. There is nothing more important that we can wish for our readers than continued growth, understanding, and pleasure in the processes of reading and teaching reading. It is with this wish that we conclude our book.

Reading textbook samples

Beginning and low levels

1   "Who's Calling?"
2   "Dish Soap for Dinner"

Intermediate level

3   "Modern Fathers Have Pleasures and Problems"

Advanced level

4   "Our Future Stock"

Superior level

5   "Theoretical Perspectives on Societies"

Text without exercises

6   "More Men Infiltrating Professions Historically Dominated by
    Women"

Reading textbook sample 1

Getting Ready to Read

Developing New Concepts and Vocabulary

Study Pictures 1, 2, 3, and 4, and study the new words and phrases.

PICTURE 1

laugh

phrases
ask ____ out
make a date

PICTURE 2

phrases
hang up
go out with ____

Reprinted with permission from *Spaghetti Forever: A Low-Intermediate Reader in English* by Jean Bodman and Judith McKoy. © 1988 by Heinle & Heinle.

PICTURE 3

phrase

pick ____ up

PICTURE 4

dance

cheer

scream

Using the Vocabulary

Say something about Pictures 1, 2, 3, and 4. Use the new words and phrases.

Thinking and Questioning

Study this picture and the new words.

cover

background

privacy

1. Say something about this picture. Use the new words.
2. Look at the picture again. Think of two questions, and write them here:

Who _____ ?

Why _____ ?

Reading

Study these new words and phrases. Then read the story.

area	happen	phrases	____ 'll be right with ____.
busy	⚠ nuts	Just a minute.	have a date
Daddy	watch	Let me see.	⚠ Big deal.
fine		Shh!	

Who's Calling?

The phone rings at the Lewises' house.

Ben: Hello?
Frank: Hello, is your mother there?
Ben: Uh . . . who's calling, please?
Frank: Frank Standish.

Ben covers the phone with his hand.

Ben: MOM! It's for you. A man!
Sarah: A man?
Ben: Yeah. Someone named Frank Standish.
Sarah: Oh! Just a minute.

Ben uncovers the phone.

Ben: Mr. Standish?
Frank: Yes?
Ben: She'll be right with you.
Frank: Thank you.

Pause for a moment. . . .

Who are the people in the story?

What is happening?

Story Question 1: Write a question you have about the story.

_____ ?

Now continue reading.

Sarah picks up the phone.

Sarah: Hello?
Frank: Hello, Sarah? This is Frank.
Sarah: Frank! It's nice to hear from you.
Frank: Yes . . .
Sarah: How are you?
Frank: Fine. Just fine. Uh . . .
Sarah: Where are you calling from?
Frank: Brighton.
Sarah: Oh.
Frank: Yes, I just bought a house on Glenwood Avenue.
Sarah: Glenwood Avenue? In Brighton? That's a beautiful area.
Frank: Yes. Well, now that I live so close to you . . .
Sarah: Yes?
Frank: . . . would you like to get together sometime?
Sarah: That would be nice, Frank.
Frank: Good. Well . . . I'm real busy this week, but . . . what about dinner?
Maybe next Friday, or uh . . . Saturday?
Sarah: Um . . . let me see . . . just a minute, Frank.

Pause for a moment. . . .

Why is Frank calling?

What do you think Sarah will say?

How do you think Sarah feels?

Story Question 2: Write a question you have about the story.

_____ ?

Now continue reading.

The children are now standing around the phone.

Ben: What's happening?
Carol: It's Mom's boyfriend.
Tina: Is he asking you out?
Carol: Mom, say yes.

Sarah covers the phone.

Sarah: Come on, kids. I'd like a little privacy here.
Ben: She wants privacy! Woooooo!
Sarah: Benjamin!

The children walk away laughing.

Sarah: Frank?
Frank: Yes.
Sarah: Saturday is fine.
Frank: Great. Okay! Saturday then. I'll pick you up at 7:00?
Sarah: Well . . .
Frank: If that's too early . . .
Sarah: No! 7:00 is fine.

In the background Carol and Tina are cheering. Sarah covers the phone.

Sarah: Shh!
Frank: Sarah? Sarah, are you there?

Pause for a moment. . . .

How do the children feel?

What do you think will happen next?

Story Question 3: Write a question you have about the story.

_____ ?

Now continue reading.

Frank: Sarah?
Sarah: Oh, sorry, Frank. It's my children. They're talking.
Frank: Oh. So, about Saturday . . .
Sarah: It'll be nice to see you again. Nineteen years is a long time.
Frank: Yes. Well, see you next Saturday . . . at 7:00.
Sarah: Okay. Thanks for calling.
Frank: Goodbye.
Sarah: Goodbye. Oh, Frank?

Sarah listens, but Frank is not on the phone anymore.

Pause for a moment. . . .

At the end of the phone call, Sarah has a question. What do you think she wants to ask Frank?

_____ ?

Now continue reading.

Sarah hangs up the phone. She looks at the children.

Carol: Well?
Sarah: Well?
Carol: Are you going out with him?
Sarah: Maybe . . .

Sarah leaves the room. Carol and Tina look at each other. They laugh, and then they scream and dance around the room together. Ben watches them.

Ben: You two are nuts.
Tina: Aren't you happy that Mom has a date?
Ben: Big deal.
Carol: It is. This is her first date since Daddy died.
Ben: Big deal.

Comprehension Activities

Reviewing the Story

Each question has two parts. Study this example.

A. Sarah's Feelings

Part 1: How does Sarah feel about her date?

____ She does not want to see Frank.

✓ She seems happy.

____ She is sad.

Part 2: How do you know your answer is correct?

I think it is correct because Sarah says to Frank,

____ "Oh, sorry, Frank. It's my children."

____ "Nineteen years is a long time."

✓ "It'll be nice to see you again."

Now you answer the questions. Check the correct answers.

B. Ben's Feelings

Part 1: At the end of the story, how does Ben feel about his mother's date?

____ He seems very happy.

____ He seems angry.

____ He seems a little upset.

Part 2: How do you know your answer is correct?

I think it is correct because

____ Ben tells his sisters, "You two are nuts."

____ Ben begins to dance around with his sisters.

____ Ben tells his sisters to stop dancing and screaming.

Using Your Story Questions

Work with a classmate. Read the Story Questions that you wrote while you were reading the story. Then read the Story Questions that your classmate wrote.

1. Try to answer your Story Questions. Can you answer all of them? Check one:

   I can answer ____ one ____ two ____ three ____ none.

2. Try to answer your classmate's Story Questions. Can you answer all of them? Check one:

   I can answer ____ one ____ two ____ three ____ none.

Remember, sometimes you cannot answer good questions right away. Sometimes you have to read more of the story to get the information you need.

Summarizing the Story

The following sentences are about Sarah's phone call. Read all the sentences. Then check the *four* sentences that give you the most important information about the story. The first two important sentences are checked for you. You check the other two.

____ The phone rings.

____ Ben answers the phone.

✓ Frank, an old friend of Sarah's, calls to ask her for a date.

✓ Frank has just moved and now lives close to Sarah.

____ Sarah's kids want to know what Frank wants.

____ They are laughing and making a lot of noise.

____ Sarah tells Frank she will see him on Saturday.

____ Carol asks, "Well?" when Sarah gets off the phone.

____ After Frank and Sarah hang up, Carol and Tina begin to scream and dance.

____ Ben says, "Big deal."

Discuss your choices with your classmates. Do you agree?

Making a Guess

1. Why are the girls happy?

_____

_____

2. What do you think will happen next in the story?

_____

_____

Wondering About the Story

What do you want to know about the story? Write a question here:

_____ ?

Vocabulary Practice

Making Associations

When people are happy, what do they usually do? Circle the words.

laugh	cheer	dance
cry	watch	sit
hang up	scream	sleep

Discuss your answers with your classmates.

Using New Vocabulary

Circle the best word or phrase to make a story. The first best choice is circled for you.

Peter is (calling) / cheering his friend, Ann. He wants to ask her out / pick her up for Saturday night and take her to a date. / a school dance. Peter likes to hang up / go out with Ann because she likes to laugh / cheer and have a good time.

When Peter asks her if she wants to go, she says, "Yes, but just a minute. / big deal. I have to ask my parents first." Peter watches / waits for her. When she comes back to the phone, she tells Peter, "It's okay. Everything is busy. / fine. They say I can go."

Peter says he will go out with her / pick her up at her house at 5:00 on Saturday. Ann says, "That will be nuts. / great. I'm dying to go to this dance."

More Difficult Practice—
Understanding Figurative Language: Sarcasm

Read these lines from the story:

> Tina: Aren't you happy that Mom has a date?
> Ben: Big deal.

Check the correct answer.

What does Ben mean when he says "Big deal?"

___ He does not think his mother's date is important.

___ He thinks his mother's date is wonderful.

___ He thinks his mother's date is very important.

More Difficult Questions—
Discussing the Story

In this story, Sarah tells Frank that she will go on a date with him. This is her first date since her husband died. Tina and Carol seem happy, but Ben is upset and says, "Big deal."

1. Do you think that Ben should say what he thinks? Check one:

   ___ Yes ___ No

2. Why or why not?

_____

_____

Reading textbook sample 2

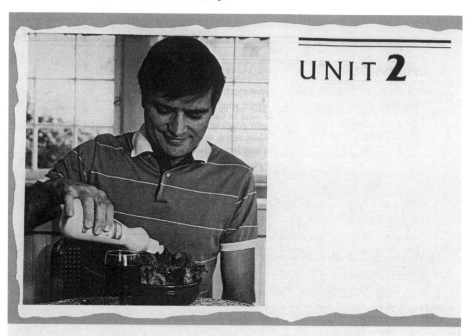

UNIT **2**

1. PRE-READING

Look at the picture.

- What is the man eating?
- What is the man putting on his salad?

2. VOCABULARY

Complete the sentences. Find the right words. Circle the letter of your answer.

1. The dish soap was a _____ from a soap company.
   a. letter
   b. free sample
   c. mailbox

2. The company wanted people to _____ the soap.
   a. try
   b. eat
   c. mail

3. There was a picture of two lemons on the _____.
   a. soap company
   b. label
   c. salad

4. What can we learn from Joe's story? Read labels _____.
   a. fast
   b. happily
   c. carefully

From *True Stories in the News: A Beginning Reader* by Sandra Heyer, copyright © 1987 by Longman Publishers. Reprinted with permission.

Dish Soap for Dinner

JOE came home from work and opened his mailbox. In his mailbox he found a yellow bottle of soap—soap for washing dishes.

The dish soap was a free sample from a soap company. The company mailed small bottles of soap to thousands of people. It was a new soap with a little lemon juice in it. The company wanted people to try it.

Joe looked at his free bottle of soap. There was a picture of two lemons on the label. Over the lemons were the words "with Real Lemon Juice."

Joe was happy. "I'm going to eat a salad for dinner," he thought. "This lemon juice will taste good on my salad." He put the soap on his salad and ate it.

Soon Joe felt sick. He wasn't the only person who got sick. A lot of people thought the soap was lemon juice. They put the soap on fish, on salads, and in tea. Later they felt sick, too. Some people had stomachaches. Some people went to the hospital. Luckily, no one died from eating the soap.

What can we learn from Joe's story? Read labels carefully. And don't eat dish soap for dinner!

3. COMPREHENSION

UNDERSTANDING THE MAIN IDEA

Circle the letter of the best answer.

1. "Dish Soap for Dinner" is about
   a. reading labels carefully.
   b. many people in the hospital.
   c. free samples from soap companies.

2. Another good title for this story is
   a. "A Day at the Hospital."
   b. "Soap and Salad."
   c. "Joe's Mailbox."

FINDING INFORMATION
Read the questions. Find the answers in the story. Write the answers.

1. Did Joe find a letter or a free sample in his mailbox?

   Joe found a free sample in his mailbox.

2. Was the free sample from a soap company or from a food company?

   _____

3. Did the soap have tomato juice or lemon juice in it?

   _____

4. Did Joe put the soap on his dishes or on his salad?

   _____

5. Did some people have stomachaches or headaches?

   _____

6. Did some people go to the supermarket or to the hospital?

   _____

UNDERSTANDING DETAILS
Read the sentences. One word in each sentence is not correct. Find the word and cross it out. Write the correct word.

1. In his mailbox Joe found a yellow bottle of ~~beer.~~ *soap*

2. The dish soap was a free ticket from a soap company.

3. It was a new soap with a little apple juice in it.

4. The company wanted people to eat it.

5. There was a picture of two bananas on the label.

6. Joe put the soap on his dishes.

7. Soon Joe felt fine.

8. Some people had backaches.

9. Some people went to the library.

4. DISCUSSION

Labels often have important warnings. The warnings say, "Be careful!"
Look at these pictures and read the warnings. Draw a line and connect the
warning with its meaning.

1. May cause drowsiness.

2. May be harmful or fatal if
   swallowed.

3. Flammable.

a. This is poison. Do not eat or
   drink this. You can die.

b. Do not smoke or use matches
   here. This can burn easily.

c. You can feel sleepy.

Look for bottles and cans with warnings on the label. Copy the warnings.
Bring the warnings to class and discuss them.

5. WRITING

Read this story. It is in the present tense. Write the story again in the past
tense.

Joe comes home from work and opens his mailbox. In his mailbox he
finds a free sample of dish soap. The dish soap has a little lemon juice in it.
Joe looks at his bottle of soap. There is a picture of two lemons on the
label. Over the lemons are the words "with Real Lemon Juice."
Joe thinks the soap is lemon juice. He puts it on his salad and eats it.
Soon he feels sick. Poor Joe!

*Joe came home from work and opened
his mailbox.*

Modern Fathers Have Pleasures and Problems

Reprinted with permission from *Explorations: An Interactive Approach to Reading* by Alison Rice and Susan Stempleski. © 1988 by Heinle & Heinle.

Pre-reading

WORK WITH A GROUP

1. Talk about the fathers and children in the pictures. Write down any vocabulary words that are new for you.

   _____

2. What is each father doing?

   a. Picture 1 _____

   b. Picture 2 _____

   c. Picture 3 _____

   d. Picture 4 _____

   Do fathers in your country do these things too?

3. Together, make a list of the things a man should do to be a good father.

4. The next article is "Modern Fathers Have Pleasures and Problems." Check (✔) the things you think this article will talk about.

   ☐ Fathers in the past
   ☐ Good and bad things about being a father
   ☐ Mothers and children
   ☐ What fathers do at work
   ☐ Why fathers are doing more at home

> Read the article. See whether your guesses are correct. Then compare your list from Exercise 3 with the things that James Hogan and Harlan Swift do. Are these men good fathers?

Modern Fathers
Have
Pleasures and Problems

James Hogan, 38, became a father 18 months ago. When his daughter was born, he quit his full-time job. He wanted to have more time to spend with his child.

"I wanted to be a real father to my daughter," says Hogan of Washington, D.C.

At first, Hogan had a lot of problems. "I had a lot to learn about babies," he says. "For example, I didn't know how to change a diaper and I wasn't sure how to hold a baby."

There are thousands of fathers like Hogan in the United States today. These "liberated dads" are spending more time with their children—holding them, feeding them, playing with them, and changing their diapers.

There are many reasons for this change. One reason is that modern men have more free time away from work. Another reason is that more married women with children work outside the home. These mothers are too busy to do all the housework and take care of the children alone. Their husbands have to help them.

Modern fathers are enjoying the change. James Hogan spends 25 to 30 hours per week with his daughter. He says he isn't sorry he left his job. "I wanted more time to be with my daughter, and now I have it," he says.

Another father who is enjoying the change is Harlan Swift, a 34-year-old engineer and father of two. "Spending time with the kids is the most important thing in my life. I enjoy every minute I'm with them," Swift says.

Not many men can afford to quit work when they become fathers. They don't have enough money. Combining a full-time job and home life is difficult. You need a lot of energy. As Harlan Swift says, "I never have enough time to do everything."

Modern fathers will need to learn to balance work at home with their jobs outside the home. They will also need to learn new skills. Like James Hogan, many men are uncomfortable holding babies or changing diapers. That is not going to change overnight.

1 Scanning

Read the questions. Then look at the article "Modern Fathers Have Pleasures and Problems" to find the answers as quickly as possible.

1. James Hogan became a father _____ months ago.
   a) 8   b) 18   c) 28

2. Hogan comes from _____ .
   a) New York   b) Chicago   c) Washington, D.C.

3. Harlan Swift is _____ years old.
   a) 24   b) 34   c) 38

4. He has _____ children.
   a) two   b) three   c) four

5. He is an _____ .
   a) engineer   b) artist   c) architect

2 Comprehension
WORK WITH A PARTNER

1. TRUE OR FALSE? Decide if the statements below are true (T) or false (F). Write the sentence from the story that supports your answer. If the article doesn't give the answer, write *It doesn't say*.

EXAMPLE: James Hogan has a son. ___F___
When his daughter was born, he quit his full-time job.

1. Hogan knew a lot about babies before he had one. _____

2. Hogan left his job because he was unhappy at work. _____

3. Modern men work more hours a week than their fathers did. _____

4. In the past, fewer women than today worked outside the home. _____

5. James Hogan spends only two or three hours with his daughter every day. _____

6. A lot of men begin to work part-time when they have children. _____

7. Harlan Swift could use a 26-hour day. _____

---

8. The author thinks that in a few years most men will be comfortable with babies. _____

---

2. MAKING INFERENCES. Circle *all* of the answers that you think are correct. Explain your answers.

1. James Hogan thinks that
   a) a father should spend a lot of time with his child.
   b) fathers are more important than mothers.
   c) it's difficult to take care of a baby.

2. Harlan Swift
   a) likes being with his children.
   b) doesn't have a lot of energy.
   c) thinks that his job is more important than his children.

3. The author of this article thinks that
   a) modern women are lazy.
   b) many men in the future will work part-time.
   c) men today spend more time with their children than men in the past.

③ *Finding the Facts*

Answer the following questions with information from the article "Modern Fathers Have Pleasures and Problems."

1. What are "liberated dads" doing with their children?
   a. *They're spending more time holding them.* _____
   b. _____
   c. _____
   d. _____

2. Why are fathers doing more with their children?
   a. _____
   b. _____

3. What do modern fathers have to learn?
   a. _____
   b. _____

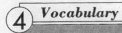

Vocabulary

1. GETTING THE MEANING FROM CONTEXT. Match the underlined word in each sentence with the definition from the list in the box.

> a) abilities that come from education or experience
> b) eight hours a day, five days a week
> c) free to try things they never did before
> d) have enough money
> e) give equal time to

1. _____ Some parents want to spend more time with their children, so they stop working <u>full-time</u>. That way, they can be at home in the afternoons.

2. _____ Unfortunately, most people aren't rich. They can't <u>afford</u> to stop working.

3. _____ Modern fathers are "<u>liberated</u>." They can do things with their children that men in the past thought only women should do.

4. _____ It's difficult for modern parents to <u>balance</u> all the different parts of their lives—jobs, housework, children—and still find time to relax.

5. _____ Many men don't have childcare <u>skills</u>. They don't know how to take care of young children.

WORD FORMS

2. Choose the form of the word that completes each sentence.

1. combines   combination
      verb   noun
   a. Being a successful parent is a _____ of hard work and good luck.

   b. A good school _____ academic, social, and physical education.

2. easy   ease
     adjective noun
   a. Experienced parents usually take care of their own children with

   _____ .

   b. However, it isn't _____ to care for a sick child.

3. energy   energetically
     noun   adverb
   a. Children have a lot of _____ .

   b. The young couple cleaned their house _____ because their friends were coming for a visit.

4. enjoy   enjoyable
     verb   adjective
   a. Most families _____ taking a vacation in the summer.

   b. Going to the beach is _____ and inexpensive.

Henry is a newspaper columnist. He gives people advice about their problems. Here are two letters asking for help. Student A will read the letter on this page. Student B will read the letter on the next page.

Student A's letter

Helpful Henry

DEAR HENRY,

We don't know what to do about our daughter. She is twenty-two years old and won't look for a job. She says we have to take care of her for the rest of her life.

She graduated from college last year. Now all she does is eat like an elephant, sleep, read, watch TV, and listen to records.

We asked two doctors for help. They said that there was nothing wrong with her. The police cannot help because she is not a criminal.

What should we do about her? We are not millionaires, and we are tired of . . .

FEEDING AN ELEPHANT

Now ask your partner the following questions about his/her letter.

1. Who is the letter about?
2. What is the problem?
3. What else do you know about the young man?
4. Does the mother dislike her son's girlfriend?
5. What does the mother want her son to do?
6. What advice does she want from Henry?
7. What advice would you give her?

Student B's letter

DEAR HENRY,

I am worried sick about my son. He is eighteen years old and a senior in high school. Yesterday he told me that he wants to marry his girlfriend. She is sixteen.

I want him to get married. But I want him to graduate from high school and go to college first. My son wants to get married right away. He says he is going to quit school and find a full-time job. (Right now he has a part-time job in a supermarket.)

My son's girlfriend is lovely. But they are both too young to get married. I want my son to complete his education first. What should I do?

WORRIED MOTHER

Now ask your partner the following questions about his/her letter.

1. Who is the letter about?
2. What is the problem?
3. What else do you know about the young woman?
4. Who did the parents speak to about their problem?
5. Did they get any help from these people?
6. What advice do they want from Henry?
7. What advice would you give them?

6 ***Discussion***

WORK WITH A PARTNER

Talk about the advice you and your partner gave those parents. Do you agree with each other? Would parents in your countries have these problems?

Reading textbook sample 4

OUR FUTURE STOCK

About the Selection:

In the first lesson you had an opportunity to explore some of your thoughts about change and about the future of your field or occupation. Now you will have a chance to compare your predictions for the future with those of experts who have studied these issues in depth. The following reading selection is from the popular science magazine *Omni.* In 1982 the editors of *Omni* gathered information from various U.S. government agencies and industry experts. They used this information to develop a picture of what the work force and the economy of the future may look like. This selection is an excerpt from the article reporting their predictions. As you read through it, consider whether the changes mentioned here are similar to those you wrote about in lesson 1.

The First Reading

Before You Read: Anticipating the Topic

Look at the title and graphics. *Stock* often refers to an investment or an accumulation of something for future use. Judging from the subtitles and the pictures, what do you think *stock* refers to in this case? _____

What type of future developments does this excerpt seem to focus on?

_____

Based on the results of your brainstorming in lesson 1, write two to three sentences about the kinds of careers and workplace changes one could "put stock in" (expect; have faith in) for the future.

_____

_____

As You Read: Looking for the General Ideas

First read the article quickly to discover its main points and general organization. Then do the activities that follow. Later, in your second reading, you can go through the entire article more carefully or focus in on

Brown, H. Douglas, *Challenges: A Process Approach to Academic English,* © 1991, pp. 7, 11–18. Reprinted by permission of Prentice-Hall, Inc., Englewood Cliffs, N.J.

particular sections to pick up the specific details and development of the main points. You will see that two or three quick, purposeful readings will be more efficient and productive than one slow, detailed reading.

Don't worry about vocabulary! As you read, you will find words you do not know. Don't worry about these. Either guess their meanings or skip them entirely. *Do not* look up any words in the dictionary at this time. To do so would only slow you down and prevent you from focusing on the key points. Vocabulary exercises will follow.

OUR FUTURE STOCK:
A Survey of Jobs, New Technology, and the World Economy in the Next Millenium

[1]   During the next 50 years an incredible array of new technologies is expected to move from the lab to the world of business. We are already seeing evidence of this today. Robots are replacing humans on the production lines. Microcomputers have become fixtures in offices. Biofactories are beginning to manufacture batches of engineered human insulin. . . . The coming decades promise to be especially volatile[1] and exciting for American business. The expected upheaval will profoundly change not only our lives but also those of our children and grandchildren.

[2]   For the more developed nations, this era of turmoil will be marked by economic difficulties, problems with waste and pollution, and continually dwindling[2] resources. By contrast, the Third World countries will spearhead a new industrial age with the same fervor and energy that characterized American industrial expansion in the days of Vanderbilt, Carnegie, Morgan and Rockefeller . . .

Job Markets and Careers

[3]   The technological revolution that will prevail[3] for the remainder of this century will create jobs and professions that as little as five years ago were nonexistent. These newly developed markets will demand of workers an understanding of sophisticated technical communications systems as well as an increased technical expertise. By the year 2001 basic skills that once were vital to business will be rendered obsolete. The spot welder on the automobile production line, the clerk typist in an office, the field worker on a farm will go the way of the steamboat pilot and the blacksmith.

[4]   The most significant trend in years to come will be the shift from

---

[1] **volatile:** changeable

[2] **dwindling:** becoming smaller and smaller (in amount)

[3] **prevail:** occur as the most important feature

formation-type jobs (factory work, office typing, and general clerical work) to information-type jobs (programming, word processing, and supervising technical machinery).[4] The American economy will witness the demise of the blue-collar worker as automation and robotics become more prevalent, heralding the rise of the steel-collar worker. Such traditional blue-collar employers as General Motors and U.S. Steel have already begun to automate their factories – a fact reflected in the swollen[5] unemployment rolls in our industrial states.

5   By contrast, office and service jobs will be abundant, but only for those prepared to improve their technical skills. Again it will be automation that will displace many of the low-skilled and semiskilled workers in the present economy.

6   In fact, the era of the paperless office has already begun. It has been promoted by two principal developments: computers that process business information and the explosive growth of telecommunications systems and products. This office revolution not only has changed how work is done and information is handled but has redefined the function of everyone who works in an office, from the corporate executive down to the lowliest clerk . . .

7   For the job hunter of 2020, scanning[6] classified ads will be a quick education in how drastically[7] the workplace will have changed. He or she is likely to see openings for such positions as biological historians, biofarming experts, computer art curators, fiberoptics technicians, robot retrainers, space traffic controllers, and teleconferencing coordinators, to cite but a few.

8   There will always be farms, but by the next century farmworkers as we know them will be scarcer. The business of farming will become ever more complex. With computerized operations and robot harvesters, there will be no need for unskilled labor. The farm will be a place for people with training as electronic technicians, bioengineers, and computer programmers. Indeed, the human farmworker someday may be simply the person with the phone number of the nearest robot repairman.

---

[4] **formation-type jobs:** jobs which result in the actual "formation" of a material product, such as a car, manually typed report, and so on.

  information-type jobs: jobs which focus on the electronic processing of information, whether that information is used in an office or business setting or used to control machines which then produce material goods and services. Note that this information may never take concrete material form; it can be processed and stored electronically in our computer systems, transmitted from one place to another by complex electronic telecommunications systems, and read on a computer screen rather than on separate sheets of paper.

[5] **swollen:** enlarge; having got bigger

[6] **scanning:** looking over or reading quickly (often to find specific information)

[7] **drastically:** severely; suddenly

Reprinted with permission from *The Omni Future Almanac,* copyright © 1982 Omni Publications, Pharos Books, New York, NY 10166.

After You Read

• Identifying the Main Idea

DIRECTIONS: Choose the answer that best expresses the main idea.

1. Based on paragraphs 1 and 2, choose the statement that best expresses the main idea of the article.
   a. Industrialized nations will face many problems in the years ahead.
   b. New technological developments will greatly change our lives and the lives of our children.
   c. Robots will replace humans on factory production lines.
   d. Change is everywhere.

2. The main idea for the section "Job Markets and Careers" is:
   a. Our future world will be very different from today's world.
   b. Farmwork will be largely automated and computerized in the future.
   c. There will be more office jobs and fewer factory jobs in the future.
   d. New technology will create many new jobs and professions and will make many old ones outdated.

• Guessing Vocabulary from Context

When you encounter unfamiliar vocabulary in an English reading selection, what is your typical response? Do you bring out your bilingual or English monolingual dictionary to look up the word? Do you then spend precious moments looking through all the definitions to decide which one fits? Have you ever finally decided on a definition only to realize that you have forgotten what you were reading and must begin the sentence or paragraph all over again?

Over-reliance on a dictionary not only slows down your reading but may interfere with your comprehension as well. A better strategy is to use the context, the words and sentences surrounding a particular word, to help you guess that word's meaning. Usually the guesses you make will be accurate enough for you to understand the author's ideas. When they are not, or when the terms require an exact technical definition, you can use your English dictionary as a back-up resource.

DIRECTIONS: The following exercise contains words taken from the reading selection. Use the new context to select the most appropriate meaning.

1. Just as the invention of the automobile <u>rendered</u> horse-drawn carriages <u>obsolete</u> in modern cities, so the use of computers and word processors will make the common typewriter much <u>scarcer</u> in offices of the future.

render obsolete: a. cause it to be outdated and no longer useful
                      b. cause it to increase in price
                      c. cause it to change

scarcer: a. more common
                      b. more efficient
                      c. more rare

2. Because business computers are becoming more and more complex, many office workers have had to get new training to handle these <u>sophisticated</u> electronic systems.

sophisticated: a. complex
                    b. business
                    c. worldly

3. Computers are even becoming more <u>prevalent</u> in American schools and homes; perhaps in another twenty years every school-age child in the United States will be able to operate a computer.

prevalent: a. large
              b. common
              c. expensive

4. Some automobile factories have begun to <u>automate</u> their assembly lines by using robots instead of human workers. This <u>automation</u> will increase the amount of money needed for machinery but will decrease the cost of labor.

automate: a. to increase the number of human workers
              b. to produce a greater variety of products
              c. to operate or control something by machine rather than by human labor

automation: the noun form of *automate,* referring to the process of automating

5. Unlike white-collar workers, who usually work in an office, <u>blue-collar workers</u> may be found in many different work settings. For example, they may work outdoors to construct a new highway, or they may assemble new cars in an auto factory or repair damaged ones in a mechanic shop.

blue-collar workers: a. business executives
                           b. secretaries
                           c. manual laborers

6. The early industrial revolution contributed to the <u>demise</u> of the feudal lords and the rise of the bourgeoisie. Likewise, the new technological

may <u>herald</u> major social and economic changes in the societies of the future.

demise: a. creation
           b. loss of power
           c. gain in power

herald: a. introduce
           b. end
           c. respond to

7. Blue-collar workers were originally given this name because of the blue workshirts they often wore. Given this information and the preceding vocabulary clues, reread paragraph 4. Can you guess what or who the "steel-collar workers" are who are replacing the blue-collar workers? Write your answers in the space provided.

steel-collar workers: _____

The Second Reading

Before You Read: Knowing Your Purpose

In the first reading you were looking for the main ideas of the article; this time, your purpose is to see how these ideas are supported. You might want to think about the following questions as you read:

1. What is the main change that will take place in the work force?
2. What types of jobs will be affected by this change?
3. What are some specific examples of the jobs and careers we might expect to see in the future?

After You Read

- Understanding the Author's Plan

In order to better understand what you read, it is often helpful to consider the author's plan of organization and method of development. In the following exercise, the purpose of each paragraph in the section "Job Markets and Careers" is explained in the left-hand column.

DIRECTIONS: Read each explanation and then answer the comprehension questions to the right.

Author's Plan

Paragraph 3: states the main idea for this section: The new technological revolution will create many new jobs and make old jobs obsolete.

Paragraph 4: expands the main idea by defining the principal trend in the job market.

Paragraphs 4–8: discuss specific types of work and the expected developments in each.

Paragraph 4: examines factory work.

Paragraphs 5–6: discuss office work.

Paragraph 7: introduces other new occupations of the future.

Paragraph 8: discusses farmwork.

Comprehension Questions

1. What kind of knowledge will the new jobs require workers to have?
2. What will happen to many of the existing jobs and skills?
3. Do the authors give examples of outdated jobs? What are they?
4. What is the most important change taking place in the American job market?
5. What will cause the "demise of the blue-collar worker?" Why?
6. What has been the result of the automation which has already occurred in General Motors and U.S. Steel factories?
7. Will office and service jobs be plentiful or scarce in the future?
8. What kind of workers will be needed to fill these positions?
9. What is meant by the "paperless office?"
10. What two major developments have contributed to the growth of the paperless office?
11. How do the examples given in paragraph 7 show the "drastic" change in the workplace? Choose one example and explain.
12. Why will farmworkers as we know them be scarcer in the next century?
13. Who will perform the unskilled labor on the farms?

We can see that the authors have established a specific purpose for each paragraph. Recognizing the function of each paragraph helps us to understand the ideas presented in a reading.

• A Deeper Look: Discussion Questions

DIRECTIONS: Discuss the following questions in small groups. Compare your answers with those of your classmates.

1. The authors of "Our Future Stock" predict a greater demand for technically skilled labor and a decreased demand for unskilled labor. How do you think this will affect employment in industrialized nations? Have these effects already been seen in some areas?

2. How can the problem of displaced workers be resolved? Give examples.

3. In paragraph 2, the authors say, ". . . the Third World countries will spearhead a new industrial age . . ." In a later section (not included in this textbook) they discuss several factors that will contribute to this advance in Third World countries. These factors include:
   - large populations
   - large amounts of unused resources
   - (in some cases) conservative governments that are opposed to labor legislation and antipollution laws.

   Do you agree that these factors may contribute to rapid economic development in many developing countries? Why or why not? If possible, give examples of specific countries to support your view.

4. Have the technological advances mentioned in this article affected your nation or area? In what ways? What will these changes mean for your future?

5. Some critics of the new technology argue that if humans rely on computers and robots, we will become mentally lazy; we will lose our artistic creativity and our ability or desire to invent new ways of doing things. Do you agree? Why or why not?

- Becoming an Efficient Reader: Scanning

   To scan is to read quickly to locate specific information or details. On . . . page [233] is an imaginary Help Wanted section of the classified ads for the year 2020. The jobs listed in this section are based on the predictions made in the previous article and on other sources. The form of this ad section is similar to that used in many U.S. newspapers.

DIRECTIONS: Answer the following questions by scanning the Help Wanted ads. First, observe how the information is organized in the ads. Then, read each question carefully to understand what is being asked. To locate the information you need, move your eyes quickly over the printed page, paying particular attention to bold headlines and key words. Finally, write the answers in the spaces provided.

1. What is the date of this ad section?
2. Where is there a position open for a space traffic controller? How many jobs are available?
3. In order to be hired as the robot psychologist at West Docks Engineering Corporation, what experience must you have? Is this same experience required for the position at Robopsyche Institute?
4. If you enjoy working on a team with other robot psychologists, which position would you apply for?
5. If you are looking for training in a space-related field, which position would you apply for?
6. What benefits are available for new salespeople at Compu-Sales, Inc.? Is on-the-job training offered for this position?
7. What job is listed as a temporary position? How long will the job last? Is there a possibility that there will be a permanent job with this company in the future?
8. If you are a teleconferencing coordinator (TC) and you speak several languages, where might you apply for a job? What languages are required?
9. Which TC position requires experience with TeleTech Systems?
10. What position is available at Hayward State University? What qualifications are needed?

HELP WANTED: JOB OPPORTUNITIES   September 15, 2020

ROBOT PSYCHOLOGIST

needed for scientific crew at West Docks Engineering Corp.

Responsibilities: to provide counseling and reprogramming to research robots suffering from directive overload and primary order conflict.

Qualifications: Must be independent and self-sufficient; able to get along without human companionship. B.S. in robotic psychology and experience with En500 Series robots required. Process resume to CompuStation 6Z, Entry #435592.

Are you a ROBOT PSYCHOLOGIST

looking for a CHANGE?

Are you tired of working in isolation for a single company? Join the qualified professional team at ROBOPSYCHE INSTITUTE.

a recently established research facility located in sunny San Jose, California. Enjoy working with stimulating colleagues while you receive excellent salary and career advancement opportunities.

All you need is a Master's degree in robotic psychology and a cooperative, energetic personality. We will provide additional training and on-the-job experience.

Process your resumé today to Robopsyche Institute, CompuStation 5C, Entry #41156.

TEMPORARY ROBOT RETRAINERS NEEDED *NOW!*

600 Series-2Z3 Domestic Robots must be reprogrammed for new duties in a major San Francisco Hotel.

4-week deadline!

Programming degree and experience required. Good salary now with chance for permanent position to follow.

Call immediately. Elizabeth Cortex, personnel manager, 415-999-6443.

SALES/MARKETING. San Francisco-based firm is expanding business-computer operations. Needs 4 creative and energetic salespeople.

Qualifications: At least 2 years experience in computer sales; knowledge of "Value Star" and related business software.

Duties: Responsible for initiating new sales contacts and handling existing valued clients.

Benefits: Base salary + commission, health and dental insurance.

Apply now: Send resumé and current earnings statement to COMPU-SALES, Inc. CompuStation 9, Entry #6725

SPACE TRAFFIC CONTROLLER: 6 positions available for experienced space traffic controllers at the new space port in Santa Clara Valley. Excellent salary and benefits. Process resumé to CompuStation 9, Entry #4413.

SALES MANAGER: GFC, Inc. Agriculture Division. Knowledge of robot harvesters and agricultural operations software required. B.S. in Agricultural Management preferred. Send resumé and salary history to GFC, Inc., CompuStation 15, Entry #2195.

LOOKING FOR ADVENTURE?

Become a Space Geographer! On Oct. 9, Astro Travel, Inc. will begin a 4-month training session for space geographers: 3 months on-the-ground training in a classroom and 1 month actual space travel. Tuition includes travel expenses. Job placement guaranteed.

Call 773-1212 for more information.

continued

TELECONFERENCING COORDINA-TOR is being sought by major L.A.-based law firm. Must have experience with TeleTech systems, and T.C. training certificate. Call (213) 592-6312 for details.

TELECONFERENCING COORDINA-TOR: Trans-Po Bank and Trust Co. Energetic, efficient T.C. needed for international business conferences. Fluency in Spanish, Japanese, and English is a must. Experience with TeleTech systems preferred. Salary and benefits negotiable. Call (415) 599-6432.

UNIVERSITY PROFESSOR OF HISTORY FIELD: Early space exploration. Ph.D. in History with a concentration in international space programs. Send resumé and related publications to History Dept. Hayward State University, CompuStation 7, Entry #7924-0116.

Reading textbook sample 5

Theoretical Perspectives on Societies

Prereading

DISCUSSION

Directions: Read the following questions. Be prepared to discuss them.

1. This selection discusses two theories that describe the nature of societies: functionalism and conflict theory. Assuming that these are opposing theories, what do you think are the basic ideas behind each of them?

2. The selection describes an extended comparison, or metaphor, comparing society to a living organism. In what ways do you think a society is like a living thing?

3. What is the purpose of using citations, that is, giving authors' names and dates of their works, in a scholarly text?

4. Sociology is the study of society: its institutions, its groups, its relationships. What is the purpose of such study?

5. What are some things that hold a society together? What are some things that tear a society apart? Could issues that hold one society together tear another society apart? Give examples.

Romstedt, K., & McGory, J. (1988). *Reading Strategies for University Students,* pp. 100–102, 107–111. Reprinted with the permission of the authors.

PREVIEW
PART 1: FUNCTIONALISM

Directions: Find the paragraph in which the following topics are discussed. Then write the number of the paragraph beside each topic.

_____ **a.** Functionalism has received some criticism.

_____ **b.** Functionalism is founded on biology.

_____ **c.** Examples of functional and dysfunctional societies are discussed.

_____ **d.** The definition of functionalism is given.

_____ **e.** A society must meet basic needs in order to be functional.

_____ **f.** A society has primary and secondary functions.

Now read the following phrases and sentences. Write the number of the paragraph in which you find each phrase or sentence.

_____ **a.** "Society is in many ways similar to a living organism."

_____ **b.** "Emile Durkheim is often thought of as the father of functionalism as we know it today."

_____ **c.** "The real functions of a unit of social structure may not be the same as its 'official,' or intended, functions."

_____ **d.** "The most forceful criticism . . ."

_____ **e.** "Charles Darwin . . . explain(ed) evolution in terms of natural selection."

PREVIEW
PART 2: CONFLICT THEORY

Directions: Find the paragraph in which the following topics are discussed. Then write the number of the paragraph beside each topic.

_____ **a.** Conflict theory may be explained in terms of Marxist sociology.

_____ **b.** A central part of conflict theory involves a power struggle between the strong and the weak.

_____ **c.** There are leaders within a society who dominate or rule that society.

_____ **d.** Many conflict theorists believe that societies are held together by force.

_____ **e.** There is a disagreement among conflict theorists.

_____ **f.** Even though there is much disagreement among sociologists, they agree that there is something important in each perspective of conflict theory as well as in functionalism.

Now read the following words, phrases, and sentences. Write the number of the paragraph in which you find each word, phrase, or sentence.

_____ **a.** "Conflict theory is not nearly so unified a viewpoint as functionalism."

_____ **b.** " . . . is that human beings are sociable but conflict-prone animals."

_____ **c.** "proletariat"

_____ **d.** "best-known book"

_____ **e.** "A major assumption"

_____ **f.** "Conflict theory, on the other hand, focuses on the strains and tensions in life."

READING
THEORETICAL PERSPECTIVES ON SOCIETIES

Now let us return to the two major theoretical perspectives on societies, functionalism and conflict theory. . . . Here we shall explore these perspectives in more detail and see how they are used to analyze the operation of societies.

Functionalism

1   Functionalism took on its basic form in the nineteenth century. In many ways, this was the century of biology. Knowledge of the human body, of microscopic forms of life, and of plants and animals around the world kept increasing. In one of the greatest achievements of the century, Charles Darwin drew on this vast body of new knowledge to explain evolution in terms of natural selection. Biology had never before enjoyed such high prestige. Excited by these steps forward, social thinkers naturally began to apply some of the concepts of biology to society.

2   Auguste Comte and Herbert Spencer proposed the most basic idea of functionalism: *Society is in many ways similar to a living organism.* There are three aspects of this idea: First, society, like a living thing, has structure. An animal is made up of cells, tissues, and organs; society is likewise made up of structures such as groups, classes, and institutions. Second, like an organism, society is a system that has certain needs to be satisfied if the system is to survive. Societies must, for example, be able to get food and resources from the surroundings and distribute them to their members. Third, like the parts of a biological organism, the parts of a social system seem to work together in an orderly way to maintain the well-being of the whole. Spencer and his followers said that the natural tendency of systems is toward equilibrium or stability, and that each part of society has a function that adds to this stability. Thus, in formal terms functionalism views society as a complex system made up of parts that function to fulfill the needs of the whole so as to maintain stability.

3   Later, scholars took the basic idea of functionalism – that society is similar to a living organism – and refined and added to it. Émile Durkheim is often thought of as the father of functionalism as we know it today. In his work he made heavy use of functionalist terms drawn from biology. He saw society as a special kind of organism, one ruled by a consensus of moral values. Functionalism was also the major perspective of the British founders of the branch of anthropology called "cultural anthropology."

4   In the United States, the sociologist Talcott Parsons was the leading figure in making functionalism into a general yet systematic theory for sociological analysis. A society, he said, will remain functional – that is, maintain its order and stability – if it can meet four basic needs (Parsons,

Source: David Popenoe, *Sociology,* 10/e, © 1995, pp. 87–89. Reprinted by permission of Prentice Hall, Upper Saddle River, New Jersey.

1951; Parsons & Smelser, 1956). These four needs, sometimes called *functional requisites,* are the achievement of goals, adjustment to the environment, the integration of the various parts of society into a whole, and control of deviance from accepted norms. Parsons (1951) placed special emphasis on the need to integrate the parts of a society, which he felt required that people believe in and follow their society's *shared values.* These shared values, he said serve as a kind of "glue" holding society together. If too many people reject these values, social stability will break down.

5   Robert Merton (1968) refined Parsons' functionalism and made it more useful for guiding empirical research. He began by focusing on the function of a given unit of social structure. Earlier theorists often explained the presence of a part by saying that it adds to the maintenance of the whole. It was difficult, however, for them to see any social unit as harmful to the whole. If a unit of social structure existed, they thought, it must be functional. But Merton pointed out that not all parts of a social system need be functional. A unit of structure is *dysfunctional* when it prevents society, or one of its parts, from meeting its needs.

6   Religion is functional when it binds together the members of a society; an army is functional when it protects a society from harm; a political machine is functional when it helps to integrate immigrant groups into a society by providing them with needed information about government and social services. But religion that promotes political strife, as in Northern Ireland, is dysfunctional. So are an army that drains resources from other pressing social needs, such as health or education, and a political machine that relies on graft and creates corruption in public life.

7   It is also important to point out that the "real" functions of a unit of social structure may not be the same as its "official," or intended, functions. Besides its intended or **manifest functions,** a unit of social structure also has unrecognized, unintended **latent functions.**

8   One manifest function (intended purpose) of colleges and universities, for instance, is to educate young people and prepare them for specialized roles in society. A latent function (unintended purpose) may be to keep a large part of the population (students) out of the job market and so prevent strains on the economy.

9   Functionalism has been criticized on many grounds, but mainly that its view of society is inherently conservative. Because it stresses shared values and views society as composed of parts that function together for the benefit of the whole, functionalism seems to leave little room for people who do not share society's values or who try to change them. Critics charge that it gives little attention to dissent and social conflict. By focusing so heavily on order, stability, and consensus, functionalism may even distort the true nature of societies. Unlike the parts of an organism, argue the critics, the parts of society do not always function together for the benefit of the whole. Some societal parts are in conflict; some parts benefit at the expense of others.

10   The most forceful criticism of functional theory has come from a group called conflict theorists. They agree that the functional perspective may be valuable in studying stable societies. But a look around the

world today suggests that societies are rising and falling at a rapid rate, and conflict is not the exception but the rule.

Conflict Theory

11   *Conflict theory* is not nearly so unified a viewpoint as functionalism. It is, instead, a varied body of theories that has been given the conflict label only in recent years. Perhaps the one common belief of all conflict theorists is that societies are always in a state of conflict over scarce resources. One of the most important scarce resources is power. Therefore, conflict theorists argue, society is best viewed as an arena in which there is a constant struggle for power.

12   A major assumption of many conflict theorists is that, rather than being held together by the "glue" of shared values, societies and social order are maintained by force. The more powerful members of society are able, partly through the use of force, to get the less powerful members of the society to conform to their values. One of the main concerns of conflict theorists, therefore, has been to pick out the dominant groups in society and to discover how they maintain their dominance – and, in fact, how they achieved their power in the first place.

13   Sometimes "conflict theory" means simply Marxist sociology. Marxist sociologists emphasize economic forces in societies, in contrast to functionalism's emphasis on shared cultural values. And they stress the constant struggle between economic classes of people. Marx identified two classes: the working class, or *proletariat,* and the owners of the means of production, or *bourgeoisie.* He predicted that the conflict between these two classes would lead to the revolutionary overthrow of capitalist societies, with classless society as the final outcome (Marx, 1848). That this prediction has not yet come to pass, however, does not mean that the basic class struggle had ended in most capitalist societies. Neo-Marxist conflict theorists continue to follow Marx in emphasizing that most societies are torn by conflict and struggle between economic classes. They say that social progress will occur only when the power of the capitalists – the dominant class – is diminished (Braverman, 1974).

14   But the term "conflict theory" typically includes many non-Marxist sociologists as well. Perhaps the best known of living conflict theorists is the German sociologist Ralf Dahrendorf (1958, 1959), who is now head of the London School of Economics. Dahrendorf attacks the basic premise of functionalism, that society is orderly. He regards that premise as almost utopian (1958) and directs attention to society's "ugly face" – that of conflict. In contrast to Marx, he sees conflict as more a struggle for power than a class conflict over economic resources. But like Marx, he views society as always verging on instability and change. Indeed, he maintains that the study of social change, not social order, should be the main focus in the analysis of society (1959).

15   The founding father of conflict theory in the United States was C. Wright Mills. Mills felt that he was working in a Marxist tradition, but there is also much in his thought that comes from the work of Max Weber. In addition, Mills's work comes out of midwestern populism and its battle against the "big interests" in American life. In his best-known book, *The Power Elite* (1956), Mills tried to discover who really rules in America. He concluded that America is dominated by leaders from three spheres that are more and more related: top management of the big corporations, key officials in government, and the top ranks of the military. Moreover, these leaders are easily interchanged. Corporate executives often join the government, and retired generals are elected to the boards of large corporations. Thus, Mills felt, a small and very centralized group makes most of the major decisions in our society about war and peace, money and taxes, civil rights and responsibilities.

16   The ideas developed by Mills are central to much of conflict theory today (e.g., Domhoff, 1967, 1978, 1980). Despite their visible signs of success, conflict theorists note, the people who make up the "power elite" are often less aware of their power than they are of other people's resistance to it. To deal with this resistance and to keep public resentment within bounds, those in power try to blur the line between themselves and the masses. Nonetheless, the masses are aware of their powerlessness, and they resent it. The tension between the strong and the weak becomes the breeding ground for social conflict. The people who benefit most from the social order as it is will seek to preserve it. Those who are deprived will work to change it. And the conflict resulting from the opposition of these groups can lead to radical social change.

17   An important younger theorist closely connected with the conflict perspective is Randall Collins. Collins clearly sees himself following in the footsteps of Max Weber, who strongly opposed Karl Marx on many issues. The basic insight of conflict theory, Collins says, "is that human beings are sociable but conflict-prone animals" (1975, p. 59). The term "conflict theory" also has been used to refer to the work of scholars such as Lewis Coser (1956, 1967). (Coser, however, rejects the label.) Building on the work of Georg Simmel, Coser has studied the process of social conflict in all its forms. He has not tried to develop a "theory of society."

18   Conflict theories differ among themselves not only in what areas of social conflict they choose to emphasize but also in their views on the role of social science in society (Wallace & Wolf, 1980). Some conflict theorists, especially those working in the Marxist tradition, feel a moral obligation not only to criticize society but also actively to promote social change. These sociologists reject the principle of ethical neutrality, . . . the principle that social scientists should do only scientific work and not fight political and moral battles. Other conflict theorists – such as Ralf Dahrendorf, Randall Collins, and Lewis Coser – hold a more traditional view. They

feel that the main aim of the social services is explanation rather than social activism and that social scientists must strive to be objective about political events.

[19]   The issue of the role of the social sciences in society provokes some of the most bitter debate between conflict theorists (at least those who reject the principle of ethical neutrality) and functionalists. Otherwise, most sociologists today, no matter what their own views, accept that each perspective has something important to offer – that each is looking at a different aspect of society. Functionalism looks at the way people work together in everyday life. It gives some important answers to the question: Why are people who have their own special needs and interests often so cooperative with one another? Conflict theory, on the other hand, focuses on the strains and tensions in life, on the lack of equality in societies, and on breakdowns in social order. Just as functionalism may sometimes err in seeing more cooperation and order than actually exists, conflict theories may err in seeing social conflict as *the* major form of social interaction. But both perspectives point up aspects of our social existence that are basic and universal, as we will explore further in many of the chapters to follow.

References

Braverman, H. 1975. *Labor and Monopoly Capital.* New York: Monthly Review Press

Collins, Randall. 1975. *Conflict Sociology.* Orlando, FL: Academic Press

Coser, Lewis. 1956. *The Functions of Social Conflict.* New York: Free Press

Coser, Lewis. 1967. *Continuities in the Study of Social Conflict.* New York: Free Press

Dahrendorf, Ralf. 1958. "Out of utopia: Toward a reorganization of sociological analysis." *American Journal of Sociology* 64:115–127

Dahrendorf, Ralf. 1959. *Class and Class Conflict in Industrial Society.* Palo Alto, CA: Stanford University Press

Domhoff, G. William. 1967. *Who Rules America?* Englewood Cliffs, NJ: Prentice-Hall

Domhoff, G. William. 1978. *Who Really Rules?* New Brunswick, NJ: Transaction Books

Domhoff, G. William (ed.). 1980. *Power Structure Research.* Beverly Hills: Sage

Marx, Karl, and Friedrich Engels. 1969. *The Communist Manifesto.* Baltimore: Penguin Books. (Originally published in 1848.)

Merton, Robert K. 1968. *Social Theory and Social Structure* (enl. ed.). New York: Free Press

Mills, C. Wright. 1956. *The Power Elite.* New York: Oxford University Press

Parsons, Talcott. 1951. *The Social System.* Glencoe, IL: Free Press

Parsons, Talcott, and Neil J. Smelser. 1956. *Economy and Society.* New York: Free Press

Wallace, R., and A. Wolf. 1980. *Contemporary Sociological Theory.* Englewood Cliffs, NJ: Prentice-Hall
– From David Popenoe, *Sociology.* Prentice-Hall, 1983.

Postreading

TRUE OR FALSE

Directions: *Decide if each of the following statements is true (T) or false (F) based on the selection.*

_____ **1.** Sociologists have been influenced by theories in biology.

_____ **2.** Karl Marx believed that society is similar to a living organism.

_____ **3.** "Stability" is the foundation of conflict theory as we know it today.

_____ **4.** While many sociologists in the United States explained societies in terms of functionalism, cultural anthropologists in England attempted to explain societies in terms of conflict theory.

_____ **5.** The four functional requisites are obtaining goals, adjusting to the environment, integrating the various parts of society into a whole, and controlling the less powerful members of a society.

_____ **6.** An example of a dysfunctional structure in society is a military which uses up the money necessary for social welfare programs.

_____ **7.** A latent function is one that is unknown to the members of society.

_____ **8.** Most conflict theorists believe that societies are always struggling over scarce resources.

_____ **9.** *Bourgeoisie* refers to the working class of people and *proletariat* refers to the owners of production.

_____ **10.** As Marx predicted, the conflict between the workers and owners of production, resulted in an overthrow of the capitalist society in England, leaving a classless society.

_____ **11.** Social change, according to conflict theorists, is due to instability caused by conflict.

_____ **12.** Conflict theorists view members of societies as independent whereas functionalists view them as being dependent on one another.

READING WORKSHEET

Directions: *After you have completed the true-or-false exercise, answer the following questions. You may refer to the selection if necessary.*

1. What is the purpose of paragraph 1? _____

_____

2. In the last sentence of paragraph 1, what does *these steps forward* refer to? _

_____

3. Why is functionalism described in terms of biology? _____

_____

4. In the definition of functionalism given in the text, what are the "parts" that make up a society? _____

_____

5. How did Émile Durkheim's idea of functionalism differ from those of Auguste Compte and Herbert Spencer? _____

_____

6. Paragraphs 2 through 5 are related to a particular sentence in paragraph 1. Which sentence is it and what is its function? _____

_____

7. Who was Talcott Parsons? _____

_____

8. According to Parsons, what needs must be met in order to maintain a functional society? _____

_____

9. How did Robert Merton's theory of functionalism differ from that of Parsons?

_____

_____

10. What is the purpose of paragraph 6? _____

_____

11. What is the major topic discussed in paragraph 6? _____

_____

12. What is the meaning of the prefix *dys-*? _____

_____

13. In your own words, define *latent function* and *manifest function*. Give an example of each. _____

_____

14. According to functionalist theory, what is the major purpose of a society? __

_____

15. What relationship do paragraphs 9 and 10 have to the next section of the reading, "Conflict Theory"? _____

_____

16. Whereas functional theorists believe society is held together by "glue," conflict theorists believe society is held together by _____

_____

17. According to conflict theorists, what causes conflict within a society? _____

_____

18. In the phrase *to get the less powerful members of the societies to conform to their values* (paragraph 12), what does *their* refer to? _____

_____

19. According to Karl Marx, where does the main conflict in society lie? _____

20. In your own words, what does Marx think will happen to capitalist societies?

21. In paragraph 13, why are the terms *proletariat* and *bourgeoisie* in italics? __

22. What type of organization is used in the discussion of Mills's conflict theory?
   a. comparison/contrast
   b. cause and effect
   c. chronological order
   d. all of the above
   e. both b and c

23. In *The people who benefit most from the social order as it is will seek to preserve it* (paragraph 16), what does *it* refer to? _____

24. What "positive" feature of society has Randall Collins attributed to conflict theory? _____

25. In what ways do conflict theories differ among themselves? _____

INFERENCE AND RESTATEMENT

Directions: *Decide whether each of the following is a restatement (R), an inference (I), or false statement (F) according to the selection. If the sentence is a restatement, locate the original in the selection and give the paragraph number where it is found.*

_____ **1.** Sociologists have developed two major theories concerning the relationship among groups within a society.

_____ **2.** Functionalism takes a kinder view of human societies than does conflict theory.

_____ **3.** Dissent is an important element of all societies that all sociological theories consider.

_____ **4.** Marxist sociologists do not believe that capitalism is a workable system because it forces individuals or groups to compete for resources needed by all the members of a society.

_____ **5.** It is the understood primary objective of a university to provide the opportunity for higher education to the population.

_____ **6.** According to conflict theory, powerful people who desire to keep their power want less powerful people to be aware of it and to respect it.

_____ **7.** According to conflict theory, the people who have the most power are those who have the support of groups that control the resources of the society.

_____ **8.** According to C. Wright Mills, decisions about important matters that affect the society as a whole often are made by the most powerful group.

_____ **9.** According to conflict theory, the natural tendency of society is toward stability.

_____ **10.** The focus of conflict theory is the struggle between those who have power and those who do not.

OUTLINING

Directions: *Below is a partial outline of the "Functionalism" section from the selection. Reread that section and complete the outline.*

I. Functionalism

    **Defines society as _____

    _____

    A. _____

        _____

        _____

        1. _____

        2. Both have certain needs that must be fulfilled.

        3. _____

    B. Émile Durkheim, the father of functionalism, says society is ruled by a consensus of moral values.

    C. Talcott Parsons _____

        _____

        1. _____

        2. _____

        3. _____

        4. Control of deviance

    D. _____

        _____ dysfunctional parts of society.

        1. _____ aspects of society

            a. Religion: _____

            b. Military: protecting society

            c. _____

        2. Dysfunctional _____

            a. _____

            b. _____

            c. _____: creating corruption

VOCABULARY FROM CONTEXT

Directions: *Using your own knowledge and information from the text, answer the following questions. Refer to the selection while you work. Don't be afraid to guess.*

1. prestige (paragraph 1)
   Notice the tone of this sentence (*enjoyed, high*).

   Prestige means _____

2. dissent (paragraph 9)
   In this line, the word is linked to social conflict.

   Dissent means _____

3. verging (paragraph 14)
   Like Karl Marx, Ralf Dahrendorf sees society as constantly "verging on instability and change." Look at Marx's theory in paragraph 13. Notice the words *predicted* and *lead.*

   Verging means _____

4. to blur the line (paragraph 16)
   If an important powerful person wants to win the sympathy and support of the powerless people, will he make a sharp distinction between himself and potential supporters?

   To blur the line means _____

5. provokes (paragraph 19)
   What in the organization of the sentence gives you a clue to the meaning of this word?

   Provokes means _____
   _____

6. strains (paragraph 19)

   Strains means _____
   How do you know? What clues are there in the sentence itself and/or the paragraph? _____
   _____

Reading textbook sample 6

As the women's movement grows in America, men too are being freed from traditional roles. Today you see more and more men in the delivery room when their children are being born. You see American men changing diapers, taking paternity leaves, and gaining custody of their children in divorces.

Another change in men's roles has occurred in the types of professions available to them. Traditional "female" jobs such as kindergarten teacher, nurse, and secretary are now opening up to men. The following article examines this phenomenon and its effect on the professions that men have begun to "infiltrate."

MORE MEN INFILTRATING PROFESSIONS HISTORICALLY DOMINATED BY WOMEN

By CAROL HYMOWITZ

When Donald Olayer enrolled in nursing school nine years ago, his father took it hard. "Here's my father, a steelworker, hearing about
5 other steelworkers' sons who were becoming welders or getting football scholarships," Mr. Olayer recalls. "The thought of his son becoming a nurse was too much."
10 Today, Mr. Olayer, a registered nurse trained as an anesthetist, earns about $30,000 a year at Jameson Memorial Hospital in New Castle, Pa. His father, he says,
15 has "done an about-face. Now he tells the guys he works with that their sons, who can't find jobs even after fours years of college, should have become nurses."
20 That's not an unusual turnabout nowadays. Just as women have gained a footing in nearly every occupation once reserved for men, men can be found today working routinely in a wide variety of 25 jobs once held nearly exclusively by women. The men are working as receptionists and flight attendants, servants, and even "Kelly girls." 30

The Urban Institute, a research group in Washington, recently estimated that the number of male secretaries rose 24% to 31,000 in 1978 from 25,000 in 1972, while the 35 number of male telephone operators over the same span rose 38%, and the number of male nurses, 94%. Labor experts expect the trend to continue. 40

Job Availability Cited

For one thing, tightness in the job market seems to have given men an additional incentive to take
45 jobs where they can find them. Although female-dominated office and service jobs for the most part rank lower in pay and status, "they're still there," says June
50 O'Neill, director of program and policy research at the institute. Traditionally male blue-collar jobs, meanwhile, "aren't increasing at all."
55 At the same time, she says, "the outlooks of young people are different." Younger men, with less rigid views on what constitutes male or female work "may not feel
60 there's such a stigma to working in a female-dominated field."

Although views have softened, men who cross the sexual segregation line in the job market may still
65 face discrimination and ridicule. David Anderson, a 36-year-old former high school teacher, says he found secretarial work "a way out of teaching and into the business
70 world." He had applied for work at 23 employment agencies for "management training jobs that didn't exist," and he discovered that "the best skill I had was being able to
75 type 70 words a minute."

He took a job as a secretary to the marketing director of a New York publishing company. But he says he could "feel a lot of people
80 wondering what I was doing there and if something was wrong with me."

Mr. Anderson's boss was a woman. When she asked him to fetch coffee, he says, "the other
85 secretaries' eyebrows went up, and one snidely said, 'Oh, there goes Kay's new boy.'" Sales executives who come in to see his boss, he says, "couldn't quite believe that I
90 could and would type, take dictation, and answer the phones."

Occasionally, men in traditionally female jobs may find themselves treated as sex objects.
95 Anthony Shee, a flight attendant with US Air Inc., says some women passengers flirt brazenly. "One lady felt compelled to pat me on the rear when I walked down
100 the aisle," he says, "and she was traveling with her husband."

On the other hand, the males sometimes find themselves mistaken for higher-status profes-
105 sionals. Mr. Shee has been mistaken for a pilot. Mr. Anderson, the secretary, says he found himself being "treated in executive tones whenever I wore a suit."
110 In fact, the men in traditional female jobs often move up the ladder fast. Mr. Anderson actually worked only seven months as a secretary. Then he got a higher
115 level, better-paying job as a placement counselor at an employment agency. "I got a lot of encouragement to advance," he says, "including job tips from male executives
120 who couldn't quite see me staying a secretary."

Experts say, for example, that while men make up only a small fraction of elementary school
125 teachers, a disproportionate number of elementary principals are

men. Barbara Bergmann, an econ-
omist at the University of Mary-
130 land who has studied sex segregation at work, believes that's partly
because of "sexism in the occupa-
tional structure" and partly because men have been raised to as-
135 sert themselves and to assume responsibility. Men may also feel
more compelled than women to advance, she suspects.

Donald Olayer, the nurse, is typical. Almost as soon as he grad- 140
uated from nursing school, he
says he decided "not to stay just
a regular floor nurse earning
only $12,000 a year." Now he
can look forward to earning three 145
times that much, "enough to support a family on," he says, and he
also has "much more responsibility."

References

Aebersold, J. A. (1984). The relationship between reading ability in a foreign language and proficiency in that foreign language and reading ability in the native language. Doctoral dissertation, University of Michigan, Ann Arbor.

Alderson, C. J. (1984). Reading: A reading problem or a language problem? In C. J. Alderson & A. H. Urquhart (Eds.), *Reading in a Foreign Language* (pp. 1–27). New York: Longman.

Anderson, N. J. (1991). Individual differences in strategy use in second language reading and testing. *Modern Language Journal, 75,* 460–72.

Anderson, N. J.; Bachman, L.; Perkins, K.; & Cohen, A. (1991). An exploratory study into the construct validity of a reading comprehension test: Triangulation of data sources. *Language Testing, 8*(1), 41–66.

Anderson, R. C.; Reynolds, R. E.; Schallert, D. L.; & Goetz, E. T. (1977). Frameworks for comprehending discourse. *American Educational Research Journal, 14*(4), 367–81.

Anderson, R. C., & Shifrin, Z. (1980). The meaning of words in context. In R. J. Spiro, B. Bruce, & W. Brewer (Eds.), *Theoretical Issues in Reading Comprehension* (pp. 331–48). Hillsdale, NJ: Lawrence Erlbaum.

Bachman, L. (1991). What does language testing have to offer? *TESOL Quarterly, 25*(4), 671–704.

Barnett, M. (1989). *More than Meets the Eye: Foreign Language Reading Theory and Practice.* Englewood Cliffs, NJ: CAL & Prentice-Hall.

Barrett, M. E., & Datesman, M. K. (1992). *Reading on Your Own: An Extensive Reading Course.* Boston: Heinle & Heinle.

Baudoin, E. M.; Bober, E. B.; Clarke, M. A.; Dobson, B. K.; & Silberstein, S. (1988). *Reader's Choice* (2nd ed.). Ann Arbor: University of Michigan Press.

Benedetto, R. A. (1985). Language ability and the use of top-level organizational strategies. Paper presented at the annual meeting of the National Reading Conference. ERIC Document Reproduction Service, No. ED 266 437.

Bierce, A. (1977). An occurrence at Owl Creek bridge. In *The Stories and Fables of Ambrose Bierce* (18–28). Owings Mills, MD: Stemmer House.

Bloom, B. (1956). *Taxonomy of Educational Objectives, Handbook 1: Cognitive Domain.* New York: David McKay.

Bormuth, J. R. (1969). An operational definition of comprehension instruction. In K. S. Goodman & J. T. Fleming (Eds.), *Psycholinguistics and the Teaching of Reading* (pp. 48–78). Newark, DE: International Reading Association.

Bowen, J. D.; Madsen, H.; & Hilferty, A. (1985). *TESOL: Techniques and Procedures.* New York: Newbury House.

Brinton, D. M.; Snow, M. A.; & Wesche, M. B. (1989). *Content Based Second Language Instruction.* New York: Harper & Row.

Brown, D. S. (1988). *A World of Books: An Annotated Reading List for ESL/ EFL Students.* Washington, DC: TESOL.

Brown, D. S. (1994). *Books for a Small Planet: A Multicultural/Intercultural Bibliography for Young English Language Learners.* Alexandria, VA: TESOL.

Brown, H. D. (1987). *Principles of Language Learning and Teaching.* Englewood Cliffs, NJ: Prentice-Hall.

Brown, H. D. (1994). *Teaching by Principles: An Interactive Approach to Language Pedagogy.* Englewood Cliffs, NJ: Regents/Prentice-Hall.

Brown, J. D. (1988). *Understanding Research in Second Language Learning: A Teacher's Guide to Statistics and Research Design.* New York: Cambridge University Press.

Brown, J. D. (1995). *The Elements of Language Curriculum: A Systematic Approach to Program Development.* Boston: Heinle & Heinle.

Bruder, M. N., & Henderson, R. T. (1986). *Beginning Reading in English as a Second Language.* Englewood Cliffs, NJ: Prentice-Hall.

Burton, J., & Agor, G. (Eds.). (1994). Special Issue on Teacher Research. *TESOL Journal, 4*(1).

Canale, M., & Swain, M. (1980). Theoretical bases of communicative approaches to second language teaching and testing. *Applied Linguistics, 1*(1), 1–47.

Candlin, C. N. (1984). Preface. In J. C. Alderson & A. H. Urquhart (Eds.), *Reading in a Foreign Language* (pp. ix–xiii). New York: Longman.

Cantoni-Harvey, G. (1987). *Content Area Instruction: Approaches and Strategies.* Reading, MA: Addison-Wesley.

Carrell, P. L. (1984a). Evidence of formal schema in second language comprehension. *Language Learning, 34*(2), 87–112.

Carrell, P. L. (1984b). The effects of rhetorical organization on ESL readers. *TESOL Quarterly 18*(3), 441–69.

Carrell, P. L. (1988). Some causes of text-boundedness and schema interferences in ESL reading. In P. Carrell, J. Devine, & D. E. Eskey (Eds.), *Interactive Approaches to Second Language Reading* (pp. 101–13). New York: Cambridge University Press.

Carrell, P. L. (1989). Metacognitive awareness and second language reading. *Modern Language Journal, 73*(2), 121–34.

Carrell, P. L.; Devine, J.; & Eskey, D. (Eds.). (1988). *Interactive Approaches to Second Language Reading.* New York: Cambridge University Press.

Carrell, P. L.; & Eisterhold, J. (1983). Schema theory and ESL reading pedagogy. *TESOL Quarterly, 71*(4), 553–73.

Carrell, P. L.; Pharis, B. G.; & Liberto, J. C. (1989). Metacognitive strategy training for ESL reading. *TESOL Quarterly, 23*(4), 647–78.

Carroll, M. (1994). Journal writing as a learning and research tool in the adult classroom. *TESOL Journal, 4*(1), 19–23.

Carson, J.; Carrell, P.; Silberstein, S.; Kroll, B.; & Kushn, P. (1990). Reading–writing relationships in first and second language. *TESOL Quarterly, 24*(2), 245–66.

Carter, R., & Long, M. N. (1991). *Teaching Literature.* New York: Longman.

Clarke, D. F., & Nation, I. S. P. (1980). Guessing the meanings of words from context: Strategies and techniques. *System 8*(3), 211–20.

Clarke, M. A. (1979). Reading in Spanish and English. *Language Learning, 29,* 121–50.

Clarke, M. A. (1980). The short-circuit hypothesis of ESL reading – or when language competence interferes with reading performance. *Modern Language Journal, 64,* 203–9.

Clarke, M. A., & Silberstein, S. (1977). Toward a realization of psycholinguistic principles in the ESL reading class. *Language Learning, 27*(1), 135–54.

Clennell, C. (1994). Investigating the use of communication strategies by adult second language learners: A case for trusting your own judgment in research. *TESOL Journal, 4*(1), 32–5.

Climate clues lie below ocean. (1993). *Ann Arbor News,* C5, June 28.

Cochran-Smith, M., & Lytle, S. L. (1993). *Inside/Outside: Teacher Research and Knowledge.* New York: Teachers College Press.

Cohen, A. (1994). *Assessing Language Ability in the Classroom* (2nd ed.). Boston: Heinle & Heinle.

Collie, J., & Slater, S. (1987). *Literature in the Language Classroom: A Resource Book of Ideas and Activities.* Cambridge: Cambridge University Press.

Connor, U. (1995). *Contrastive Rhetoric.* New York: Cambridge University Press.

Cumming, A. (Ed.). (1981). Age of arrival and immigrant second language learning in Canada: A reassessment. *Applied Linguistics, 2,* 132–49.

Cumming, A. (1994). Alternatives in TESOL research: Descriptive, interpretive, and ideological orientations. *TESOL Quarterly, 28*(4), 673–704.

Dagostino, L., & Carifio, J. (1994). *Evaluative Reading and Literacy: A Cognitive View*. Boston: Allyn & Bacon.

Davey, E. (1983). Think aloud – Modeling the cognitive processes of reading comprehension. *Journal of Reading, 27*, 44–7.

Davies, A., & Widdowson, H. G. (1973). Reading and writing. In J. P. B. Allen & S. Pit Corder (Eds.), *The Edinburgh Course in Applied Linguistics* (pp. 156–201). London: Oxford University Press.

Devine, J. (1987). General language competence and adult second language reading. In J. Devine, P. L. Carrell, and D. E. Eskey (Eds.), *Research in Reading English as a Second Language* (pp. 73–86). Washington, DC: TESOL.

Devine, J. (1988a). A case study of two readers: Models of reading and performance. In J. Devine, P. L. Carrell, & D. E. Eskey (Eds.), *Research in Reading in English as a Second Language* (pp. 127–39). Washington, DC: TESOL.

Devine, J. (1988b). The relationship between general language competence and second language reading proficiency: Implications for teaching. In P. L. Carrell, J. Devine, & D. E. Eskey (Eds.), *Interactive Approaches to Second Language Reading* (260–77). Washington, DC: TESOL.

Devine, J. (1993). The role of metacognition in second language reading and writing. In J. G. Carson & I. Leki (Eds.), *Reading in the Composition Classroom: Second Language Perspectives* (pp. 105–27). Boston: Heinle & Heinle.

Dickinson, E. (1942). There's a certain slant of light. In M. D. Bianchi & A. L. Hampson (Eds.), *Poems by Emily Dickinson,* #258 (p. 108). Boston: Little Brown.

Dole, J.; Valencia, S.; Gree, E. A.; & Wardrop, J. (1991). Effects of two types of prereading instruction on the comprehension of narrative and expository text. *Reading Research Quarterly, 26*(2), 142–59.

Draper, C. G. (1993). *Great American Short Stories 1: An ESL/EFL Reader.* Englewood Cliffs, NJ: Regents/Prentice-Hall.

Duff, A., & Maley, A. (1990). *Literature.* Oxford: Oxford University Press.

Ehrman, M. E., & Oxford, R. L. (1990). Adult language learning styles and strategies in an intensive training setting. *Modern Language Journal, 74*, 311–27.

Ellis, R. (1986). *Understanding Second Language Acquisition.* New York: Oxford University Press.

Ely, C. (1989). Tolerance of ambiguity and use of second language learning strategies. *Foreign Language Annals, 22*, 437–45.

English, F. (1992). *Deciding What to Teach and Test: Developing, Aligning, and Auditing the Curriculum.* Newbury Park, CA: Corwin Press.

Eskey, D. (1988). Holding in the bottom: An interactive approach to the language problems of second language readers. In P. Carrell, J. Devine, & D. Eskey (Eds.), *Interactive Approaches to Second Language Reading* (pp. 223–38). New York: Cambridge University Press.

Faltis, C. (Ed.). (1995). Special issue on alternative assessment. *TESOL Journal 5*(1).

Faltis, C. (Ed.). (1996). Special issue on self-assessment: Guiding learners to assess their strategies and abilities to communicate. *TESOL Journal 5*(3).

Fanselow, J. (1992). *Contrasting Conversations: Activities for Exploring our Beliefs and Teaching Practices.* New York: Longman.

Field, M. L. (1984). Teaching Literature in China. *Language Learning and Communication 3*(3), 387–96.

Field, M. L., and Aebersold, J. A. (1990). Cultural attitudes toward reading: Their implications for reading teachers working with ESL/bilingual readers. *Journal of Reading, 33*(6), 406–10.

Flower, L. (1990). Introduction. In L. Flower et al., *Reading to Write: Exploring a Cognitive and Social Process.* New York: Oxford University Press.

Foley, K. S. (1993). Talking journals. *TESOL Journal, 3*(1), 37–8.

Foucault, M. (1979). *Discipline and Punish.* New York: Vintage Books.

Gardner, D. (1996). Self-assessment for self-access learners. *TESOL Journal, 5*(3), 18–23.

Goodman, K. (1967). Reading: A psycholinguistic guessing game. *Journal of the Reading Specialist, 6,* 126–35.

Gower, R., & Pearson, M. (1987). *Reading Literature.* Burnt Mill, UK: Longman.

Grabe, W. (1986). The transition from theory to practice in teaching reading. In F. Dubin, D. Eskey, and W. Grabe (Eds.), *Teaching Second Language Reading for Academic Purposes* (pp. 25–48). Reading, MA: Addison-Wesley.

Grabe, W. (1988). Reassessing the term "interactive." In P. L. Carrell, J. Devine, & D. E. Eskey (Eds.), *Interactive Approaches to Second Language Reading* (pp. 56–70). New York: Cambridge University Press.

Grabe, W. (1991). Current developments in second language reading research. *TESOL Quarterly, 25*(3), 375–406.

Graves, M. F.; Cooke, C. L.; & Laberge, M. J. (1983). Effects of previewing difficult short stories on low ability junior high school students' comprehension, recall, and attitudes. *Reading Research Quarterly, 18*(3), 262–76.

Green, C., & Green, J. M. (1993). Secret friend journals. *TESOL Journal, 21*(3), 20–3.

Grellet, F. (1984). *Developing Reading Skills: A Practical Guide to Reading Comprehension Skills.* Cambridge: Cambridge University Press.

Handscombe, J. (1993a). The search for researchers begins. *Elementary Education Newsletter, 15*(2), 2–3.

Handscombe, J. (1993b). The search for researchers continues. *Elementary Education Newsletter, 15*(3), 4–5.

Hatch, E. M. (1983). *Psycholinguistics: A Second Language Perspective.* Rowley, MA: Newbury House.

Haynes, M. E. (1989). Individual differences in Chinese readers of English: Orthography and reading. Doctoral dissertation, Michigan State University.

Heath, S. B. (1983). *Ways with Words: Language, Life and Work in Communities and Classrooms.* New York: Cambridge University Press.

Heath, S. B. (1993). Inner city life through drama: Imagining the language classroom. *TESOL Quarterly, 27*(2), 177–92.

Heaton, J. B. (1975). *Writing English Language Tests.* Burnt Mill, UK: Longman.

Heaton, J. B. (1990). *Classroom Testing.* Burnt Mill, UK: Longman.

Hewett, N. M. (1990). Reading, cognitive style and culture: A look at some relationships in second-language acquisition. In A. Labarca & L. Bailey (Eds.), *Issues in L2: Theory as Practice/Practice as Theory* (pp. 62–87). Delaware Symposium 7. Norwood, NJ: Ablex.

Hosenfeld, C.; Arnold, V.; Kirchofer, J.; Laciura, J.; & Wilson, L. (1981). Second language reading: A curricular sequence for teaching reading strategies. *Foreign Language Annals, 14*(5), 415–22.

Huckin, T.; Haynes, M.; & Coady, J. (Eds.). (1993). *Second Language Reading and Vocabulary Learning.* Norwood, NJ: Ablex.

Hughes, A. (1989). *Testing for Language Teachers.* Cambridge: Cambridge University Press.

James, M. O. (1987). ESL reading pedagogy: Implications of schema-theoretical research. In J. Devine, P. L. Carrell, & D. E. Eskey (Eds.), *Research in Reading in English as a Second Language* (pp. 175–88). Washington, DC: TESOL.

Jensen, L. (1986). Advanced reading skills in a comprehensive course. In F. Dubin, D. E. Eskey, & W. Grabe (Eds.), *Teaching Second Language Reading for Academic Purposes* (pp. 103–24). Reading, MA: Addison-Wesley.

Johnson, P. (1982). Effects on reading comprehension of building background knowledge. *TESOL Quarterly, 16,* 503–16.

Kaplan, R. B. (1966). Cultural thought patterns in inter-cultural education. *Language Learning, 16,* 1–20.

Kaplan, R. B. (1987). Cultural thought patterns revisited. In U. Connor & R. B. Kaplan (Eds.), *Writing across Languages: Analysis of L2 Tests* (pp. 9–12). Reading, MA: Addison-Wesley.

Kebir, C. (1994). An action research look at the communication strategies of adult learners. *TESOL Journal, 4*(1), 28–31.

Kirschner, M.; Wexler, C.; & Spector-Cohen, E. (1992). Avoiding obstacles to student comprehension of test questions. *TESOL Quarterly, 26*(3), 537–56.

Kletzien, S. B. (1991). Strategy use by good and poor comprehenders reading expository text of differing levels. *Reading Research Quarterly, 26*(1), 67–84.

Li, X-M. (1992). A celebration of tradition or self? An ethnographic study of teachers' comments on student writing in America and China. Doctoral dissertation, University of New Hampshire.

Littlewood, W. T. (1984). *Foreign and Second Language Learning: Language Acquisition Research and Its Implications for the Classroom.* Cambridge: Cambridge University Press.

Lorch, R. J., Jr., & O'Brien, E. J. (Eds.). (1995). *Sources of Coherence in Reading.* Hillsdale, NJ: Lawrence Erlbaum.

MacLean, M., & d'Anglejan, A. (1986). Rational cloze and retrospection: Insights into first and second language reading comprehension. *Canadian Modern Language Review, 42,* 814–26.

Madsen, H. S. (1983). *Techniques in Testing.* New York: Oxford University Press.

Maria, K., & Hathaway, K. (1993). Using think alouds with teachers to develop awareness of reading strategies. *Journal of Reading, 37*(1), 12–18.

McLaughlin, B. (1978). The monitor model: Some methodological considerations. *Language Learning, 28,* 309–32.

Mikulecky, B. S. (1990). *A Short Course in Teaching Reading Skills.* Reading, MA: Addison-Wesley.

Murphy, T. (1994–5). Tests: Learning through negotiated interaction. *TESOL Journal, 4*(2), 12–16.

Nation, I. S. P. (1990). *Teaching and Learning Vocabulary.* New York: Newbury House.

Nevo, N. (1989). Test-taking strategies on a multiple-choice test of reading comprehension. *Language Testing, 6*(2), 199–215.

Nunan, D. (1988). *The Learner-Centered Curriculum.* Cambridge: Cambridge University Press.

Nunan, D. (1989). *Understanding Language Classrooms: A Guide for Teacher-Initiated Action.* New York: Prentice-Hall.

Nunan, D. (1992). *Research Methods in Language Learning.* New York: Cambridge University Press.

Nuttall, C. (1983). *Teaching Reading Skills in a Foreign Language.* London: Heinemann.

Omaggio, A. C. (1986). *Teaching Language in Context: Proficiency-Oriented Instruction.* Boston: Heinle & Heinle.

Omaggio, A. C. (1983). *Proficiency-Oriented Classroom Testing.* Washington, DC: Center for Applied Linguistics.

Oxford, R. S. (1990). *Language Learning Strategies: What Every Teacher Should Know.* New York: Cambridge University Press.

Parry, K. (1992). *Reading for a Purpose.* New York: St. Martin's Press.

Patterson, L.; Snata, C. M.; Short, K.; & Smith, K. (Eds.). (1993). *Teachers Are Researchers: Reflection and Action.* Newark, DE: International Reading Association.

Pearson, P. D., & Johnson, D. D. (1978). *Teaching Reading Comprehension.* New York: Holt, Rinehart & Winston.

Peters, C. W. (1978). Assessing reading performance at a secondary level through the utilization of a cognitive self-rating scale. In P. D. Pearson & J. Jansen (Eds.), *Reading: Disciplined Inquiry in Process and Practice* (pp. 161–65). Clemson, SC: National Reading Conference.

Peyton, J. K., & Reed, L. (1990). *Dialog Journal Writing with Nonnative English Speakers: A Handbook for Teachers.* Alexandria, VA: TESOL.

Pressley, M.; Ghhatala, E.; Woloshyn, V.; & Pirie, J. (1990). Sometimes adults miss the main ideas in text and do not realize it: Confidence in responses to short-answer and multiple-choice comprehension questions. *Reading Research Quarterly, 25*(3), 232–49.

Pritchard, R. (1990). The effects of cultural schemata on reading processing strategies. *Reading Research Quarterly, 25*(4), 273–95.

Purves, A. C., & Hawisher, G. (1986). Viewpoints: Cultures, test models and the activity of writing. *Research in the Teaching of English, 20*(2), 174–97.

Rando, W. C., & Menges, R. J. (1991). How practice is shaped by personal theories. In *College Teaching: From Theory to Practice* (pp. 7–14). New Directions for Teaching and Learning 45. San Francisco: Jossey-Bass.

Richard-Amato, P. A. (1988). *Making It Happen.* New York: Longman.

Richards, J. C. (1990). *The Language Teaching Matrix.* New York: Cambridge University Press.

Richards, J. C., & Lockhart, C. (1994). *Reflective Teaching in Second Language Classrooms.* New York: Cambridge University Press.

Richards, J. C., & Rodgers, T. S. (1986). *Approaches and Methods in Language Teaching: A Description and Analysis.* New York: Cambridge University Press.

Reid, J. (1995). *Learning Styles in the ESL/EFL Classroom.* Boston: Heinle & Heinle.

Robinson, G. L. (1985). *Cross-cultural Understanding: Processes and Approaches for Foreign Language, English as a Second Language, and Bilingual Educators.* New York: Pergamon Press.

Roller, C. (1990). Commentary: The interaction between knowledge and structure variables in the processing of expository prose. *Reading Research Quarterly, 25*(2), 79–89.

Rosenthal, N. E. (1993). Diagnosis and treatment of seasonal affective disorder. *Journal of the American Medical Association, 270*(22), 2717–20.

Royer, J. M., & Carlo, M. S. (1991). Transfer of comprehension skills from native to second language. *Journal of Reading, 34*(6), 450–55.

Rumelhart, D. E. (1977). Toward an interactive model of reading. In S. Dornic (Ed.), *Attention and Performance VI* (pp. 575–603). Hillsdale, NJ: Lawrence Erlbaum.

Samway, C. D. (1994). But it's hard to keep field-notes while also teaching. *TESOL Journal, 4*(1), 47–48.

Sarig, G. (1987). High-level reading in the first and in the foreign language: Some comparative process data. In J. Devine, P. L. Carrell, & D. E. Eskey (Eds.), *Research in Reading in English as a Second Language* (pp. 107–120). Washington, DC: TESOL.

Scarcella, R., & Oxford, R. (1992). *The Tapestry of Language Learning: The Individual in the Communicative Classroom.* Boston: Heinle & Heinle.

Segalowitz, N. (1986). Skilled reading in the second language. In J. Vaid (Ed.), *Language Processing in Bilinguals: Psycholinguistic and Neuropsychological Perspectives* (pp. 3–19). Hillsdale, NJ: Lawrence Erlbaum.

Shih, M. (1992). Beyond comprehension exercises in the ESL academic reading class. *TESOL Quarterly, 26*(2), 289–318.

Shohamy, E. (1993). *The Power of Tests: The Impact of Language Tests on Teaching and Learning.* National Foreign Language Center Occasional Papers. Washington, DC: National Foreign Language Center at Johns Hopkins University.

Shohamy, E., & Reves, T. (1985). Authentic language tests: Where from and where to? *Language Testing, 2*(1), 48–59.

Short, M., & Candlin, C. (1989). Teaching study skills for English literature. In M. Short (Ed.), *Reading, Analyzing and Teaching Literature* (pp. 178–203). New York: Longman.

Showalter, E. (1985). Feminist criticism in the wilderness. In E. Showalter (Ed.), *The New Feminist Criticism: Essays on Women, Literature and Theory* (pp. 243–70). New York: Pantheon.

Silberstein, S. (1994). *Techniques and Resources in Teaching Reading.* New York: Oxford University Press.

Smith, R., & Barrett, T. C. (1974). *Teaching Reading in the Middle Grades.* Reading, MA: Addison-Wesley.

Spolsky, B. (1985). The limits of authenticity in language testing. *Language Testing, 2*(1), 31–40.

Stanoich, K. (1990). Concepts of developmental theories of reading skill: Cognitive resources, automaticity, and modularity. *Developmental Review, 10,* 72–100.

Steffensen, M. S., & Joag-Dev, C. (1984). Cultural knowledge and reading. In J. C. Alderson & A. H. Urquhart (Eds.), *Reading in a Foreign Language* (pp. 48–61). New York: Longman.

Steinbeck, J. (1954). The chrysanthemums. In P. Covici (Ed.), *The Portable John Steinbeck* (pp. 56–69). New York: Viking Press.

Stodard, S. (1991). *Text and Texture: Patterns of Cohesion.* Norwood, NJ: Ablex.

Tutor, E. (1992). Personal note.

van Lier, L. (1994). Some features of a theory of practice. *TESOL Journal, 4*(1), 6–10.

Wallace, C. (1992). *Reading.* New York: Oxford University Press.

Zhang, J. (1993). Reading-portfolio assessment. In R. R. Day (Ed.), *New Ways in Teaching Reading* (pp. 212–13). Alexandria, VA: TESOL.

Index

Boldface page numbers indicate where defined terms are located.